D1592994

How I Love Your Torah, O LORD!

How I Love Your Torah, O LORD!

Studies in the Book of Deuteronomy

Daniel I. Block

CASCADE *Books* · Eugene, Oregon

HOW I LOVE YOUR TORAH, O LORD!
Studies in the Book of Deuteronomy

Cascade Books
A Division of Wipf and Stock Publishers
199 W. 8th Ave., Suite 3
Eugene, OR 97401

www.wipfandstock.com

ISBN 13: 978-1-61097-342-7

Cataloging-in-Publication data:

Block, Daniel Isaac, 1943–.

How I love your torah, o Lord! : studies in the book of Deuteronomy / Daniel I. Block.

xxviii + 242 p. ; 23 cm. Includes bibliographical references and indexes.

ISBN 13: 978-1-61097-342-7

1. Bible. O.T. Deuteronomy—Criticism, interpretations, etc. 2. Ten Commandments—Criticism, interpretations, etc. 3. Shema. I. Title.

BS1275.52 B57 2011

Manufactured in the U.S.A

*This book is dedicated
to my doctoral students and research assistants
who have inspired me with their love for the Torah*

Jenny Lowery
Timothy Wu
Richard Holland
D. Jeffrey Mooney
Jason DeRouchie
Gregory Smith
Kenneth Turner
James Harriman
Bryan Cribb
Rebekah Josberger
Steven Guest
J. Nathan Elliott
Philip Marshall
Myrto Theocharous
Christopher Ansberry
Jerry Hwang
Charles Trimm
Jason Gile
A. Rahel Schafer
Matthew Newkirk
Matthew Patton
Daniel Owens
Carmen Imes
Austin Surls

Contents

     Anthem (Deuteronomy 32) • 162

     Excursus B: Text-Critical Issues in Deuteronomy 32:43 • 185

     Bibliography • 189

     Index of Modern Authors • 213

     Index of Selected Subjects • 217

     Index of Scripture References • 221

Illustrations

Tables

Preface

G IVEN THE UBIQUITOUS PRACTICE in contemporary worship, it comes as a surprise to many to learn that in the Old Testament people would never have had the *chutzpah* to tell God they love him.[1] Equally surprising to many is the contrasting discovery of unrestrained expressions of love for the Torah, particularly in Ps 119. The title of this volume is inspired by Ps 119:97: מָה־אָהַבְתִּי תוֹרָתֶךָ כָּל־הַיּוֹם הִיא שִׂיחָתִי, "How I love your Torah! All day long it is my meditation."[2] Within the context of the Psalter, this statement sounds like the psalmist's response to the characterization of the "privileged man" (אַשְׁרֵי־הָאִישׁ) in Ps 1:1–2:

בְּתוֹרַת יְהוָה חֶפְצוֹ   In the Torah of YHWH he delights,

וּבְתוֹרָתוֹ יֶהְגֶּה יוֹמָם וָלָיְלָה   and in his Torah he meditates day and night.

But what is the Torah in which the blessed person delights? Some interpret הַתּוֹרָה, as "the Law," as opposed to "the Psalms" and "the Prophets" (Luke 24:44), the five books of the Pentateuch. While the laws in and of themselves may not be a cause for delight, they are embedded in gospel narratives and punctuated by motive clauses that constantly draw at-

---

1. The verb אָהֵב, "to love, to demonstrate covenant commitment in action that serves the interest of the other," never appears with a first person subject with God as the object. Neither Ps 18:1 nor 116:1 contradicts this observation. In Ps 18:1 the psalmist intentionally avoids the statement, preferring an extremely awkward construction involving the only occurrence in the entire Old Testament of the qal form of רחם, which in piel means "to show pity, have compassion," and always expresses the disposition of a superior to an inferior in need. Psalm 116:1 does indeed use the verb אָהֵב with a first person subject, but the Hebrew translates literally, "I love because YHWH has heard my voice." As in 1 John 4:19, the verb lacks an object.

2. See also Ps 119:113, 163; cf. 165. The verb אָהֵב with first person subject is also used with other designations for YHWH's revealed will: his מִצְוֹת, "commands" (119:47, 48, 127); עֵדֹת, "[covenant] stipulations" (119:119, 167); פִּקּוּדִים, "precepts" (119:159); אִמְרָה, "word, declaration" (119:40).

tention to YHWH's acts of grace. However, it is doubtful the expression had come to function as a designation for the Pentateuch by the time the psalm was written. Some interpret the word תּוֹרָה narrowly as "law" (Greek ὁ νόμος), finding here a reference to the 613 laws of the Pentateuch, as identified by the Jewish scholar Maimonides. However, apart from the gospel represented by the surrounding narratives and the motive clauses, by itself the law becomes a burden to be borne, rather than a cause for delight. Some interpret תּוֹרַת יְהוָה, "the Torah of YHWH," broadly as Scripture,[3] that is, all the inspired writings of the Old Testament, if not also including the New Testament. The word תּוֹרָה is often used of "instruction" generally, and in the rest of Scripture we discover many reasons to delight, though we have also added a preponderance of prophetic texts, which announce judgment and call for lamentation and confession, rather than for celebration. Furthermore, the expression תּוֹרַת יְהוָה, "the Torah of YHWH," is never used in the generic sense of "instruction"; it always refers to the Sinai revelation and/or the book of Deuteronomy.[4] Indeed in the other *Torah* psalms (Pss 19, 119) the word is used in the very specific sense of the revealed will of God—alongside other expressions (מִצְוֹת, "commands"; חֻקִּים, "ordinances"; מִשְׁפָּטִים, "judgments"; עֵדֹת, "[covenant] stipulations"; פִּקּוּדִים, "precepts"; אִמְרָה, "word") embodied in the Pentateuch. Some interpret תּוֹרַת יְהוָה, "the Torah of YHWH," as a reference to the Psalter itself. Accordingly, Ps 1:2 is understood as an exhortation for readers to meditate on the Psalter as Scripture, and to find there divine guidance and inspiration in the life of faith.[5] While rarely admitted, this is how many Christians treat the Psalms.[6] At worst they reject and at best they neglect the rest of the Old Testament, particularly the constitutional materials of the Pentateuch. Finding great inspiration and delight in the book of Psalms, they elevate it above the rest of the Old Testament. Although this interpretation might be supported by the division of the Psalter into five books, each of which ends with a doxology (1–41, 42–72, 73–89, 90–106, 106–50)—as if the Psalter is a replacement

3. For example, Gerald Wilson (*Psalms*, 96) argues that תּוֹרָה "implies the traditional commandments of God in the Torah—commandments Israel is expected to obey—as well as the life-giving guidance God gives elsewhere in Scripture."

4. Exod 13:9; 2 Kgs 10:31; 1 Chr 16:40; 22:12; 2 Chr 12:1; 17:9; 31:3–4; 34:14; 35:26; Ezra 7:10; Neh 9:3; Isa 5:24; Jer 8:8; Amos 2:4.

5. Childs, *Introduction to the Old Testament as Scripture*, 513–14.

6. Symbolized by the inclusion of the Psalms at the back of Gideon New Testaments.

for the Pentateuch—this is without warrant in the Scriptures, and flies in the face of Jewish tradition, which views the Torah (Pentateuch) as having unrivaled authority within the Hebrew Bible.

Although each of these interpretations has its advocates, in the end it seems best to interpret תּוֹרַת יְהוָה, "the Torah of YHWH," as the book of Deuteronomy. First, every element of Ps 1 identified by scholars as evidence of wisdom influence may be derived from Deuteronomy. The vocabulary is Deuteronomic (אַשְׁרֵי occurs in Deut 33:29); the notion of choosing between two ways, the way of blessing and the way of retribution, is explicit in Deut 11:26–28 and 30:15–20; the word תּוֹרָה as authoritative divine revelation is most at home in Deuteronomy; the didactic/teaching function is in perfect accord with the genre of Deuteronomy, which presents itself as Moses' final pastoral addresses to his people. Second, the genre of most of the material in the Psalter does not obviously fit the category of תּוֹרָה, which normally means "authoritative instruction," given by a superior to inferiors (God to human beings; parents to children; teachers to students). Few of the psalms are cast as instruction. Most represent personal or communal responses to the ways of God, whether those ways are reported in the Torah or in the personal experience of the psalmists. The direction of speech tends to be upward to God, rather than downward from God. These are primarily the words of people to God, rather than the words of God to people. Third, Ps 1 echoes YHWH's exhortation to Joshua in Josh 1:8, which marks the beginning of the Prophets section of the Hebrew Bible, suggesting that those responsible for the Psalter particularly and the third division of the Hebrew Bible generally intentionally sought to highlight adherence to the Torah as the key to whatever issues are raised in the following books. This canonical stitching with exhortations to Torah piety is reinforced in the last verses of Malachi, which call the people back to the Torah of Moses.

Of course, this does not mean the psalmists were not inspired or that the psalms do not contain the truth of God, or that the Psalms are not Scripture in the full sense of the word.[7] It means rather that we should interpret the psalms that follow, not as Torah in the same sense as Deuteronomy and the Pentateuch, but as prayers and hymns that guide the believer in how to respond to the Torah, learning the righteousness called for by God in his covenant with his people and applying it to every

7. The New Testament writers clearly recognized the psalmists as inspired: Acts 1:16; 2:25, 34; 4:25; Rom 11:9; Heb 4:7.

conceivable circumstance of life. Indeed Christians have no right to seek inspiration from the Psalter if they will not take the book of Deuteronomy seriously as their authoritative Scripture. For Jesus and Paul this was the favorite book of the Old Testament; and so it should be for us. It represents the heart of biblical revelation.

If we are to interpret the entire Psalter as a Davidic/royal document, as some have argued,[8] not only is David presented as the embodiment of covenant righteousness as advocated by the Deuteronomic Torah, but Ps 1 also offers a royal reader a guide on how to read the Torah. The "blessed man," who "walks in the counsel," "stands in the path," and "sits in the seat" (Ps 1:1), is not "everyman," but a high official. In Ps 1:2–3 the call to meditate (הָגָה) in the Torah of YHWH "day and night" and the promise of success for those who do (הִצְלִיחַ) clearly echo Josh 1:8. However, although Joshua is never treated as royalty, in the latter text YHWH seems to apply to him the instructions for a king provided by Moses in Deut 17:14–20. Instead of offering a normal job description of the king that would have placed him within the ancient Near Eastern context (his roles as military leader, judicial authority, and patron of the cult), Moses' prescriptions concern only his relationship to the Torah:

> When he sits on the throne of his kingdom, he shall write for himself in a written document (סֵפֶר) book a copy of this Torah, in the presence of the Levitical priests. And it shall accompany him, and he shall read in it all the days of his life, that he may learn to fear YHWH his God by keeping all the words of this Torah and these statutes, and doing them, so that his heart does not rise above his brothers, and that he does not turn aside from the [Supreme] Command, either to the right hand or to the left, so that he may continue long in his kingdom—he and his children—in the midst of Israel. (vv. 18–20)

In this text הַתּוֹרָה הַזֹּאת, "this Torah," refers to Moses' speeches in the book of Deuteronomy,[9] addresses that he committed to writing, handed to the Levitical priests as custodians of the Torah to be placed beside the ark of the covenant, and then charged them to read every seven years at Sukkoth (Festival of Booths, Deut 31:9–13). Remarkably, the Deuteronomic Torah

---

8. See Waltke, "Canonical Process Approach to the Psalms," 3–19; Waltke, *Old Testament Theology*, 872–74.

9. Similarly Miller ("Deuteronomy and the Psalms," 11) who writes, "[F]or the Psalter, the *law is Deuteronomy*" (italics his).

is the only part of the Pentateuch that is accompanied with instructions for its liturgical use—it is to be read regularly in the hearing of the entire community.

Nevertheless, in keeping with Deut 17:18–20 and Josh 1:8, Ps 1 addresses primarily a royal reader, presenting the prince/king instructions on how to read the Torah for himself and thereby nourish his own soul, offer him guidance for life, and secure the success of his tenure.[10] The 150 psalms that follow reflect the responses of persons who are immersed in the Torah and for whom reading the Torah is the staple of life (cf. Ps 119). However, inasmuch as the king was perceived as the exemplary embodiment of covenant righteousness for God's people, it also offers us insight into how we should read the Torah. The book of Deuteronomy is the heart of the Torah, which priests were to teach and model,[11] which psalmists praised,[12] to which the prophets appealed,[13] by which faithful kings ruled[14] and righteous citizens lived. In short, this book provides the theological base for virtually the entire Old (and New) Testament and the paradigm for much of its literary style.

The essays in this volume arise out of my ten-year meditations on the book of Deuteronomy. Although Pss 1:2 and 119:97 use different expressions for these ruminations,[15] in context they belong to the same semantic field. While we normally associate meditation with devotional reading, for me the articles that follow represent deep literary and theological meditations that have been personally incredibly inspiring and transformative. We have attempted to produce a stylistically coherent

---

10. On which, see Grant, *King as Exemplar*.

11. Deut 33:10; 2 Chr 15:3; 19:8; Mal 2:6, 9; cf. Jer 18:18; Ezek 7:26; Ezra 7:10.

12. Pss 19:7–14; 119; etc.

13. Isa 1:10; 5:24; 8:20; 30:9; 51:7.

14. 1 Kgs 2:2–4; 2 Kgs 14:6; 22:11; 23:25.

15. Ps 1:2 uses הָגָה, which refers naturally to the sounds made by creatures—the cooing of doves (Isa 38:14; 59:11; Nah 2:8), the growl of lions (Isa 31:4)—but is also used of the sound of human utterance, whether private audible reading (Josh 1:8; Ps 1:2), rebellious plotting (Ps 2:1), or oral speech/proclamation (Pss 35:28; 37:30; 71:24; 115:7). Elsewhere in the Psalms this word is used of meditations on YHWH himself (Ps 63:7 [Eng 6]) or his deeds (77:13 [Eng 12]; 143:5). Psalm 119:97 uses the rare noun, שִׂיחָה, "meditation" (elsewhere only in Job 15:4), but it is cognate to a common denominative verb, שִׂיחַ, "to muse, complain, talk about." This is the psalmists' preferred expression for "muse" (77:7) or meditate upon (77:13//הָגָה); 119:15, 23, 27, 48, 78, 148, 145:5, though it may also be used of oral praise, singing (Ps 105:2 = 1 Chr 16:9).

volume, though reproducing them more or less as originally published precludes a smoothly flowing series of chapters. The articles included here represent literary and theological meditations on specific texts—arranged according to their order in Deuteronomy. For more general essays on hermeneutical, theological, and ethical issues raised by Deuteronomy, readers may consult the companion volume, *The Gospel according to Moses: Theological and Ethical Reflections on the Book of Deuteronomy*.

Each essay in this collection was written to stand on its own. Since they were originally presented orally and in print in widely different contexts, readers of the entire volume may notice some repetition. Commitments to the publishers of the earlier versions precluded eliminating redundancies with cross-references and summary statements when material presented earlier resurfaces. Unless otherwise indicated, generally the English translations of biblical texts are my own. I have tried to be consistent in rendering dates as BCE ("before the common era") and CE ("common era"), which Christians may also interpret as "before the Christian era" and "Christian era," respectively. The presentation of the divine name—represented by the Tetragrammaton, יהוה—is a particular problem for scholars. The practice of rendering the divine name in Greek as κύριος (= Hebrew אֲדֹנָי, "Adonay") is carried over into English translations as "LORD," which reflects the Hebrew יהוה, and distinguishes it from "Lord," which reflects Hebrew אֲדֹנָי. But this creates interpretive problems, for the connotations and implications of referring to someone by name or by title are quite different. Traditionally, when rendered as a name, English translations have vocalized יהוה as "Jehovah," which combines the consonants of יהוה with the vowels of אֲדֹנָי. Today non-Jewish scholars generally render the name as "Yahweh," recognizing that "Jehovah" is an artificial construct. Grateful that YHWH expressly revealed his name to his people and invited them to address him by name (e.g., Exod 3:13–15), but recognizing the uncertainty of its original vocalization and in deference to Jewish sensibilities regarding the name, in this volume the divine name is rendered simply with the English letters of the tetragrammaton, YHWH (except in direct quotations of English versions or secondary authors).

Behind the voice of Moses in the book of Deuteronomy we hear the voice of YHWH, for Moses repeatedly declares that all his instructions were given as YHWH his God had charged him. But YHWH, the God of Moses and Israel, is incarnate in Jesus Christ.[16] When Moses speaks of YHWH, he speaks of Jesus (cf. Luke 24:44). Deuteronomy was not only Jesus' favorite book in the Old Testament (judging by the frequency of quotations); he also stands behind the Torah left for our meditation and nurture by Moses. Although I do not expect all who read my essays to agree with me on all points of interpretation, I hope that all will recognize my love for the Torah of Moses, which is the Torah of YHWH. And I pray that my work will help many discover anew in the book of Deuteronomy the divinely breathed, hence living and transforming, Scripture of which Saint Paul, the New Testament Moses, spoke in 2 Tim 3:16. May we, like the apostle, find in the "Book of the Torah of Moses" a sure and effective source for teaching, reproof, correction, training in righteousness, and equipping God's people for every good work to the glory of God.

16. Cf. Rom 10:13; 1 Cor 1:31; 2:16; 2 Cor 10:17; Phil 2:10–11. For further discussion of this matter, see Block, "Who do Commentators say 'the Lord' is?"

Acknowledgments

ALTHOUGH I AM RESPONSIBLE for this collection of essays on the book of Deuteronomy, this volume is the work of a community of friends and scholars who have inspired, nurtured, pushed, and corrected me and each other. Whereas in an earlier phase of my vocation I lived with Ezekiel in Babylon, for the past decade I have lived with Moses on the plains of Moab. However, the adventure represented by this volume began more than a quarter century ago, when I taught a Hebrew exegesis course on Deuteronomy for the first time. No matter how technical our explorations, when we read the Scriptures we must stand before the biblical text with reverence and awe, and let the voice of God transmitted through his authorized spokespersons penetrate our hearts and minds.

However, this conversation has not been a one-way monologue; it has been a lively dialogue. Sometimes when I read Deuteronomy and I hear the voice of Moses, I don't understand what I am hearing, and I ask for clarification. Sometimes what I hear sounds so different from what my ears have been trained to hear and my mind has been taught to accept. This leaves me puzzled and confused. Sometimes I hear the message clearly, but I don't like what I hear and I protest. The word of God challenges my theology and my understanding of piety. Sometimes I hear Moses pleading with me to abandon my idols and to follow the Lord more fully, and I resist his plea. But his voice exposes my self-centeredness and my hypocrisy. I do not love the Lord with all my heart and mind, with all my being, and with all my resources, and I certainly do not love my neighbor as myself. But thank you, Moses, for revealing to me the way of freedom and forgiveness; for reminding me of God's relentless pursuit of his people, and of his lavish grace.

Along the way, while Moses has been speaking to me, there have been many who have aided him by supporting me in my research on this remarkable book. This volume of essays is dedicated to two dozen students who have walked with me as I have walked with Moses. Many of these have sat through my lectures and seminars and offered welcome insights into the book, and helped me refine the ways in which I communicate my discoveries. Many have performed mundane tasks for me, scouring databases and libraries for secondary materials that might aid in our interpretation, or proofreading drafts for factual errors and stylistic infelicities. Specifically, I must acknowledge the assistance of Daniel Owens, whose diligence and extraordinary computer skills have saved me countless hours and immeasurable frustration and facilitated preparation of this first volume of essays for Cascade Books, and Jason Gile, who read the page proofs and assisted in indexing, along with Austin Surls and my wife Ellen.

Since most of the essays in this volume have been published elsewhere, I must express my deep gratitude to editors of journals and publishers of books for their grace and willingness to let us reprint what they had made available earlier. In keeping with our promise, we have acknowledged the original place of publication on a separate page below, as well as at the beginning of each reprinted article. The versions presented here retain the essence of the original publication. Naturally, to produce a coherent volume and to follow the stylistic standards of Cascade Books, we have had to modify these essays stylistically—some more than others. Where needed, we have corrected errors of substance or form in the original, and in a few minor details my mind has changed. But readers should find no dissonance between the present forms of these essays and the original publications.

Special thanks are due to Robin Parry and Christian Amondson, for their enthusiasm for this project and the efficiency with which they have handled all the business and editorial matters. From the first conversation at the annual meeting of the Society of Biblical Literature in Atlanta, they have encouraged us and offered all the help we needed to produce it to their specifications. I am grateful to the administrators and my faculty colleagues at Wheaton College, for the unwavering institutional support and encouragement they offer, not only by creating a wonderful teaching environment, but also for providing the resources for our research. I am deeply grateful to Bud and Betty Knoedler, who have given so generously to underwrite my professorial chair. It is a special grace to know them not only as supporters of Wheaton College, but also as personal friends.

Ellen and I are grateful for their daily prayers on our behalf. I eagerly also acknowledge Ellen, the delight of my life, who has stood by me as a gracious friend and counselor for more than four decades. Without her love and wisdom, the work represented here would either never have been finished, or it would have taken a different turn.

Finally, we must give praise to God. Unlike others who serve gods of wood and stone, that have eyes but don't see, ears but don't hear, and mouths but don't speak, we have a God who speaks. By his grace he revealed himself to Israel by name and by deed, and by his grace he revealed to them his will (Deut 4:6–8). This God, who introduced himself to Israel as YHWH, has introduced himself to us in the person of Jesus Christ. If in the Torah of Deuteronomy we hear his voice, this is a supreme grace, mediated by Moses. But this grace has been surpassed in Jesus Christ. He does not merely mediate the grace of God; he embodies it (John 1:16–17), for he is YHWH incarnate (John 1:23). To him be ultimate praise and glory.

Credits

I HEREBY GRATEFULLY ACKNOWLEDGE PERMISSION to republish articles that have appeared elsewhere:

Chapter 1: "The Grace of Torah: The Mosaic Prescription for Life (Deut 4:1–8; 6:20–25)," was previously published in *Bibliotheca Sacra* 162 (2005) 3–22.

Chapter 3: "Bearing the Name of the LORD with Honor," was previously published in *Bibliotheca Sacra* 168 (2011) 20–31.

Chapter 4: "How Many Is God? An Investigation into the Meaning of Deuteronomy 6:4–5," was previously published in *Journal of the Evangelical Theological Society* 47 (2004) 193–212.

Chapter 5: "The Joy of Worship: The Mosaic Invitation to the Presence of God (Deut 12:1–14)," was previously published in *Bibliotheca Sacra* 162 (2005) 131–49.

Chapter 6: "The Burden of Leadership: The Mosaic Paradigm of Kingship (Deut 17:14–20)," was previously published in *Bibliotheca Sacra* 162 (2005) 259–78.

Chapter 7: "The Privilege of Calling: The Mosaic Paradigm for Missions (Deut. 26:16–19)," was previously published in *Bibliotheca Sacra* 162 (2005) 387–405.

Abbreviations

AB	Anchor Bible
ABD	*Anchor Bible Dictionary*. Edited by D. N. Freedman. 6 vols. Garden City, NY: Doubleday, 1992.
AHw	*Akkadisches Handwörterbuch*. Edited by W. von Soden. 3 vols. Wiesbaden: Harrassowitz, 1965–81
AJT	*Asia Journal of Theology*
ANET	*Ancient Near Eastern Texts Relating to the Old Testament*. Edited by James B. Pritchard. 3rd ed. Princeton: Princeton University Press, 1969
AnOr	Analecta orientalia
AOAT	Alter Orient und Altes Testament
ASORDS	American School of Oriental Research Dissertation Series
ASV	American Standard Version
AUSS	*Andrews University Seminary Studies*
AV	Authorized Version
BA	*Biblical Archaeologist*
BAR	*Biblical Archaeology Review*
BASOR	*Bulletin of the American Schools of Oriental Research*
BDB	Brown, F., S. R. Driver, and C. A. Briggs. *A Hebrew and English Lexicon of the Old Testament*. Oxford: Oxford University Press, 1907
BECNT	Baker Exegetical Commentary on the New Testament
Bib	*Biblica*
BN	*Biblische Notizen*
BR	*Biblical Research*
BRev	*Bible Review*
BSL	Biblical Studies Library
BWANT	Beiträge zur Wissenschaft vom Alten und Neuen Testament
BZ	*Biblische Zeitschrift*

BZAW	Beihefte zur Zeitschrift für die alttestamentliche Wissenschaft
CAD	*The Assyrian Dictionary of the Oriental Institute of the University of Chicago.* Chicago: Oriental Institute, 1956–2011
CBOT	Coniectanea biblica Old Testament Series
CBQ	*Catholic Biblical Quarterly*
COS	*The Context of Scripture.* Edited by W. W. Hallo. 3 vols. Leiden: Brill, 1997–2002
DCH	*Dictionary of Classical Hebrew.* Edited by D. J. A. Clines. Sheffield: Phoenix, 1993–
DDD	*Dictionary of Deities and Demons in the Bible.* Edited by K. van der Toorn, B. Becking, and P. W. van der Horst. Rev. ed. Leiden: Brill, 1999
DJD	Discoveries in the Judaean Desert
DNWSI	*Dictionary of the North-West Semitic Inscriptions.* J. Hoftijzer and K. Jongeling. 2 vols. Leiden: Brill, 1995
EA	El-Amarna tablets. According to the edition of J. A. Knudtzon. *Die El-Amarna-Tafeln mit Einleitung un Erläuterungen.* Leipzig: J. C. Hinrichs, 1908–1915. Reprint, Aalen: Otto Zeller, 1964. Supplemented in A. F. Rainey, *El-Amarna Tablets 359–379.* 2nd ed. AOAT 8. Neukirchen-Vluyn: Neukirchener, 1978
EAJT	*East Asia Journal of Theology*
EncJud1	*Encyclopaedia Judaica.* 1st ed. 16 vols. Jerusalem: Keter, 1972
EncJud2	*Encyclopaedia Judaica.* 2nd ed. 22 vols. Edited by F. Skolnik. Farmington Hills, MI: Gale, 2007
EQ	*Evangelical Quarterly*
ErIsr	*Eretz-Israel*
ESV	English Standard Version
ETL	*Ephemerides theologicae lovanienses*
ExpTim	*Expository Times*
HALOT	Koehler, L., W. Baumgartner, and J. J. Stamm, *The Hebrew and Aramaic Lexicon of the Old Testament.* Translated and edited under the supervision of M. E. J. Richardson. 4 vols. Leiden: Brill, 1994–1999
HCSB	Holman Christian Standard Bible

HdO	Handbuch der Orientalistik
HSM	Harvard Semitic Monographs
HSS	Harvard Semitic Studies
HUCA	*Hebrew Union College Annual*
ICC	International Critical Commentary
IDB	*The Interpreter's Dictionary of the Bible.* Edited by G. A. Buttrick. Nashville: Abingdon, 1964
Int	*Interpretation*
ISBE	*International Standard Bible Encyclopedia.* Rev. ed. 3 vols. Grand Rapids: Eerdmans, 1976–86
JAOS	*Journal of the American Oriental Society*
JB	Jerusalem Bible
JBL	*Journal of Biblical Literature*
JBLMS	Journal of Biblical Literature Monograph Series
JBTh	*Jahrbuch für Biblische Theologie*
JCS	*Journal of Cuneiform Studies*
JETS	*Journal of the Evangelical Theological Society*
JHS	*Journal of Hellenic Studies*
JJS	*Journal of Jewish Studies*
JNES	*Journal of Near Eastern Studies*
JQR	*Jewish Quarterly Review*
JSOT	*Journal for the Study of the Old Testament*
JSOTSup	Journal for the Study of the Old Testament Supplement Series
JTI	*Journal of Theological Interpretation*
KAI	*Kanaanäische und aramäische Inschriften.* H. Donner and W. Röllig. 2nd ed. Wiesbaden: Harrassowitz, 1966–69
LCC	Library of Christian Classics
LCL	Loeb Classical Library
LSJ	Liddell, H. G., R. Scott, and H. S. Jones. *A Greek-English Lexicon.* 9th ed., with revised supplement. Oxford: Oxford University Press, 1996
NAC	New American Commentary
NAS	New American Standard
NCB	New Century Bible
NIBC	New International Biblical Commentary
NICNT	New International Commentary on the New Testament
NICOT	New International Commentary on the Old Testament

NIDOTTE	*New International Dictionary of Old Testament Theology & Exegesis*. Edited by Willem VanGemeren. 5 vols. Grand Rapids: Zondervan, 1997
NIGTC	New International Greek Testament Commentary
NIV	New International Version
NIVAC	New International Version Application Commentary
NJB	New Jerusalem Bible
NJPSV	Tanakh: The Holy Scriptures: The New JPS Translation according to the Traditional Hebrew Text
NLT	New Living Translation
NRSV	New Revised Standard Version
NSBT	New Studies in Biblical Theology
NTL	New Testament Library
OBO	Orbis biblicus et orientalis
OBT	Overtures to Biblical Theology
OTL	Old Testament Library
OTS	Old Testament Studies
RHR	*Revue de l'histoire des religions*
RSV	Revised Standard Version
SAA	State Archives of Assyria
SBAB	Stuttgarter biblische Aufsatzbände
SBB	Stuttgarter biblische Beiträge
SBLDS	Society of Biblical Literature Dissertation Series
SBLSCS	Society of Biblical Literature Septuagint and Cognate Studies
SBLWAW	Society of Biblical Literature Writings from the Ancient World
SBS	Stuttgarter Bibelstudien
SBT	Studies in Biblical Theology
SBTJ	*The Southern Baptist Theological Journal*
SBTS	Sources for Biblical and Theological Study
ScrHier	Scripta hierosolymitana
SE	*Studia Evangelica*
STDJ	Studies on the Texts of the Desert of Judah
TDNT	*Theological Dictionary of the New Testament*. Edited by G. Kittel and G. Friedrich. Translated by G. W. Bromiley. 10 vols. Grand Rapids: Eerdmans, 1964–76.

THAT	*Theologisches Handwörterbuch zum Alten Testament.* Edited by E. Jenni, with assistance from C. Westermann. 2 vols. Munich: Kaiser, 1971–76
TDOT	*Theological Dictionary of the Old Testament.* Edited by G. J. Botterweck and H. Ringgren. Translated by J. T. Willis, G. W. Bromiley, and D. E. Green. 15 vols. Grand Rapids: Eerdmans, 1964–76
TLOT	*Theological Lexicon of the Old Testament.* Edited by E. Jenni, with assistance from C. Westermann. Translated by M. E. Biddle. 3 vols. Peabody, MA: Hendrickson, 1997
TNIV	Today's New International Version
TOTC	Tyndale Old Testament Commentaries
UBL	Ugaritisch-Biblische Literatur
VTSup	Vetus Testamentum Supplement Series
WBC	Word Biblical Commentary
WMANT	Wissenschaftliche Monographien zum Alten und Neuen Testament
WOO	Wiener Offene Orientalistik
WTJ	*Westminster Theological Journal*
WUNT	Wissenschaftliche Untersuchungen zum Neuen Testament
ZAW	*Zeitschrift für die alttestamentliche Wissenschaft*
ZTK	*Zeitschrift für Theologie und Kirche*

1

The Grace of Torah

The Mosaic Prescription for Life (Deut 4:1–8; 6:20–25)[1]

T HE POWER OF GOD'S "word" is seen in the Old Testament in several ways. First, it is God's utterance that called the universe into existence. Stated repeatedly in Gen 1, this is eloquently summarized in Ps 33:6: "By the word of YHWH the heavens were made, and by the breath of his mouth all their host."

Second, the "word" is the divine utterance that determines the course of history, as in Isa 44:24–28:

> Thus says the Lord, your Redeemer, who formed you from the womb: "I am the Lord, who made all things, who alone stretched out the heavens, who spread out the earth by myself, who frustrates the signs of liars and makes fools of diviners, who turns wise men back and makes their knowledge foolish, who confirms the word of his servant and fulfills the counsel of his messengers, who says of Jerusalem, 'She shall be inhabited,' and of the cities of Judah, 'They shall be built, and I will raise up their ruins'; who says to the deep, 'Be dry; I will dry up your rivers'; who says of Cyrus, 'He is my shepherd, and he shall fulfill all my purpose'; saying of Jerusalem, 'She shall be built,' and of the temple, 'Your foundation shall be laid.'" (ESV)

This is also expressed in Isa 46:9–11:

1. This essay was previously published in *Bibliotheca Sacra* 162 (2005) 3–22.

"I am God, and there is no other; I am God, and there is none like me, declaring the end from the beginning and from ancient times things not yet done, saying, 'My counsel shall stand, and I will accomplish all my purpose,' calling a bird of prey from the east, the man of my counsel from a far country. I have spoken, and I will bring it to pass [or, make it happen]; I have purposed, and I will do it." (ESV)

Third, God's "word" is powerful in calling people to life or verbally declaring their death. An example of the first of these is Ezek 16:3–7:

Thus says the Lord God to Jerusalem: "Your origin and your birth are of the land of the Canaanites; your father was an Amorite and your mother a Hittite. And as for your birth, on the day you were born your cord was not cut, nor were you washed with water to cleanse you, nor rubbed with salt, nor wrapped in swaddling cloths. No eye pitied you, to do any of these things to you out of compassion for you, but you were cast out on the open field, for you were abhorred, on the day that you were born. And when I passed by you and saw you wallowing in your blood, I said to you in your blood, 'Live!' . . . I made you flourish like a plant of the field. And you grew up and became tall and arrived at full adornment. Your breasts were formed, and your hair had grown; yet you were naked and bare." (ESV)

An illustration of the latter (declaring death) is Ps 90:3. "You return a person to the dust, by simply saying, 'Return, O member of the human race!'"

All these statements have to do with the power of God's *oral* word. This article, however, focuses on the power of his *written* word, by noting two little-known texts in Moses' farewell addresses to his people on the plains of Moab. The first, Deut 4:1–8, appears near the end of his first address; the second, Deut 6:20–25, near the beginning of his second address. In looking at these passages two important hermeneutical principles are illustrated. First, in interpreting a biblical text the most important clues to its meaning must be derived from the immediate literary context. Second, biblical texts must always be interpreted in the light of the broader cultural context from which they derive.

What Mean These Laws?

In his second farewell pastoral address to his people Moses raised an important question. "When your son asks you in time to come, 'What is the meaning of the covenant stipulations and the ordinances and the laws that YHWH our God has commanded you?' . . ." (Deut 6:20, author's translation).

The form in which Moses cast the question arose out of the everyday experience of parents trying to raise their children. I shall never forget one evening when my family was eating supper. As is often the case with teenagers, we were engaged in a rather warm discussion. Suddenly our son burst out, "Why do we have to live in such a prehistoric family?" While his motives left something to be desired, I took this as a compliment. At least he recognized that our household was run by countercultural norms!

The point Moses raised is that succeeding generations would not experience what the people in his audience shared, either of YHWH's revelation at Sinai or the present discourses about that revelation on the plains of Moab. Therefore it was necessary for that and all subsequent generations to be intentional in transmitting their faith to the next generation. As in every social context and every age, children watch the way their parents live, and especially when faced with the challenge of competing cultures, they are curious about the nature and rationale behind their own traditions. Moses assumed that the children would ask their parents for an explanation of their way of life.

The specific question Moses anticipated here concerns the covenant stipulations (עֵדֹת), ordinances (חֻקִּים), and regulations (מִשְׁפָּטִים) that YHWH had commanded Israel to observe. These three expressions represent the will of God as it had been revealed primarily at Horeb and to a lesser degree *en route* to the Promised Land. They point to all the moral, ceremonial, and civil regulations God prescribed as the appropriate response to his salvation and the privilege of covenant relationship. As illustrated so impressively in Lev 19, this revelation did not divide life into the sacred and the ordinary. When children of Israelite parents would observe how their parents conducted their private and family lives, how they carried on their social and economic relations, how they worshiped, how they conducted themselves within the family, then they would inquire about the meaning of it all. Of course, the children's question did not call for a detailed exposition of each of the 613 laws in the Pentateuch but rather an explanation of the significance of the entire package.[2] In short, "Why is it that our lives are governed by this set of principles?" and "What is the significance of this set of laws?"

If we were asked today, "What is the significance of the stipulations, the ordinances, and laws that God commanded the Israelites to observe?" we would probably respond with different answers. Reading the Mosaic laws, some probably shake their heads in bewilderment, wondering whether there is any point to these laws. An example is Lev 19:19. "You shall keep my statutes. You shall not let your cattle breed with a different kind. You shall not sow your field with two kinds of seed, nor shall you wear a garment of cloth made of two kinds of material." Another example is Lev 11:3–6. "Whatever parts the hoof and is cloven-footed and chews the cud, among the animals, you may eat. Nevertheless, among those that chew the cud or part the hoof, you shall not eat these: The camel, because it chews the cud but does not part the hoof, is unclean to you. And the rock badger, because it chews the cud but does not part the hoof, is unclean to you. And the hare, because it chews the cud but does not part the hoof, is unclean to you."

If we are not actually bewildered by these kinds of laws, we may still feel sorry for the Israelites. What a burden they were called on to bear! Surely many Israelites must have looked with envy on other nations that were not saddled with these requirements.

Some people with cultural and antiquarian interests, especially those interested in the history of law and culture, might say these laws offer readers today an interesting window into the society of ancient Israel. Readers familiar with the Near Eastern legal world of the second millennium BCE might even conclude that these laws represent a significant advance on those found in the Law Code of Hammurabi, king of Babylon in the nineteenth century BCE.

My suspicion, however, is that many of us would not have answered the question in either of these ways. When asked about the significance of the Law for Israel, many Christians today would answer that for Israel the Law was the way of salvation. They say that whereas after the Cross

---

2. Maimonides, twelfth-century CE Jewish scholar and philosopher, was one of the first to point out that the number of laws in the Pentateuch total 613. See Reines, "Commandments, The 613," 760–83; see also Lev, *Sepher Mitzvoth*. The laws are helpfully reproduced by Sailhamer, in *Pentateuch as Narrative*, 481–516.

people are saved by grace, people under the old covenant were saved by keeping the Law.

The problem with this explanation is that it flies in the face of Paul's explicit statements that even in the Old Testament people (like Abraham) were justified by faith rather than through obedience to the Law (Rom 4; Gal 3:1–12). In fact, many view the Mosaic law not as a way of salvation but as the way of death. And they quote Paul to buttress their position, for he wrote in Rom 4:15, "The law brings wrath," and in Rom 7:6, "But now we have been released from the Law, having died to that by which we were bound" (NASB). According to Gal 3, "all who rely on works of the law are under a curse" (v. 10), and "the law is not of faith" (v. 12), and "Christ redeemed us from the curse of the law" (v. 13). Also Paul wrote in verses 23–24, "Before faith came, we were kept in custody under the Law, being shut up to the faith which was later to be revealed. Therefore the Law has become our tutor" (NASB). And in 4:21–31 Paul wrote that Mount Sinai (who is Hagar) bears children who are slaves, in contrast to Jerusalem, our mother, who has borne free children.

These verses seem to offer a clear answer to the question that Moses raised: The significance of the Law lies in its power to bind those who are under the Law, to subject them to the curse and the wrath of God, and to demonstrate their desperate need of a Savior. While on the surface this seems to be the way the New Testament perceives the Law, it raises serious questions about both the justice and mercy of God. How and why would God rescue the Israelites from the burdensome and death-dealing slavery of Egypt (Exod 20:2) only to impose on them an even heavier burden of the Law, which they were unable to keep and which would sentence them to an even more horrible fate—damnation under his own wrath?

Moses' First Answer

Moses answered this question in two ways. First, he stated that *knowledge of the will of God is the supreme privilege of the covenant people of God.* One of the most important guidelines for biblical hermeneutics is to interpret Scripture with Scripture. And this is what we are doing when we appeal to Paul for the answer to Moses' question. But sometimes we move too quickly to later texts, especially the New Testament, and we forget the primacy of the immediate context in determining the meaning of a statement in Scripture. The fact is that Moses had already given a partial answer to the question he raised in Deut 6:20. In 4:1–8 he had offered a remarkable commentary on the significance of the Law.

> And now, O Israel, listen to the statutes and the rules that I am teaching you, and do them, that you may live, and go in and take possession of the land that the Lord, the God of your fathers, is giving you. You shall not add to the word that I command you, nor take from it, that you may keep the commandments of the Lord your God that I command you. Your eyes have seen what the Lord did at Baal-peor, for the Lord your God destroyed from among you all the men who followed the Baal of Peor. But you who held fast to the Lord your God are all alive today. See, I have taught you statutes and rules, as the Lord my God commanded me, that you should do them in the land that you are entering to take possession of it. Keep them and do them, for that will be your wisdom and your understanding in the sight of the peoples, who, when they hear all these statutes, will say, "Surely this great nation is a wise and understanding people." For what great nation is there that has a god so near to it as the Lord our God is to us, whenever we call upon him? And what great nation is there, that has statutes and rules as righteous as all this law [read Torah] that I set before you today? (ESV)

In these verses Moses made three points. First, the Torah he was teaching is normative and canonical by definition (vv. 1–2). By warning his hearers not to add anything to his word, he declared that *only* what he (on behalf of YHWH) prescribed was normative. By warning them not to delete anything from his word, he declared that *all* that he (on behalf of YHWH) prescribed was normative.[3] As Moses again stated later, everything he said was binding on Israel (12:32).[4] But this was no outra-

---

3. Moses' warning against adding to or deleting his utterances follows a widespread ancient Near Eastern tradition of warnings (often curses) against altering documents attested in the epilogue to Hammurabi's Law Code (*ANET*, 178) and in treaty texts. Esarhaddon's Succession Treaty reads, "Whoever changes, disregards, transgresses or erases the oaths of this tablet or [dis]regards . . . this treaty and transgresses its oath, [*may the guardian(s) of*] this treaty tablet, king of the gods, and the great gods, my lords [. . .]" (Parpola and Watanabe, *Neo-Assyrian Treaties and Loyalty Oaths*, 44–45; cf. *ANET*, 538). For Hittite examples in treaties and edicts, see Beckman, *Hittite Diplomatic Texts*, 86, 112, 167, 175. Such formulations were also attached to ancient Greek and Roman treaties (Weinfeld, *Deuteronomy and the Deuteronomic School*, 262, for discussion and bibliography), as illustrated by 1 Macc 8:30 (the treaty between Judas Maccabeus and the Romans). Rev 22:18–19 echoes the wording of Deut 4:2.

4. Related expressions of this notion are given in Prov 30:6 and Eccl 3:14.

geous claim. As YHWH's authorized spokesman, Moses hereby presented
the obverse of the privilege of Israel's high calling. YHWH, their divine
Suzerain, who by grace had rescued them from the bondage of Egypt, and
who by grace had called Israel to covenant relationship with Himself, and
who by grace was calling on them to represent him to the world, retained
the exclusive right to define the appropriate response to the grace he had
lavished on them. Total acceptance of the will of the divine Benefactor
would be the correct and reasonable response.

Second, Moses affirmed that obedience to the Torah was the key to
life (4:3–4). The people standing before him had seen with their own eyes
the importance of obedience. In fact they were living proof of the principle. Adopting a method he would employ repeatedly in his addresses
(e.g., 30:15–20) and that the wisdom literature frequently employed,[5]
Moses declared that obedience to YHWH is a matter of life and death.
This was demonstrated at Baal Peor, which he took to be paradigmatic
for the nation on the move.[6] At each stage in Israel's journey the people
had been called on to decide whether they would remain true to YHWH
or not. According to Num 25:1–9, at Baal Peor a large number of those
who had survived the wilderness journey made the wrong decision by
"yoking themselves"[7] to the pagan god, Baal of Peor. Here Moses declared
YHWH's response in summary form: All those who "followed" after Baal
of Peor YHWH destroyed.[8] By contrast the people standing before Moses
were alive because they "held fast" to YHWH,[9] and were rewarded with

5. Ps 1; Prov 9:1–18; 19:16, and others.

6. Peor was a mountain in the vicinity of Mount Nebo to which Balak took Balaam
in hope of getting him to curse Israel (Num 23:28). Numbers 25:1–9 reports that later
at this same place the Israelites engaged in horrendous acts of idolatry and immorality.
Technically Baal Peor, that is, "Baal of Peor," identifies the local manifestation of Baal as
worshiped by the Moabites at this place. The first occurrence of the phrase in Deut 4:3
treats it as a place name, similar to others of this type, such as Baal Gad, Baal Hamon,
Baal Hazor, and others.

7. Num 25:3 (and Ps 106:28) uses the niphal stem of the root צמד, the noun form of
which is used of a team or yoke of draft animals.

8. According to Num 25:9, twenty-four thousand died as the result of a plague, apparently in addition to those killed by the valiant Phinehas.

9. The verb דָּבַק, which can describe a decisive commitment (Gen 2:24; Ruth 1:14),
occurs an additional four times in Deuteronomy (10:20; 11:22; 13:5[Eng 4]; 30:20).
Moses' choice of this the strongest of expressions for "sticking together" (cf. Job 29:10)
apparently answers to the expression for the idolators' "yoking themselves" to Baal Peor
(Num 25:3).

life. They were living testimony to the importance of obedience to the divine will as evidence of commitment to Him.

Third, Moses affirmed that knowledge of the Torah was the highest privilege imaginable (Deut 4:5–8). Here Moses put himself in the shoes of the nations around Israel, who would observe how Israel lived and then draw some rather remarkable conclusions—conclusions that catch many people today by surprise. If we had been responsible for verses 6–7, this is probably what *we* would have written: "You must keep the commandments and do them, for that is your duty and your obligation in the sight of the peoples, who, when they hear all these ordinances, will say, 'Surely this unfortunate nation is a sorrowful and burdened people.'" If our own context does not help us appreciate what Moses was saying, perhaps we should ask how the peoples around Israel at that time would have responded to the revelation of the will of God as the Israelites had received it. To understand the significance of the Torah, hear this prayer, written in Sumerian, dating back to the second millennium, but preserved in the library of Ashurbanipal, one of the kings of Assyria in the seventh century BCE.[10] The text—Prayer to Every God[11]—is repetitious, but to get the point we need to read the entire piece.

> May the fury of my lord's heart be quieted toward me.[12]
> May the god who is not known be quieted toward me;
> May the goddess who is not known be quieted toward me.
> May the god whom I know or do not know be quieted toward me;
> May the goddess whom I know or do not know be quieted toward me.
> May the heart of my god be quieted toward me;
> May the heart of my goddess be quieted toward me.
> May my god and goddess be quieted toward me.

10. "This prayer is addressed to no particular god, but to all gods in general, even those who may be unknown. The purpose of the prayer is to claim relief from suffering, which the writer understands is the result of some infraction of divine law. He bases his claim on the fact that his transgressions have been committed unwittingly, and that he does not even know what god he may have offended. Moreover, he claims, the whole human race is by nature ignorant of the divine will, and consequently is constantly committing sin. He therefore ought not to be singled out for punishment" (F. J. Stephens, in *ANET*, 391–92).

11. Adapted from ibid.

12. According to Stephens the Sumerian is literally, "of my lord, may his angry heart return to its place for me" (ibid.). The phrase "return to its place," a figurative expression for "settle down," suggests the imagery of a raging storm or of water boiling in a kettle.

May the god [who has become angry with me][13] be quieted toward me;
May the goddess [who has become angry with me] be quieted
     toward me.
[Lines 11–18 cannot be restored with certainty.]
In ignorance I have eaten that forbidden of my god;
In ignorance I have set foot on that prohibited by my goddess.
O Lord, my transgressions are many; great are my sins.
O my god, (my) transgressions are many; great are (my) sins.
O my goddess, (my) transgressions are many; great are (my) sins.
O god, whom I know or do not know, (my) transgressions are
     many; great are (my) sins;
O goddess, whom I know or do not know, (my) transgressions are
     many; great are (my) sins.
The transgression that I have committed, indeed I do not know;
The sin that I have done, indeed I do not know.
The forbidden thing that I have eaten, indeed I do not know;
The prohibited (place) on which I have set foot, indeed I do not know.
The lord in the anger of his heart looked at me;
The god in the rage of his heart confronted me;
When the goddess was angry with me, she made me become ill.
The god whom I know or do not know has oppressed me;
The goddess whom I know or do not know has placed suffering
     upon me.
Although I am constantly looking for help, no one takes me by
     the hand;
When I weep they do not come to my side.
I utter laments, but no one hears me;
I am troubled;
I am overwhelmed;
I cannot see.
O my god, merciful one, I address to you the prayer,
"Ever incline to me";
I kiss the feet of my goddess;
I crawl before you.
[Lines 41–49 are mostly broken and cannot be restored with
     certainty.]
How long, O my goddess, whom I know or do not know, before
     your hostile heart will be quieted?
Man is dumb; he knows nothing;
Mankind, everyone that exists—what does he know?

13. The restoration is based on line 32, after Langdon, *Babylonian Penitential Psalms*,
39–44.

Whether he is committing sin or doing good, he does not even
    know.
O my lord, do not cast your servant down;
He is plunged into the waters of a swamp; take him by the hand.
The sin that I have done, turn into goodness;
The transgression that I have committed let the wind carry away;
My many misdeeds strip off like a garment.
O my god, (my) transgressions are seven times seven; remove my
    transgressions;
O my goddess, (my) transgressions are seven times seven; remove
    my transgressions;
O god whom I know or do not know, (my) transgressions are
    seven times seven; remove my transgressions;
O goddess whom I know or do not know, (my) transgressions are
    seven times seven; remove my transgressions.
Remove my transgressions (and) I will sing your praise.
May your heart, like the heart of a real mother, be quieted toward me;
Like a real mother (and) a real father may it be quieted toward me.

Is this not a pathetic piece? And what an indictment this prayer is on the religious systems of the world around ancient Israel! To be sure, with his keen sense of sin and his awareness of ultimate accountability before his deities, this person expresses greater enlightenment than many people today. However, he could not escape the fact that he was faced with three insurmountable problems. First, he did not know which god he had offended. Second, he did not know what the offense was. Third, he did not know what it would take to satisfy the god or gods. Contrast this with Moses' statements in Deut 4:1–8. With their clear knowledge of the will of YHWH, the faithful in Israel perceived themselves as an incredibly privileged people and the envy of the nations. Unlike other peoples, whose gods of wood and stone crafted by human hands neither saw nor heard nor smelled (Deut 4:28; cf. Ps 135:15–17), YHWH hears his people when they call on him (Deut 4:7). And unlike the nations, whose idols have mouths but they do not speak (Ps 135:16), Israel's God has spoken. By his grace God has given his people statutes and judgments that are perfect in righteousness (Deut 4:8), because (A) they reveal with perfect clarity who he is, (B) they reveal with perfect clarity what sin is, and (C) they reveal with perfect clarity how that sin may be removed and a relationship of peace and confidence with him established and maintained. This explains why, when David experienced forgiveness for his sins, he could exclaim, "Oh, the joy [or, privilege] of the one whose transgression is forgiven, whose sin is covered!" (Ps 32:1, author's translation). Why would anyone give up this sparkling spring of water that leads to life for the broken cisterns of idolatry that can yield only death (cf. Jer 2:9–13)?

Moses' Second Answer

This prepares us for Moses' second answer to the question he asked in Deut 6:20: *Obedience to the will of God is the supreme delight of the covenant people of God.* Hear Moses' words in Deuteronomy 6:21–25:

> Then you shall say to your son, "We were Pharaoh's slaves in Egypt. And YHWH brought us out of Egypt with a mighty hand. And YHWH showed signs and wonders, great and grievous, against Egypt and against Pharaoh and all his household, before our eyes. And he brought us out from there, that he might bring us in and give us the land that he swore to give to our fathers. And YHWH commanded us to do all these statutes, to fear YHWH our God [or, to practice all these ordinances as an expression of the fear of YHWH our God], for our good always, that he might preserve us alive, as we are this day. And it will be righteousness for us, if we are careful to do all this commandment before YHWH our God, as he has commanded us." (ESV)

This answer to Moses' question in verse 20 has been called a "family catechism."[14] With this response Moses declared that the primary motive for an Israelite's life was not a system of rules but knowledge of the salvation YHWH wrought on their behalf by his mighty power and grace. Obedience to the revealed will of God is presented as a *response* to the glorious "gospel" of salvation, as evidence of fear or love for Him, and a mark of gratitude for all he has done for them. A life ordered by the stipulations of the Mosaic covenant was to be their response to their own history.

Four elements in these verses present the foundation of YHWH's covenant relationship with Israel and at the same time declare in a nutshell the essential elements of Old Testament theology. First, God rescued Israel from the bondage of Egypt with a mighty hand (v. 21). Second, he performed great and devastating signs and wonders in Egypt while the Israelites watched, thereby declaring them his special people (v. 22). Third,

14. Cf. Weinfeld, *Deuteronomy 1–11*, 328–29.

YHWH brought Israel out of that land in order to bring them into the land he had promised on oath to their ancestors (v. 23). Fourth, YHWH spoke to the Israelites at Sinai, revealing to them his will (v. 24).

The giving of the Law was thus a climactic moment of divine *grace*. YHWH's rescue of Israel was significant both soteriologically and judicially. He freed his chosen people from slavish vassaldom in Egypt and claimed them as his own vassals, a status symbolized by the stipulations, decrees, and laws, to which he demanded compliance. But these laws were not to be viewed as a burden laid on their shoulders that was so heavy that no one could carry it. That is not grace! That is tyranny and deceit. To Moses, receiving the revelation of God's will was a supreme *privilege*—and the more detailed the revelation the greater the privilege. The Israelites had been liberated from the bondage of Egypt that they might become the privileged servants of YHWH, in fact, his "sons" (14:1).

No wonder the Apostle John could write, after four decades of reflection on the significance of the Incarnation, "And from his fullness we have all received, grace upon grace. For the law [i.e., the Torah] was given [ἐδόθη] through Moses; grace and truth came [or, happened, ἐγένετο] through Jesus Christ" (John 1:16–17). Contrary to the interpretation of this verse suggested by the inserted adversative conjunction "but" in the King James Version, the contrast here is *not* between law and grace, but between two ways in which grace has been communicated in two climactic moments in time: first, the grace of the Torah was mediated through Moses; second, grace and truth have been personified in Christ. Moses certainly viewed the revelation of the laws at Sinai as a climactic moment of grace, as did the poet who penned Ps 119 centuries later. And this is how we should view the law of God, whether it is the law revealed in the Old Testament or the law as it is revealed in the New Testament.

When our children ask us why we have to go to church, or why we have to live by such old-fashioned standards, or why we have to put money in the offering plate, or why we feel compelled to speak up about the evils of our day, can we answer as Moses did? Many Christians say inwardly if not outwardly, "I wish I weren't a Christian. I wouldn't have to do all these things and my conscience wouldn't bother me if I swindled a little as I scratch my way to the top." We should feel sorry for people like that, people for whom the Christian life is a burden, an obligation, fixed by a code of laws.

How different was Moses' response. What is the significance of all these stipulations, laws, and regulations? They represented the glorious privilege the redeemed Israelites enjoyed in being bond servants of YHWH. The laws provided a way of saying "thank you" to God for the deliverance he gave them in the Exodus, for the delight of being his covenant people, for the privilege of receiving the Promised Land as his gift. The revelation of the Law was a supreme act of grace preceded and superseded only by the experience of the Exodus itself. It represented the climactic moment of a whole series of events by which YHWH delivered Israel from bondage. Obeying God's commands was a delight. And so today believers should delight in obeying Him.

However, some people today think of the Mosaic law as a burden, a complex series of obligations by which to earn salvation. Others think that because of their salvation, they are free to do as they please. Of course both ideas pervert the Scriptures.

In Deut 6:24–25 Moses finally answered the question, "What is the significance of the stipulations, ordinances, and laws that YHWH has commanded us?" His answer consists of four significant declarations. First, he said that YHWH had given the Israelites the Law as a visible means of demonstrating their fear for Him: "And YHWH commanded us to practice all these statutes as an expression of fear of YHWH our God."[15] Throughout the Book of Deuteronomy Moses associated knowledge of the will of God with the fear of God, as in the following paradigm:

Reading ⇨ Hearing ⇨ Learning ⇨ Fear ⇨ Obedience ⇨ Life.[16]

The relationship between fear and obedience is clearly illustrated in 10:12–13. "And now, Israel, what does YHWH your God require of you, but to fear YHWH your God, to walk in all his ways, to love him, to serve YHWH your God with all your heart and with all your soul, and to keep

15. This follows Georg Braulik's reading of לְיִרְאָה אֶת־יהוה ("Gesetz als Evangelium," 139; and Braulik, "Law as Gospel," 7). This reading understands the preposition as a lamed of reference or standard. This interpretation finds support in the way Deuteronomy associates the fear of YHWH and obedience elsewhere. The form לְיִרְאָה, "to fear" occurs eight times in the book. Four verses mention fearing YHWH before obeying him (5:29; 10:12; 17:19; 31:12); and 4:10 and 14:23 mention fear but omit references to obedience. In 6:24 Moses reversed the order of the more common wording by mentioning obedience before fear. The present sequence is illogical, unless the lamed is understood as Braulik suggests. The present construction parallels that found in 28:58.

16. This is reflected most completely in Deut 17:18–20 and 31:9–13.

the commandments and statutes of YHWH, which I am commanding you today for your good?"

For future generations the knowledge of God's will would be the key to the proper fear of God.[17] In these contexts the verb יָרֵא means not only an awed disposition toward God but also often serves as the Old Testament word for "faith" in God that is demonstrated through obedience.

Second, Moses declared that YHWH gave Israel the Law for her own good—not to be a burden or a noose around their necks but as an incredible *benefit*. It is fascinating to observe how the word טוֹב is used in Deuteronomy. On the one hand, טוֹבָה, "[the] good," is used alongside הַיָּשָׁר "the right," to identify what is good in the eyes of YHWH, namely, conduct that arises out of love for him and is in accord with his will.[18] On the other hand the noun טוֹבָה, "[the] good,"[19] and the cognate verb יָטַב, "to experience good,"[20] frequently refer to the benefactions[21] that Israel would experience from the hand of YHWH in the land he gave them.[22] In 28:1–14 Moses gave concrete expression to "that which is good," while also highlighting the link between fidelity to the divine Suzerain, as expressed in obedience to his will, by framing this declaration with determinative conditional clauses: "If you faithfully obey the voice of YHWH your God, being careful to do all his commandments that I command you today" (v. 1); "if you obey the voice of YHWH your God" (v. 2); "if you keep the commandments of YHWH your God and walk in his ways" (v. 9); "if you

17. Hence Malachi's concluding challenge to remember the Law of Moses, that is, the statutes and ordinances revealed to him for the sake of all Israel (Mal 4:4). Malachi's concern had been to expose the evidences of the absence of fear of YHWH in the postexilic community.

18. Typically this is expressed as right or good action "in the eyes of YHWH" (6:18; 12:25, 28; 13:19[Eng 18]; 21:9), in contrast to what is evil (4:25; 9:18; 17:2; 31:29) and what is right in one's own eyes (12:8). In 1:23 Moses spoke of action that was good in his eyes.

19. Deut 6:24; 8:16; 26:11; 28:12, 63; cf. 10:13.

20. Deut 4:40; 5:16, 29, 33; 6:3, 18; 12:25, 28; 19:13; 22:7.

21. These benefits are referred to substantively as בִּרְכַּת יהוה, "the blessing of YHWH" (12:15; 16:17) and the blessing that he commanded on Israel and her barns, etc. (28:8; cf. also 11:26–27; 30:1, 19), and verbally as YHWH blessing Israel directly (1:11; 2:7; 7:13; 12:7; 14:24, 29; 15:4, 6, 10, 14, 18; 16:10, 15; 23:20; 24:13, 19; 26:15; 28:8; 30:16). For discussion of the reward for fidelity expressed in terms of blessing, see Weinfeld, *Deuteronomy and the Deuteronomic School*, 310–13.

22. The geographic context is highlighted by the frequent reference to the Promised Land as "the good land/ground" (1:25, 35; 3:25; 4:21–22; 6:18; 8:7, 10; 9:6; 11:17), and descriptions of the lavish resources of the land (8:7–10; 11:8–12).

obey the commandments of YHWH your God, which I command you today, being careful to do them, and if you do not turn aside from any of the words that I command you today, to the right hand or to the left, to go after other gods to serve them" (vv. 13–14).

From Deut 28:63 it is evident that YHWH does not dispense goodness to his people grudgingly; rather this is his greatest delight. However, obedience to the will of God is the prerequisite to such blessing.

Third, Moses declared that YHWH gave Israel the Law so that she might live. Of course obedience to the Law should not be understood as a way of self-redemption, and "to live" should not be interpreted in a soteriological sense of salvation from sin and the enjoyment of eternal life with God. According to 6:21–23 the divine act of "salvation" (deliverance from Egypt) was accomplished four decades earlier. What is envisioned is Israel's continued prosperous existence in the land and the fulfillment of YHWH's mission through her.

This interpretation is reinforced by the rare use of the piel form of the verb הָיָה, "to live." The piel appears elsewhere in 20:16, where it clearly means "to let live," and in 32:39, where it means "to restore someone to life,"[23] but neither meaning makes sense here. Lohfink has convincingly argued that here, as in many other occurrences in the Old Testament, the piel means "to maintain," with the infinitive construct assuming YHWH as the subject.[24] By his grace YHWH revealed to his people his will, which, if they would follow it, would result in his sustaining them alive, even as he was doing at the present moment. This accords with Deuteronomy's general emphasis on obedience to the Law as the key to a meaningful life,[25] not to mention the positive role of the Law in other Old Testament texts as well.[26]

Fourth, YHWH gave Israel the Law so that she might be confident of his approval. The fact that Deut 6:25 represents the climax of Moses' response to the children's question is signaled not only by its location at the center of this chiasm but also by the emphatic grammatical construction,

23. In this verse YHWH is the subject of אֲחַיֶּה, which is the antonym of אָמִית, "to slay, put to death."

24. Lohfink, "Deuteronomy 6:24," 111–19. Lohfink finds this usage of the piel in Neh 9:6; Pss 33:19; 41:3; Eccl 7:12; and Jer 49:11 and a cognate semantic analogue in the D stem of Akkadian *Balāṭu*, "to live" (ibid., 118).

25. Cf. Deut 4:1–4; 5:33; 8:1–3; 11:9; 16:20; 22:7; 30:16; 31:9–13; 32:46–47.

26. Lev 18:5; Neh 9:29; Pss 19:7–14; 119.

"And righteousness it will be for us if . . ." In the Old Testament the term
צְדָקָה, usually translated "righteousness," bears a variety of meanings,
ranging from "innocence" to "acquittal, justification" and "salvation."
The word occurs six times in Deuteronomy. In 33:21 Moses spoke of "the
righteousness of YHWH," which he equated with "his laws [מִשְׁפָּטָיו] with
Israel." This suggests that the word refers to the objective standards of
faith and conduct as determined by YHWH and outlined in the covenant
stipulations.[27] Elsewhere in Deuteronomy צְדָקָה denotes behavior that
conforms to the norms as established and represented in the stipulations of YHWH's covenant.[28] In 9:4–6 צְדָקָה is associated with "integrity"
(יֹשֶׁר לֵב, literally, "straightness or rightness of heart"), whose opposite
is represented by רִשְׁעָה, "wickedness, rebellion" (v. 5), קְשֵׁה עֹרֶף, "stiff-
neckedness, recalcitrance" (v. 6), and מָרָה, "to rebel" (v. 7).[29] In 24:13 the
act of returning before nightfall a cloak that a poor person had given as a
pledge is presented as a concrete illustration of covenant "righteousness."

According to 6:20–25, when a member of the covenant community
conscientiously obeyed the Law, YHWH accepted that as evidence of that
person's righteousness. This statement is among the most fundamental in
the Old Testament for understanding the relationship between human
works and human righteousness.

Two extremes must be avoided. The first is the notion that Moses
viewed obedience to the commandments as the *basis* of covenantal relationship. Moses had just declared (in vv. 21–23) that Israel's position as
the people of YHWH rested entirely on his saving actions, independently
of any Israelite merit. And in 9:1–24, especially verses 1–6, YHWH stated
that he had called Israel to himself and was about to give them the land in
spite of their unrighteousness. A second extreme to be rejected is the idea
that one may enjoy relationship with God to the full without obedience
to his commandments, as if a state can exist without concrete evidence

27. In 4:8 Moses observed that none of the nations possessed "ordinances" (חֻקִּים) and
"laws" (מִשְׁפָּטִים) as "righteous" (צַדִּיקִם) as the entire Torah that Moses was presenting to
his people. Following his own example in 1:16, in 16:18–20 Moses charged the people to
appoint judges who would serve the people with "righteous judgment" (מִשְׁפַּט־צֶדֶק), and
"righteous pronouncements" (דִּבְרֵי צַדִּיקִם). Indeed their single professional commitment
should be the pursuit of righteousness (צֶדֶק).

28. This probably accounts for the rendering of the word in 6:25 as ἐλεημοσύνη,
"charity, alms," in the Septuagint and *misericors*, "merciful," in the Vulgate.

29. In "the Song of YHWH" (usually referred to as "the Song of Moses") God in Deut
32:4 is characterized as "righteous and straight" (צַדִּיק וְיָשָׁר).

of that state. Genesis 15:6 provides a close analogue to the present text, except that there Abraham's faith was accounted to him as righteousness. However, it does not contradict this interpretation.[30] Elsewhere Abraham demonstrated his righteousness with obvious acts of obedience (cf. Jas 2:18–24). In both Gen 15:6 and Deut 6:25 צְדָקָה designates the loyalty of the human vassal before his divine Suzerain demonstrated in response acceptable to the Suzerain:[31] trust in YHWH's promises in the first instance[32] and scrupulous obedience to YHWH's commands in the second.[33]

Moses' point here was that the Israelites should demonstrate their loyalty to YHWH by adherence to the supreme commandment and by concrete acts of obedience to the detailed injunctions. When these arose out of genuine faith/fear, YHWH accepted them as proof of righteousness and responded with blessing and life. Conversely, he assumed that in the absence of obedience, faith was lacking and the covenant relationship rejected, to which YHWH responded with the curse and death.

Application

The significance of Deut 6:20–25 for Christians today is considerably greater than the length of the passage would suggest. First, it highlights the

30. The Targums translate צְדָקָה in 6:25 as "merit, credit." This meaning of the Aramaic צדקה is attested in extrabiblical inscriptions. (1) A seventh-century BCE Nerab Inscription reads, "Because of my righteousness/merit before him [i.e., the god], he afforded me a good name and lengthened my days." See the translation by Gibson, *Aramaic Inscriptions*, 97; see also Hoftijzer and Jongeling, *Dictionary of North-West Semitic Inscriptions*, 1:965. (2) A fifth-century BCE papyrus inscription from Elephantine in Egypt reads, "You will have merit before Yhwh the god of the heavens more than the person who offers him" (Cowley, *Aramaic Papyri*, 114, 118).

31. Contra Gibson (*Aramaic Inscriptions*, 82), in both of these contexts צדק bears the nuance of loyalty toward an overlord, comparable to that found in the eighth century BCE Samalian Aramaic inscription of Panamuwa II (*KAI* 215), where צדקה/צדק occurs three times (ll. 1, 11, 19) with this meaning. Note especially line 19: "Because of the loyalty [צדק] of my father and because of my loyalty [צדק], my lord [Tiglath-Pileser, king of Assyria] has caused me to reign [on the throne] of my father." For the translation, see *COS*, 2:159–60.

32. The idiom "to believe in/trust in" (Gen 15:6) is used in parallelism with בָּטַח, "to trust," in Job 39:11–12; Ps 78:22; and Mic 7:5.

33. In Deut 9:23 these two notions are linked not only with each other but also with rebellion. "And when YHWH sent you from Kadesh-barnea, saying, 'Go up and take possession of the land that I have given you,' then you rebelled [מְרָה] against the commandment of YHWH your God and did not believe [הָאֱמַנְתֶּם] him or obey [שְׁמַעְתֶּם] his voice." In 1:26, 43, מְרָה occurs as an expression of rebellion against YHWH.

importance of deliberate strategies for transmitting the faith. The Israelite regulations for ethics and worship offered many reasons to arouse the curiosity of outsiders and the uninitiated within the community. Moses hereby prescribed a method whereby the memory of YHWH's saving actions could be kept alive from generation to generation. As Judg 2 testifies, with the loss of the memory of his saving grace, apostasy and the Canaanization of culture followed close behind. The New Testament includes exhortations to pass on the faith from generation to generation (e.g., 2 Tim 2:2), and Jesus deliberately transformed the Passover, as prescribed in Exod 12–13, into YHWH's Supper in order for his followers to keep alive the memory of his saving actions: "Do this in remembrance of me" (Luke 22:19; 1 Cor 11:24). The communion meal offers Christians an opportunity to keep the memory of Christ's sacrifice fresh in their own minds and answer curious questions by outsiders and children. Like the Israelite system of regulations and laws, questions regarding this rite present a glorious opportunity for gospel witness.

Second, Deut 6:20–25 teaches clearly the relationship between law and grace within the divine plan of salvation and sanctification. The Scriptures are consistent in asserting that no one may perform works of righteousness sufficient to merit the saving favor of God. In the words of Isaiah, "All of us have become like one who is unclean, and all our righteous acts are like a polluted garment. We all fade like a leaf, and our iniquities, like the wind, take us away" (Isa 64:6).[34] And in the words of David, "Against you, you only, have I sinned and done what is evil in your sight, so that you are proved right when you speak and justified when you judge. Surely I was sinful at birth, sinful from the time my mother conceived me" (Ps 51:6–7, NIV). And in the New Testament Paul wrote, "All have sinned and fall short of the glory of God" (Rom 3:23).

However, within the gospel of salvation by grace alone through faith alone, YHWH graciously reveals the standard of righteousness by which his redeemed people may live and be confident of his approval. There is no conflict here between Law and grace. The Law was a gracious gift for Israel. It gave them an ever-present reminder of YHWH's deliverance, his power, his covenant faithfulness, and the way of life and prosperity.

But how is this perspective to be reconciled with Paul's statements regarding the death-dealing effect of the Law in contrast to the life that

---

34. Compare the repeated assertions of the psalmists that apart from a proper relationship with YHWH there is no one who does good (Ps 14:1, 4; 53:1, 3).

comes by the Spirit (Rom 2:12–13; 4:13–15; 7:6, 8–9; 8:2–4; 2 Cor 3:6; Gal 3:12–13, 21–24; 5:18)? In answering this question several important considerations must be kept in mind.

First, Moses' statement about the life-giving and sustaining effects of the Law is consistent with his teaching in Deut 30:15–20 and is consistent with the teaching of the Old Testament elsewhere. In Lev 18:5 YHWH declared, "Keep my decrees and laws, for the man who obeys them will live by them. I am YHWH" (NIV). Similar statements occur in Ezek 20:11 and 13 and Neh 9:29. The Psalter begins with an ode to the life-giving nature of the Law (1:1–6), and Ps 119 is devoted entirely to the positive nature of the Law. References to the relationship between life and keeping the Law are common (vv. 17, 40, 77, 93, 97, 116, 144, 156, 159, 175). The basic Old Testament stance is summarized by Habakkuk in 2:4, which in context is best interpreted, "As for the proud one, his person [נֶפֶשׁ, soul] is not right on the inside; but the righteous in his faithfulness shall live." Ezekiel offered an extended exposition of this notion in Ezek 18:1–23. After describing the ethical behavior of a person, Ezekiel declared that the person "is righteous; he shall surely live" (v. 9). After describing the unethical behavior of that person's son he declared, "He has committed all these abominations; he shall surely die" (v. 13). Later Ezekiel said that if a wicked man turns from his wickedness and observes all YHWH's decrees, and practices righteousness and justice, "he shall surely live" (vv. 21–23).[35] The assumption in each case is that outward actions reflect a person's inner spirit,[36] on the basis of which a judgment of the person's status may be made and the sentence of life or death rendered.

Second, from a hermeneutical and theological perspective, later revelation cannot correct earlier revelation, as if there were some defect in it. Later revelation may be more precise and more nuanced, but this cannot mean that earlier revelations were false. Accordingly Paul cannot be interpreted as *correcting* Moses, as if there were some flaw in Moses' teaching, which seems to be the case if Moses declared that there was a life-giving and sustaining function of the Law (cf. Lev 18:5), and later Paul declared the opposite as a dogmatic assertion. He would thereby have failed the traditional and primary test of a true prophet, namely, agreement with Moses (Deut 18:15–22). But his statements should be

---

35. For a detailed discussion of this chapter, see Block, *Ezekiel 1–24*, 554–90.
36. This principle is also seen in Jesus' teaching in Matt 7:15–23.

interpreted not only in the light of Moses, but also as assertions made in the context of particular arguments. In both Romans and Galatians Paul was responding to those who insisted that *salvation* comes by the works of the Law, as represented by circumcision. To those who represented this view he replied that if one looks to the Law as a *way of salvation*, it will lead to death. On the other hand, if one looks to the revealed will of God as a *guide*, it yields a life of blessing. On this matter Moses and Paul are in perfect agreement. The notion of "the obedience of faith," that is, a faith that is demonstrated through acts of obedience, is common to both Testaments (cf. Rom 8:4).[37] Both Testaments attest to the same paradigm: (A) YHWH's gracious (i.e., unmerited) saving actions yield the fruit of a redeemed people. (B) A redeemed people yield the fruit of righteous deeds. (C) Righteous deeds yield the fruit of divine blessing.

Perhaps the relevance of Deut 6:20–25 for us may be captured by recasting it as follows:

> When our children ask us in days to come, what is the meaning of the ordinances and customs that we Christians observe, then we will say, "We were slaves to sin, but YHWH rescued us from the kingdom of darkness with a strong hand, through the work of Christ on the cross and by raising Jesus from the dead. Moreover he showed great and distressing signs and wonders before the prince of the powers of this world and all who follow Him. He has brought us out from there in fulfillment of his promises and in accord with his glorious plan of salvation, in order to bring us into an inheritance eternal and imperishable. So YHWH commanded us to observe his commandments as an expression of our fear and love for Christ for our good always and for our survival as his people. And it will be righteousness for us if we are careful to show that we love God with all our hearts by doing all that he commanded us. Then we will hear him say, 'Well done, good and faithful servant. Enter into the joy of your Lord.'"

---

37. For a helpful discussion of these and related issues from the New Testament perspective, see Hafemann, *Paul, Moses, and the History of Israel.*

2

Reading the Decalogue Right to Left

The Ten Principles of Covenant Relationship in the Hebrew Bible[1]

Introduction

IN THE OPENING STATEMENT of the 1968 English edition of his mono-graph, *The Ten Commandments in New Perspective*, Eduard Nielsen writes: "Of all the passages in the Old Testament the Decalogue, 'the ten commandments,' is presumably the best known to western civilization, and not least in countries which have a Lutheran tradition."[2] Many will concur with this opinion. My own roots are not Lutheran, but growing up in a Mennonite community in northern Saskatchewan I certainly was an heir to this tradition.

How is it that this 3,000-year-old document has come to hold such sway in Christian circles when much of the rest of the Torah, especially the constitutional material, is ignored at best and rejected at worst? Many interpret the Decalogue as a distinctive statement of moral truth univer-sally applicable and permanently relevant. Martin Luther elevated it to the

---

1. The title is an adaptation of the title of an essay by Clines, "The Ten Commandments, Reading from Left to Right." A similar adaptation is used in Exum and Williamson, eds., *Reading from Right to Left: Essays on the Hebrew Bible in Honour of David J. A. Clines.*

2. Nielsen, *The Ten Commandments in New Perspective*, 1. Compare the observation of James Barr in the foreword to Nielsen's work: "The Ten Commandments constitute beyond doubt the best known and most influential single passage in the whole Old Testament." For full theological exposition of the terms of the Decalogue, see Miller, *The Ten Commandments.*

status of natural law.[3] Is this how the Scriptures, particularly the Hebrew Bible, want us to treat the Decalogue? Frank Crüsemann for one does not think so. Reflecting on the Decalogue in Christian theology, ethics, and especially catechesis, he categorically rejects the notion that this document can be regarded as a summary or essential statement of the Torah, and it was never intended to play this role.[4] The purpose of this essay is to explore whether or not Crüsemann is right. I shall do so by investigating how the Decalogue is perceived within the Hebrew Bible itself.

But this is an extremely complex matter and may be pursued from several angles. Some approach the issue by tracing the evolution of the text of the Decalogue. More than seventy-five years ago, Rudolf Kittel reduced the original text to ten short sentences.[5] Others investigate the redaction history of the narratives in which the document is embedded. Many conclude that the Decalogue is a late composition created by Deuteronomistic theologians as a ten-article compendium of covenantal expectations resembling a catechism to be used in lay instruction, and which was secondarily inserted into the Sinai narratives of Exod 19–24 and 32–34.[6]

However, such efforts are fraught with uncertainty and often yield inconsistent results. I shall explore the role of the Decalogue in ancient Israel by examining its place in the biblical documents as we have them. While many reject efforts to let biblical texts make their own case, the contents and structure of the Hebrew Bible represent an early stage in the history of interpretation. My assignment is to examine this stage. I shall read the evidence with a sympathetic disposition, reading it from right to left and letting the present shapes of the texts and the shape of the

3. See further Schmidt, *Die Zehn Gebote im Rahmen alttestamentlicher Ethik*, 20–21.

4. Crüsemann, *The Torah*, 352–53.

5. See Kittel, *Geschichte des Volkes Israel*, 383–84. For variations of Kittel's reconstruction, see Nielsen, *Ten Commandments*, 78–86; Harrelson, *The Ten Commandments and Human Rights*, 33–34; Greenberg, "Decalogue (The Ten Commandments)," 524; Weinfeld, "The Decalogue: Its Significance, Uniqueness, and Place in Israel's Tradition," 12–15; Weinfeld, "The Uniqueness of the Decalogue and Its Place in Jewish Tradition," 6–8.

6. For variations of these reconstructions of the history of the narratives, see Schmidt, *Die Zehn Gebote*, 25–34; Otto, *Theologische Ethik des Alten Testaments*, 208–19; Albertz, *A History of Israelite Religion*, 214–16; Perlitt, *Bundestheologie im Alten Testament*, 83–86; Crüsemann, *The Torah*, 351–57; Phillips, "A Fresh Look at the Sinai Pericope," 25–48.

canon as a whole make their own statements.[7] My presentation will seek to answer three questions:

(A)　How does the Pentateuch (Torah) speak about the Decalogue?

(B)　How does Moses reinterpret the Decalogue in Deuteronomy?

(C)　What evidence is there elsewhere in the Hebrew Bible for a special status for the Decalogue in Israelite thought and life?

When we have answered these questions we should have a better understanding of the nature and function of this document in its original canonical context, and have a base for evaluating the history of the interpretation of this text.

A. Designations for the Decalogue in the Hebrew Bible

One of the most obvious clues to the Hebrew Bible's understanding of the Decalogue is found in the expressions used to refer to it. In the Torah we find four such expressions.

1. *The Decalogue as the Words of YHWH*

Remarkably, the Hebrew Bible never refers to the Decalogue as "the commandments."[8] Exodus 20:1 introduces the document with וַיְדַבֵּר אֱלֹהִים אֵת כָּל־הַדְּבָרִים הָאֵלֶּה לֵאמֹר, "And God spoke all these *words* saying."[9] In the covenant ratification narratives Moses distinguishes the "words" (הַדְּבָרִים) of the Decalogue from the "ordinances" (מִשְׁפָּטִים) of the "Book of the Covenant" (סֵפֶר הַבְּרִית).[10] YHWH uses this expression in

7. Contra Clines and Michael Fox, who writes, "Indeed the willingness *not* to take a text at face value is the essence of critical scholarship." See Fox, *Character and Ideology in the Book of Esther*, 148.

8. We often find the word מִצְוֹת in the context of YHWH's revelation (including within the Decalogue itself [Exod 20:6; Deut 5:10]), but the word is used more generally of the rest of the Sinai revelation, often in association with the מִשְׁפָּטִים ("judgments") and חֻקִּים ("ordinances"). In Exod 24:12 the singular מִצְוָה, refers to "the command that I have written for your instruction." See further below. If one must refer to the מִצְוֹת of the Decalogue as imperatives (which they are), there is no need to refer to the individual injunctions as "commandments," rather than "commands." The use of this archaic expression reflects and reinforces the faulty notion that the terms of the Decalogue are exceptional in genre or authority.

9. The verb דִּבֶּר, "to speak," recurs in v. 22. The noun דְּבָרִים, "words," referring to the Decalogue, recurs in 24:3, 4, 8; 34:1, 27, 28.

10. Exod 24:3, 4, 8. The term מִשְׁפָּטִים, literally "judgments," derives from 21:1, and

34:1, when he says that he will write on new tablets the "words" that were written on the tablets that Moses smashed, and even more emphatically in 34:27–28: "Write these *words* (דְּבָרִים); in accordance with these *words* I have made a covenant with you and with Israel . . . And he wrote on the tablets the *words* of the covenant, the ten *words*." This pattern continues in Deuteronomy where Moses recalls both the original revelatory event and the rewriting of the document on new tablets.[11]

As is well known, the Hebrew word דָּבָר bears a wide range of meanings: "word," "statement," "message," "object," "event." Especially when used with the cognate verb, דִּבֶּר, "to speak," the emphasis is on communication. The preference for דְּבָרִים, "words," in these narratives highlights the revelation of the Decalogue as a communicative, rather than a specifically legislative, event.

2. The Decalogue as the Ten Words

The phrase עֲשֶׂרֶת הַדְּבָרִים, "ten words," occurs for the first time in Exod 34:28 and twice more in Moses' recollection of the original events in Deut 4:13; 10:4.[12] No matter how deeply entrenched is the tradition of rendering the phrase as "the ten commandments," translators should follow the lead of LXX, which translates the expression literally as δέκα λόγους, "ten words," in Exod 34:28 and Deut 10:4, and δέκα ῥήματα, "ten declarations," in Deut 4:13. The phrase is best interpreted as shorthand for "the ten principles of covenant relationship."

This raises the question of why the Decalogue should consist of ten declarations. Why not seven, the typological number of completeness,[13] or twelve, a typological number tightly associated with Israel?[14] Admittedly,

the "Book of the Covenant" (סֵפֶר הַבְּרִית) is generally recognized to consist of 20:22—23:19. So also Ska, "From History Writing to Library Building," 165–69.

11. On the former, see Deut 4:10, 12, 36; 5:22, 28; 9:10. With reference to the latter, see Deut 10:2.

12. Like many others, Phillips insists the reference to "Ten Words" in Exod 34:28 is a Deuteronomistic phrase inserted by late Pentateuchal editors. See Phillips, "The Decalogue: Ancient Israel's Criminal Law," 10.

13. E.g., seven days of creation (Gen 1; Exod 20:11); seven pairs of clean animals and birds for sacrifice (Gen 7:2–3); seven ewe lambs used in ritual (Gen 21:28, 30); seven good and seven lean years (Gen 41), etc.

14. Note the references to Jacob's twelve sons (Gen 35:22; 42:13, 32), who become the twelve tribes of Israel (Gen 49:28; Exod 24:4), and will be represented at the covenant ratification ritual by twelve pillars (Exod 24:4), twelve stones on the high priest's breastpiece

ten also functions as a typological number in the Torah,[15] but it seems more likely that the reason for ten is mnemonic: to facilitate memorization and recitation.[16] If the number of principles intentionally corresponds to the fingers on one's hands, then the Decalogue was composed to function as a sort of catechism, summarizing the essence of covenant relationship.[17]

3. *The Decalogue as Torah*

The Pentateuch refers to the Decalogue as תּוֹרָה, *tôrâ*, only once. In Exod 24:12 YHWH invites Moses to the top of Sinai to receive written copies of the covenant document sealed in the foregoing ritual. But the construction of the clause is difficult, with three direct objects of the verb: וְאֶתְּנָה לְךָ אֶת־לֻחֹת הָאֶבֶן וְהַתּוֹרָה וְהַמִּצְוָה אֲשֶׁר כָּתַבְתִּי לְהוֹרֹתָם, translated literally "and I will give you the tablets of stone and the תּוֹרָה and the command (הַמִּצְוָה) that I have written for their instruction." Although most translations suggest the tablets contained the Torah and the Command, we should interpret the *waw* conjunctions epexegetically: "the tablets of stone, that is, the Torah, that is, the command that I have written for their instruction."[18] LXX renders תּוֹרָה as νόμος, "law," here and virtually every-

---

(Exod 28:21; 39:14), twelve staffs (Num 17:2, 6), and by twelve men sent out to scout the land (Num 13:2–16; Deut 1:23). Cf. also the twelve springs of water at Elim (Exod 15:27; Num 33:9). Ishmael also became the ancestor of twelve princes (Gen 17:20; 26:16).

15. The genealogies in Gen 5 and 11 and Ruth 4 consist of ten generations; for the sake of ten righteous in Sodom God would have spared the city (Gen 18:32); the number "ten" figures prominently in the design of the Tabernacle (Exod 26:1, 16; 27:12; 36:8, 21; 38:12); in the sacred rituals (Exod 29:40; Lev 5:11; 5:15; 6:20; 15:4; 16:29; 27:32; 28:5, 13, 21, 29; 29:4, 7, 10, 15, 23); the tithe (Lev 27:30–32; Num 18:21, 24, 26; Deut 12:17; 14:22–24, 28; 26:12, 14); and in proverbial intensifying usage (Gen 31:7, 41; Lev 26:26; Num 14:22); etc. Nielsen seems to favor this interpretation in *Ten Commandments*, 6–10. Philo (*De decalogo* 20) suggests ten is the perfect number that contains all kinds of numbers, both even and odd; it is the sum of the categories.

16. So also Harrelson, *Ten Commandments*, 9, 135.

17. Miller suggests the Decalogue functions something like the U.S. Constitution, providing the basis for later specification of the laws in the Book of the Covenant, the Holiness Code, and the so-called Deuteronomic Code [*sic*]. See "The Place of the Decalogue in the Old Testament and Its Law," 3–16; Miller, "The Sufficiency and Insufficiency of the Commandments," 23.

18. Though scholars tend to explain the complicated syntax as the result of a series of later expansions. Thus Childs, *The Book of Exodus*, 499.

where else,[19] even though this word does not mean "law." It is cognate to the last word in this sentence, the infinitive לְהוֹרֹתָם, "for their instruction." In Deuteronomy the word occurs repeatedly with precisely the same semantic range as Greek διδαχή or διδασκαλία, both of which mean "instruction, teaching," rather than law. The odd construction of Exod 24:12 highlights the close identification of the revelation with the tablets, but it also declares the genre of the text of the tablets.

Though singular, the second expression, הַמִּצְוָה, "the command," recognizes that the Decalogue does indeed consist largely of commands, but the following clause explains that these should not be interpreted like laws decreed by a king. The surrounding narrative (cf. 19:4–6), the form of the Decalogue, and the nature of the ten terms demonstrate that this document functions, not as a legal code, but as a statement of covenantal policy, as guidance for life, creating an ideal rather than decreeing law.[20] The commands are so general as to be virtually unenforceable through the judicial system. Their intention is to create a framework and ethos within which the Israelites were to live.

4. The Decalogue as the Foundational Covenant Document

The etymology of the Hebrew word בְּרִית continues to elude us. Nevertheless, its meaning is clear: it involves a solemn commitment between two parties, usually formally concluded with an oath. Covenants occur in two primary forms: parity covenants between persons/parties of equal status,[21] and suzerainty covenants involving a superior and a vassal.[22] In the Hebrew Bible בְּרִית is used of YHWH's covenants with the cosmos and its representative Noah (Gen 9:8–17), with Abraham (Gen 5:18; 17:1–14), and with David (2 Sam 7; Ps 89). It is also used with reference to the relationship that YHWH established with Israel at Sinai.[23] So

19. Of the 220 occurrences of תּוֹרָה, LXX renders 202 as νόμος.

20. Cf. Schmidt (Die Zehn Gebote, 17–18), "Die Gebote stellen also im strengen Sinne keine Rechtssätze dar, dienen nicht der Gerichtsbarkeit, sondern sind eher 'Verhältnisregeln,' Anweisungen für das Leben, mehr Ethos als Jus."

21. E.g., the covenant involving Jacob and Laban in Gen 31:44–54.

22. E.g., the covenant involving Nebuchadnezzar and Zedekiah (Ezek 17:11–21). The bibliography on "covenant" is immense. For a helpful beginning, see Williamson, "Covenant," 155.

23. Since within the context of Jer 31, the prophecy of the so-called new covenant, is thoroughly parochial, announcing finally the fulfillment of the ideals represented by

tightly linked to the covenant is the Decalogue that its contents may be referred to as דִּבְרֵי הַבְּרִית, "the words of the covenant" (Exod 34:28) and even more directly בְּרִיתוֹ, "his covenant" (Deut 4:13),[24] and the written document itself as לוּחֹת הַבְּרִית, "the tablets of the covenant" (Deut 9:9, 11, 15). As the covenant document, the Decalogue provided Israel with concrete proof of the divine Suzerain's immutable commitment to them and a constant reminder of their commitment to him. This document was stored in the Holy of Holies of the Tabernacle in a specially designed container known as the "ark of the covenant of YHWH" (אֲרוֹן בְּרִית־יְהוָה),[25] or "the ark of the covenant of God" (אֲרוֹן בְּרִית הָאֱלֹהִים),[26] or simply "the ark of the covenant" (אֲרוֹן הַבְּרִית),[27] because it contained the tablets that functioned as the primary symbol of the covenant (Deut 10:1–8; 1 Kgs 8:9).[28]

The frequent references to the Decalogue as עֵדֻת/עֵדָת reinforces its covenantal sense. Assuming a derivation from the same root as עוּד, "to testify," and עֵד, "witness," many translations continue to follow the ancient versions in translating the word as "testimony."[29] However, this interpretation is misleading, because we usually think of "testimony" as the utterances of a witness in a court of law or some less formal context.[30]

---

the covenant that YHWH made with Israel at Sinai and renewed on the plains of Moab (as reported in Deuteronomy), this should be understood as the "renewed covenant." We interpret the covenant made with Israel at Sinai to be essentially the same as the covenant made with Abraham, representing the fulfillment of YHWH's promise in Gen 17:7, and a formal elaboration of its terms, especially in revealing the appropriate ethical responses to YHWH's grace in election and redemption and in providing for the maintenance of the covenant through the ritual.

24. Following Lohfink, Braulik ("Deuteronomium 4,13 und der Horebbund," 29–33) is correct in interpreting the אֲשֶׁר particle in Deut 4:13 as an explicative, rather than relative particle: YHWH declared to Israel his covenant; that is, he charged (צִוָּה) them to apply (עָשָׂה) the ten words. However, this does not negate the function of the Decalogue as the foundational covenant document. I am grateful to my doctoral student, Jerry Hwang, for drawing my attention to Braulik's discussion.

25. Num 10:33; 14:44; Deut 10:8; 31:9, 25, 26; Josh 3:3, 11, 17; 4:7, 18; 6:8; 8:33; 1 Sam 4:3–5; 1 Kgs 3:15; 6:19; 8:1, 6; 1 Chr 15:25–29; 16:37; 17:1; 22:19; 28:2, 18; 2 Chr 5:2, 7; Jer 3:16.

26. Judg 20:27; 1 Sam 4:4; 15:24; 1 Chr 16:16.

27. Josh 3:6, 8, 14; 4:9; 6:6.

28. On the ark, see now Wilson, "Merely a Container?" 212–49.

29. Thus LXX, Vulgate, the Targums.

30. S. T. Hague (*NIDOTTE* 1:502) notes that "the translation of עֵדֻת as 'testimony' is reasonable, as long as we understand the testimony as *the law* that is the seal of the Lord's covenant with Israel."

The usage of the word as a virtual synonym for בְּרִית and the etymological link with *adê*, the Akkadian word for "covenant/treaty" and "loyalty oath,"[31] strengthen the case for interpreting עֵדוּת as "pact,"[32] and the plural form עֵדֹת as "contractual obligations, covenant stipulations," to which one committed oneself through formal legal procedures, including the oath. The word occurs three times in the phrase לֻחֹת הָעֵדֻת, "the tablets of the pact" (Exod 31:18; 32:15; 34:29), and more than a dozen times in the phrase אֲרֹן הָעֵדֻת, "the ark of the pact."[33]

Although the way the Decalogue is embedded in the narrative creates some tension,[34] the events described in Exod 19–24 constitute an elaborate covenant revelation and ratification ritual, beginning with the announcement in Exod 19:3b–5, and concluding with the covenant meal (24:9–11). When the ritual is completed YHWH invites Moses

31. On the meaning and significance of *adê*, see Parpola and Watanabe, *Neo-Assyrian Treaties and Loyalty Oaths*, XV–XXV.

32. Thus NJPSV. The plural form עֵדֹת functions as a general designation for the stipulations of the covenant, which Deut 4:45 associates with הַחֻקִּים, "the ordinances," and הַמִּשְׁפָּטִים, "the judgments, regulations." Cf. also Deut 6:17, 20; 1 Kgs 2:3; 2 Kgs 17:15; 23:3; 1 Chr 29:19; 2 Chr 34:31; Neh 9:34; Jer 44:23; Pss 25:10; 78:56; 93:5; 99:7; 119: 2–168 (twenty-two times). Note also that what Moses calls "the ark of the Covenant [of YHWH]" (אֲרֹון בְּרִית־יְהוָה, Deut 10:8; 31:9, 25–26) is elsewhere referred to as the ark of the עֵדוּת (Exod 25:22; 26:33–34; 30:6, 26; 31:7; 39:35; 40:3, 5, 21; Num 4:5; 4:16; 7:89. The present triad of terms recurs in Deut 6:20 (with עֵדֹת preceding the present pair. עֵדֹת appears between מִצְוֹת and חֻקִּים in 6:17. On the meaning and significance of עֵדוּת/עֵדֹת, see Simian-Yofre, 514–15.

33. Exod 25:22; 26:33, 34; 30:6, 26; 31:7; 39:35; 40:3, 5, 21; Num 4:5; 7:89; Josh 4:16. In addition, we encounter expressions like מִשְׁכַּן הָעֵדֻת, "the tabernacle of the pact" (Exod 38:21; Num 1:50, 53; 10:11); אֹהֶל הָעֵדֻת, "the tent of the pact" (Num 9:15; 17:22, 23; 18:2; 2 Chr 24:6); and פָּרֹכֶת הָעֵדֻת, "the veil of the pact" (Lev 24:3). Frequently the expression appears by itself functioning elliptically for אֲרֹן הָעֵדֻת, "the ark of the pact," especially when used with prepositions ("before the pact" [Exod 16:34; 27:21; 30:36; Num 17:4], "over the pact" [Lev 16:13]), or for לֻחֹת הָעֵדֻת, "the tablets of the pact" (Exod 25:21; 40:20). Two special cases occur. In Isa 8:20 הָעֵדֻת appears alongside הַתּוֹרָה probably serving as an alternative designation for the Torah (i.e., Deuteronomy), and in 2 Kgs 11:12 (= 2 Chr 23:11), as part of the investiture of Joash, Jehoiada the priest places on him the diadem (נֵזֶר) and the עֵדוּת. Here the expression may serve as a substitute for הַתּוֹרָה, "the Torah" (Moses' speeches in Deuteronomy), which the king is to copy and read for himself all the days of his life (Deut 17:18–19). See further Cogan and Tadmor, *II Kings*, 128.

34. Chapter 19 ends with Moses descending the mountain and "saying to them [the people]" (וַיֹּאמֶר אֲלֵהֶם), but the content of his speech is dropped. Chapter 20 begins with God speaking, and the content of his speech clearly presented as the Decalogue. This disjunction apparently serves the literary function of highlighting the role of YHWH and the Decalogue as divine speech.

up the mountain to receive from him the official copy of the covenant (24:12–18).[35]

The identification of the Decalogue as a covenant document, rather than a legal code, helps to explain several other features. Structurally the Decalogue incorporates at least five of the primary elements of ancient Near Eastern covenant forms:

a. The preamble identifies the suzerain (Exod 20:2a). The document opens with the divine Suzerain identifying himself by name and declaring the relational basis of the claims upon Israel that will follow: אָנֹכִי יְהוָה אֱלֹהֶיךָ, "I am YHWH your God."[36] This introduction compares with the opening lines of many Hittite treaties of roughly the same period.[37]

b. The historical prologue summarizes the history of the relationship (Exod 20:2b). Whereas in most second millennium Hittite and first millennium BCE Neo-Assyrian treaties the suzerain-vassal relationship was established by the suzerain overwhelming the vassal,[38] YHWH's relationship with Israel had its roots in his triumph over those who held the nation in bondage. This sets the stage for the stipulations that follow, which clarify

35. The official copy provided by the Suzerain is to be distinguished from the temporary copy prepared by Moses, and used in the covenant ratification procedures. According to Exod 24:1–8, following the direct revelation of the Decalogue to the people and apparently the revelation of the contents of the "Book of the Covenant" to Moses, Moses recounted (סְפֵּר) the words of YHWH (the Decalogue) and הַמִּשְׁפָּטִים ("the judgments") to the people (v. 3).

36. This is in fulfillment of YHWH's promise to Abraham in Gen 17:7: "I will establish my covenant between me and you, and your offspring after you throughout their generations, for an everlasting covenant, to be your God and the God of your descendants after you."

37. Cf. the opening of the treaty between Muwattalli II of Hatti and Alaksandu of Wikusa: "Thus says My Majesty, Great King, [King] of Hatti, Beloved of the Storm-god of Lightning; son of Mursili, Great King, Hero." As translated by Beckman, *Hittite Diplomatic Texts*, No. 13 §1.

38. Though some propagandistically highlight the overlord's grace toward the vassal. The introduction to the treaty between Suppiluliuma I of Hatti and Huqqana of Hayasa bears a striking resemblance to the preamble to the Decalogue, highlighting the superior's benevolence to his vassal and beginning the stipulations with a call for exclusive allegiance to the overlord: "I have now elevated you, Huqqana, a lowly dog, and have treated you well. In Hattusa I have distinguished you among the men of Hayasa and have given you my sister in marriage. All of Hatti, the land of Hayasa, and the outlying and central lands have heard of you. Now you, Huqqana, recognize only My Majesty as overlord" (as translated by Beckman, ibid., No. 3 §1–2).

how Israel was to respond to YHWH's gracious actions on her behalf (cf. 19:4). Significantly, the principles of the Decalogue are not addressed to the world at large or to Israel in Egypt, but to a redeemed people, as a summary of the appropriate response to grace already experienced. They are not presented as preconditions to Israel's redemption, and, contrary to some of Martin Luther's statements, they certainly are not presented as "natural law."[39]

c. The stipulations summarize the divine Suzerain's expectations of his vassal. In examining the stipulations, several features stand out. First, the preamble and the first command are presented in a relational I–you form. Second, they are cast as apodictic (categorical and unconditional) as opposed to casuistic (case-based) commands. The differences between these two kinds of commands are striking (Table 1). The former all transcend specific circumstances and most omit any reference to consequences, either good or bad.[40]

Third, although the Decalogue has binding authority for all Israelites, strictly speaking it is addressed to individual adult male heads of households. All the main verbs and pronouns are cast in the second person masculine singular. Judging by the content of the ten principles, the addressee is a father with children (Exod 20:5; Deut 5:9); the head of a household, with authority over sons and daughters, male and female slaves, livestock, and aliens within the village (Exod 5:9–10; Deut 5:14); apparently has aged parents still living with him (Exod 20:12; Deut 5:16); and is tempted to commit adultery (Exod 20:14; Deut 5:18), to testify falsely against his neighbor in legal proceedings (Exod 20:16; Deut 5:20), and to covet his neighbor's wife and his property, including house and field (Exod 20:17; Deut 5:21). Frank Crüsemann describes the addressee as a middle-aged male householder, a member of the עַם הָאָרֶץ, "people of the land," that is, the empowered citizenry.[41]

---

39. See further Schmidt, *Die Zehn Gebote*, 20–21.

40. The exceptions are the first command, which warns of the dire consequences of idolatry, and the fourth command, which presents honoring parents as a precondition to future blessing.

41. Crüsemann, *Bewahrung der Freiheit*, 28–35. For a helpful review of Crüsemann's work, see Johnstone, "The Ten Commandments: Some Recent Interpretations," 455–57.

Table 1: A Comparison of Conditional and Unconditional Law

Casuistic Law	Apodictic Law
If an ox gores a man or woman to death, the ox shall surely be stoned and its flesh shall not be eaten; but the owner of the ox shall go unpunished. (Exod 21:28)	You shall have no other gods before me. (Exod 20:3)
If you ever take your neighbor's cloak as a pledge, you are to return it to him before the sun sets, for that is his only covering; it is his cloak for his body. What else shall he sleep in? (Exod 22:26–27)	You shall not bear false witness against your neighbor. (Exod 20:16)
Features	Features
Conditional	Unconditional
Declarative mood	Imperative mood
In third (or second) person	In second person
Specific: based on actual cases, often with motive or exception clauses	General: without qualification or exception
Usually positive in form	Often negative in form
Begin with "If" or "When"	Begin with the verb (in the imperative) or negative particle + verb

But this raises the question: Whose interests does this document serve? In recent years it has become fashionable to argue the Decalogue was drafted to protect the interests of the rich and the powerful in Israel, at the expense of the poor and marginalized. David Clines argues that the addressee must be an urban middle-aged male who threatens the status and security of wealthy male property owners.[42] But this can scarcely be

42. See especially Clines, "The Ten Commandments, Reading from Left to Right," but also Rodd, *Glimpses of a Strange Land*, 87. For a feminist reading of the Decalogue,

the case. The addressee is the male property owner, who is deemed the potential threat to the community. Accordingly, this document functions as Israel's *magna carta*,[43] perhaps the world's oldest bill of rights.[44] However, unlike modern bills of rights, the Decalogue is not interested in the addressee's rights, but seeks to protect the rights of members of the addressee's household and his neighbors by reining in his propensity to abuse them. Israel was indeed a covenant community that had been freed from the bondage of Egyptian slavery,[45] but the community was under the constant threat of individual Israelites, especially those with social and economic power, behaving like little Pharaohs.[46] We may summarize briefly how each of the principles seeks to protect the right of someone else.[47]

(1)   YHWH has the right to exclusive allegiance—not only because he has triumphed over all gods (Exod 12:12; Num 33:4; Deut 4:34–35, 39), but especially because he has graciously redeemed Israel, brought her to himself, and entered into covenant relationship with her (Exod 19:4–6).

(2)   YHWH has the right to fair and honest representation. We view bearing the name to mean primarily claiming YHWH as one's God and covenant Lord; to bear it falsely (לַשָּׁוְא) means to claim this name but live as if one belongs to Baal or some other god.[48]

see Sivan, *Between Woman, Man, and God.* However, see also Jackson's critical review of her work, "A Feminist Reading of the Decalogue(s)," 542–54. Jackson rightly concludes that her "privileging of the Decalogue" is a response "to a contemporary rather than an ancient agenda" (ibid., 554).

43. Thus Pleins, *The Social Visions of the Hebrew Bible*, 47.

44. See also Wright, "Ten Commandments," 790.

45. Though we agree in general with those who treat this document as a "charter of human freedom" (Harrelson, *The Ten Commandments*, 154–65; Stamm, *The Ten Commandments in Recent Research*, 112–14; especially Crüsemann, *Bewahrung der Freiheit*), we view it from another angle with the view to seeing how it protects the next person's freedom.

46. Note the framing of the document with references to the "house of slaves" (בֵּית עֲבָדִים) in the preamble, and "your neighbor's house" (בֵּית רֵעֶךָ) in the last command—especially of the deuteronomic version.

47. The discourse features of the Decalogue favor the Roman Catholic and Lutheran numbering, rather than the traditional Reformed numbering. For a summary of the arguments, see Excursus A: "How Shall We Number the Ten Commands? The Deuteronomy Version (5:1–21)."

48. Cf. Isa 44:1–5; 2 Pet 4:12–19. For a full development of this interpretation, see

(3)   YHWH has the right to the Israelite's life and trust (Exodus version), and all the members of his household (including the livestock) have the right to humane treatment by the male head (Deuteronomy version).[49]

(4)   The addressee's parents have the right to his respect, which will mean more than pietistically verbalizing honor, but concretely caring for them in their old age and honoring them after death.

(5)   The addressee's family members and neighbors have the right to life.

(6)   The addressee's neighbor has the right to a pure marriage.

(7)   The addressee's neighbors have the right to their own property.[50]

(8)   The addressee's neighbors have the right to a true and honest reputation.

(9)   The addressee's neighbor and his wife have the right to freedom from fear of his intentions regarding them.

(10) The addressee's neighbor has the right to freedom from fear of his intentions concerning his property.[51]

In short, the Decalogue calls on the head of the household to be covenantally committed to YHWH, his household, and his neighbors, so that he will resist seeking his own advantage, and seek instead the interests of others. In so doing, the document views the householder's role, not primarily in terms of power and authority, but in terms of care and responsibility toward others. In this regard the Decalogue, the Book of the Covenant (Exod 22:20, 25; 23:12), the Holiness Code (Lev 19:9–10, 13–14, 29, 33–34) and the deuteronomic Torah exhibit remarkable coherence, for they are all concerned about the well-being of those who are at the mercy of persons with power.[52] Indeed, Jesus distills all the commands

Block, *Deuteronomy*, s.v. Deut 5:11; Block, "Bearing the Name of the LORD with Honor," 20–31 (reprinted as chapter 3 in this volume).

49. While Deuteronomy clearly grounds the rhythm of Israel's life in their own experience, the Exodus version is less humanitarian, and its link with the rest of the Decalogue less certain.

50. Assuming גָּנַב means more than "stealing a person," that is, robbing a person of his/her freedom (cf. Exod 21:16), but also includes stealing in the broader sense.

51. The division of IX and X is clear in Deuteronomy. See below.

52. Note the numerous contexts in which the plight of the widow, the fatherless, and the alien are addressed: Deut 10:18; 14:29; 16:11, 14; 24:19–21; 26:12–13; 27:19.

to two: "You shall love the Lord your God with all your heart and with all your being and with all your resources,"[53] and "You shall love your neighbor as yourself"[54] (see Figure 1).

Figure 1: Jesus' Understanding of the Decalogue

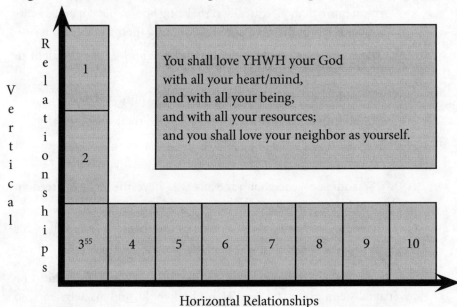

d. *The blessings and curses seek to motivate loyalty.* Hittite and Neo-Assyrian treaties, as well as the Holiness Code (Lev 26) and the deuteronomic Torah (Deut 28), gather the blessings and curses towards the end of the respective documents. Fragments of curses occur after the first and second principles (Exod 20:5, 7), and fragments of blessings occur at the end of the first and fourth principles (20:6, 12).

53. The appropriate interpretation of the Hebrew word מְאֹד, which underlies the Greek τῆς ἰσχύος σου, "your strength," in Mark 12:30.

54. For a convincing discussion of אָהַב, "love," as active and concrete demonstration of commitment to the well-being of the next person, rather than an abstract emotional expression, see Malamat, "You Shall Love Your Neighbor as Yourself," 111–15.

55. On the transitional nature of the Sabbath command, see above.

5. Provision for a Covenant Document Promotes the Fidelity of the Parties to the Covenant

The preparation of tablets inscribed with the covenant principles plays a significant role in both the Sinai narrative (Exod 24:12–18) and in Moses' recollections of these events in Deuteronomy (4:9–14; 9:15–17; 10:1–5). These tablets were made of stone,[56] and inscribed by the divine Suzerain, YHWH himself.[57] After Moses had smashed the original tablets, they were replaced with exact duplicates,[58] which provided concrete proof that YHWH had taken the Israelites back as his covenant people, and that the terms of the renewed relationship were identical to the covenant to which they had signed on originally. Longstanding tradition has it that the first of the two tablets[59] contained those commands that deal with Israel's vertical relationship to God, and that the second dealt with horizontal relationships.[60] While devotionally and homiletically interesting, this interpretation is without exegetical or contextual foundation. The need for two stone tablets accords with ancient Near Eastern practice of providing each party to a covenant with a copy of the agreement.[61]

---

56. For Calvin, the stone spoke of the permanence of the laws, in contrast to the transience of the ceremonies. *John Calvin's Sermons on the Ten Commandments*, 249.

57. Exod 24:12; 31:18; 32:16; 34:1, 28; Deut 4:13; 5:22; 9:10; 10:2, 4.

58. Exod 34:28; Deut 10:1–4; cf. Exod 32:19; Deut 9:15–17.

59. References to "two" tablets occur more than sixteen times in the Hebrew Bible: Exod 31:18; 32:15; 34:1, 4a, 4b, 29; Deut 4:13; 5:22; 9:10, 11, 15, 17; 10:1, 3; 1 Kgs 8:9; 2 Chr 5:10. To these should be added the plural references to the tablets without the numerical modifier: Exod 24:12; 32:1, 19, 28, 29; Deut 9:9; 10:2, 4, 5.

60. Calvin, *Institutes*, 2.8.11 (pp. 376, 377). The tradition dates as far back as Philo, who wrote, "We find that he divided the ten into two sets of five which he engraved on two tables (στήλαις), and the first five obtained the first place, while the other was awarded the second." Philo, *On the Decalogue (De Decalogo)*, 7.12. Similarly Josephus, *Ant.* 3.5.4, 8. On the Decalogue in Philo, see Amir, "The Decalogue according to Philo," 121–60. While New Testament scholars and theologians often use the language of "two tables," remarkably the expression also surfaces in Wright's *Old Testament Ethics*, 341.

61. For a detailed study of this issue, see Kline, "The Two Tables of the Covenant," 138–46. Hittite custom had each party deposit a copy in the treaty in the temple of the deity, where they would be under the respective god's oversight, but from where they could be retrieved and read aloud at prescribed intervals. For an example, see the treaty between Suppiluliuma I of Hatti and Shattiwaza of Mittani in *Hittite Diplomatic Texts*, 6A §13, pp. 46–47.

While the Decalogue was not the only part of the Pentateuch associated with the covenant,[62] it was recognized as the original and official covenant document, announced to the people by YHWH himself and written by his own hand (Exod 24:12; 31:18; Deut 10:1–4). However, the Decalogue did not function as a law code to be administered in the courts; it was a foundational statement of principle, creating a worldview that begins by declaring YHWH's past grace in redeeming Israel from bondage, and then offers a "sampling of several important aspects of the new life of obedience within the covenant."[63] As Exod 19:4 and the preamble to the Decalogue emphasize, Israel was not called primarily to conformity to a code of conduct, but to a relationship with their gracious redeemer.

B. The Reinterpretation of the Decalogue in Deuteronomy

The presence of two versions of the Decalogue in the Pentateuch offers a rich opportunity for intertextual and synoptic study. Although many insist the deuteronomic version antedates the Exodus version,[64] the authors of the Pentateuch intended for the deuteronomic version to be read in light of the Exodus version.[65] The two versions begin identically, but beginning with the Sabbath command they diverge significantly (see Table 2). The modifications involve deletion, addition of new features, rephrasing, and fundamental reworking of terms.

---

62. We have already noted the content of the סֵפֶר הַבְּרִית, "Book of the Covenant" and its role in the covenant ratification procedure (Exod 24:1–8). From the colophonic conclusion to the Holiness Code (Lev 17–26) in Lev 26:46 it is evident that the divine speeches of Leviticus were also considered stipulations of the covenant. And Moses' second address in Deuteronomy (Deut 4:44—26:19; 28:1–60[Eng 29:1]) is presented as a sermon on covenant relationship that was a part of a covenant renewal ceremony.

63. Thus Janzen, *Old Testament Ethics*, 92.

64. See Crüsemann, *The Torah*, 352, 355; Lang, "The Number Ten and the Antiquity of the Fathers," 218, following Hossfeld, *Der Dekalog*.

65. So also Weinfeld, *Deuteronomy 1–11*, 243 et passim.

Table 2: Synopsis of the Versions of the Decalogue in Exodus and Deuteronomy[66]

	Exodus 20:2–17	Deuteronomy 5:6–21	
2	I am YHWH your God, who brought you out of the land of Egypt, out of the house of slavery.	I am YHWH your God, who brought you out of the land of Egypt, out of the house of slavery.	6
3–6	You shall have no other gods before me. You shall not make for yourself a carved image, or any likeness of anything that is in heaven above, or that is in the earth beneath, or that is in the water under the earth. You shall not bow down to them or serve them, for I YHWH your God am a jealous God, visiting the iniquity of the fathers on the children to the third and the fourth generation of those who hate me, but showing steadfast love to thousands of those who love me and keep my commandments.	You shall have no other gods before me. You shall not make for yourself a carved image, any likeness of anything that is in heaven above, or that is on the earth beneath, or that is in the water under the earth. You shall not bow down to them or serve them; for I YHWH your God am a jealous God, visiting the iniquity of the fathers on the children to the third and fourth generation of those who hate me, but showing steadfast love to thousands of those who love me and keep my commandments.	7–10
7	You shall not carry in vain the name of YHWH your God, for YHWH will not hold him guiltless who bears his name in vain.	You shall not carry in vain the name of YHWH your God, for YHWH will not hold him guiltless who bears his name in vain.	11

66. Bold font = variation in reading; Italic font = addition

	Remember the Sabbath day, to keep it holy.	Observe the Sabbath day, to keep it holy, as YHWH your God commanded you.	
	Six days you shall labor, and do all your work, but the seventh day is a Sabbath to YHWH your God. On it you shall not do any work, you, or your son, or your daughter your male servant, or your female servant,	Six days you shall labor and do all your work, but the seventh day is a Sabbath to YHWH your God. On it you shall not do any work, you, or your son, or your daughter or your male servant, or your female servant, or your ox or your donkey	
8–11	or your livestock, or the sojourner who is within your gates.	or any of your livestock, or the sojourner who is within your gates,	12–15
	For in six days YHWH made heaven and earth, the sea, and all that is in them, and rested the seventh day.	that your male servant and your female servant may rest as well as you. You shall remember that you were a slave in the land of Egypt, and YHWH your God brought you out from there with a mighty hand and an outstretched arm.	
	Therefore YHWH blessed the Sabbath day and made it holy.	Therefore YHWH your God commanded you to keep the Sabbath day.	

12	Honor your father and your mother, that your days may be long in the land that YHWH your God is giving you.	Honor your father and your mother, as YHWH your God commanded you, that your days may be long, and that it may go well with you in the land that YHWH your God is giving you.	16
13	You shall not murder.	You shall not murder.	17
14	You shall not commit adultery.	And you shall not commit adultery.	18
15	You shall not steal.	And you shall not steal.	19
16	You shall not bear false witness against your neighbor.	And you shall not bear useless witness against your neighbor.	20
17	You shall not covet your neighbor's house; you shall not covet your neighbor's wife, or his male servant, or his female servant, or his ox, or his donkey, or anything that belongs to your neighbor.	And you shall not covet your neighbor's wife. And you shall not desire your neighbor's house, his field, or his male servant, or his female servant, his ox, or his donkey, or anything that belongs to your neighbor.	21

But how should we interpret these changes? Scholars have long observed the humanistic trajectory of Deuteronomy as a whole, especially when compared with corresponding regulations in the Book of the Covenant and the Holiness Code.[67] This trajectory is evident already in the deuteronomic version of the Decalogue, particularly the Sabbath ordinance. First, anticipating later expressions of concern for the well-being of

---

67. See Weinfeld, *Deuteronomy and the Deuteronomic School*, 282–97; Driver, *Deuteronomy*, 85.

animals,[68] Moses specifies the ox and the donkey, draft and pack animals respectively, as deserving of the Sabbath rest.[69] Second, beyond patterning human creative work after that of God the Creator, Deuteronomy portrays the Sabbath as a gift, offering all who toil an opportunity to refresh themselves. Third, instead of calling on Israelites to remember the Sabbath, it calls them to treasure the Sabbath by recalling the time when they labored for brutal Egyptian taskmasters, without Sabbath or relief.[70] The seventh-day Sabbath celebrates YHWH's special creative work in rescuing them from bondage.[71]

The adjustments to the commands on coveting follow the same trajectory. While scholars have spent a great deal of time exploring the significance of the shift from חָמַד, "to covet," to הִתְאַוָּה "to desire," in Deuteronomy,[72] the substitution of one verb with another does not appear to be nearly as consequential as the transposition of "house" and "wife," and the elevation of the command against coveting one's neighbor's wife by casting it as a completely separate command.

The Exodus commands concerning coveting consist of two statements, each involving the identical negative command, לֹא תַחְמֹד, "You shall not covet," followed by a direct object. The traditional Reformed numbering of the terms of the Decalogue treats the first statement as titular and the second as expositional, clarifying the meaning of בַּיִת, "house," in part 1.[73] This is the בֵּית אָב, "the household of the father," the domestic realm over which he exercises leadership. However, the discourse grammar of the Decalogue as a whole and syntax of these two statements in particular[74] requires distinguishing coveting the neighbor's real property (the house) from coveting the living creatures—including human beings

68. Cf. Deut 22:4, 6; 25:4.

69. This insertion may reflect the influence of the last command and/or Exod 23:12.

70. The second address repeatedly buttresses ethical and spiritual appeals with reminders of the Israelites' slavery in Egypt. Cf. Deut 15:15; 16:12; 24:18, 22.

71. YHWH's deliverance of Israel as a special creative act and his cosmic creative actions are also prominent in Pss 95 and 136.

72. Specifically whether the former forbids envious desire for what belongs to another person or prohibits taking specific actions to satisfy those desires, on which, see Chaney, "'Coveting Your Neighbor's House' in Social Context," 302–8; Rofé, "The Tenth Commandment in the Light of Four Deuteronomic Laws," 45–54.

73. For similar listings, including everything associated with the family as an economic unit, see Gen 12:5, 16; 26:14; Num 16:30, 32; Deut 11:6.

74. See n. 47 above.

and livestock—who make up the economic unit, the household.[75] Even so the deuteronomic version goes in a different direction, isolating the neighbor's wife and then treating the rest as the property of the head of the household.[76]

It seems best to interpret these changes in Deuteronomy as deliberate efforts to ensure the elevation of the wife in a family unit and to foreclose men's use of the Exodus version to justify treatment of wives as if they were mere property, along with the rest of the household possessions.[77] The Hebrew narratives are indeed rife with accounts of abusive men who treat women as property that may be disposed of at will for the sake of male honor and male ego,[78] confirming that in everyday life the Decalogue was largely ignored.

75. We should translate the last phrase in Exod 20:17, וְכֹל אֲשֶׁר לְרֵעֶךָ, either as "or anyone else belonging to your neighbor," or as "or any other [living] thing belonging to your neighbor."

76. To match the following pairs (his male and female servants; his ox and donkey), by adding "field" Deuteronomy restores a traditional pair of words. "House" and "field" appear together in Gen 39:5; Lev 25:31; Neh 5:3, 11; Isa 5:8; Jer 6:12; 32:15; Mic 2:2. LXX and Nash Papyrus add this element in Exod 20:17 as well, perhaps under the influence of Deuteronomy. The addition of "field" also restores the full complement of seven items, like the list of those who are to benefit from the Sabbath rest in Exod 20:10. Cf. Cassuto, *Commentary on the Book of Exodus*, 249. This move brings the prohibition on coveting remarkably close to the form of a similar prohibition in an Old Assyrian Treaty text (1920–1840 BCE) from Kültepe (*Kaneš*) in Anatolia: "You shall not covet a fine house, a fine slave, a fine slave woman, a fine field, or a fine orchard belonging to any citizen of Assur, and you will not take (any of these) by force and hand them over to your own subjects/servants." Kt 00/k6:62–66, as translated by Donbaz, "An Old Assyrian Treaty from Kültepe," 65.

77. References to the בַּיִת as a designation for domain frame the Decalogue: in the preamble Egypt is a "house of slavery" (בֵּית עֲבָדִים); in the last command the "house" is the domain of the male head, whose style of leadership may be as oppressive as the bondage under Pharaoh. Sivan (*Between Woman, Man, and God*, 220) interprets the transposition of "wife" and "house" in the last commands of the Decalogue as symbolic of "the interchangeability of woman with other items of property." Regarding the menial status of women in ancient Israel, Phillips speaks for many: "They [women] had no legal status, being the personal property first of their fathers, and then of their husbands" (*Ancient Israel's Criminal Law*, 70). For critical responses to this perspective, see Block, "Marriage and Family in Ancient Israel," 61–72; Wright, *God's People in God's Land*, 291–316.

78. See Trible, *Texts of Terror*. While Sivan (*Between Woman, Man, and God*, 215) rightly recognizes that these modifications reflect "scales of desires," elevating women "as the most desirable objects of coveting," the deuteronomic form is not intended to secure the welfare of men (ibid., 216–17), but to curb a weakness in men and secure the rights of one's neighbor and his wife to a healthy and secure marital relationship.

We have argued here that the Decalogue functioned as a bill of rights, seeking to protect my neighbor from my potential violation of his or her rights as a human being created as an image of God and as a member of the redeemed community in covenant relation with God and with one another. Although the principles of covenant relationship reflected in the Decalogue were determinative for the entire community, technically they addressed the heads of the households, perceiving them as the greatest threats to the well-being of society. This document recognizes that heads of households are particularly susceptible to abusing their position as a seat of power, rather than stewardship of an office that exists for the good of those in one's care.[79] In so doing the Decalogue establishes the trajectory of the rest of the book of Deuteronomy, which calls on all, especially leaders, to demonstrate love by looking out for the interests of others rather than guarding their own honor and status.[80]

C. The Status of the Decalogue in the Hebrew Bible

Both the Sinai narratives and the speeches by Moses that make up Deuteronomy highlight the special place of the Decalogue in Israel's tradition. Of all the divine revelation at Sinai and beyond, only the Decalogue was (1) spoken by YHWH directly to the people; (2) accompanied by the awe–inspiring appearance of the divine presence (Exod 19:16–25; 20:18–21; Deut 4:9–14, 36; 5:23–31); (3) written down with YHWH's own fingers (Exod 31:18); (4) presented as a closed, self-contained unit (Deut 5:22, "and he added nothing more"); (5) preserved in duplicate written form on durable tablets of stone; (6) stored in the ark of the covenant in the Holy of Holies of the Tabernacle/Temple; (7) referred to by its technical title: "The Ten Words"; (8) repeated virtually verbatim by Moses in the context of his valedictory pastoral exposition of the חֻקִּים וּמִשְׁפָּטִים, "statutes and laws"(cf. Deut 4:44–45; 5:1) on the plains of Moab. This document represented the foundation of all the other documents that came to make up Israel's constitutional treasure: the Book of the Covenant, the Holiness Code, and the deuteronomic Torah. The interrelationships among the major constitutional documents may be portrayed graphically as follows (fig. 2):

79. Contra Clines, "The Ten Commandments, Reading from Left to Right," 97–112.

80. For detailed discussion of this issue, see Block, "You Shall Not Covet Your Neighbor's Wife,'" in Block, *Gospel according to Moses*, chapter 5.

Figure 2: The Evolution of Israel's Constitutional Tradition

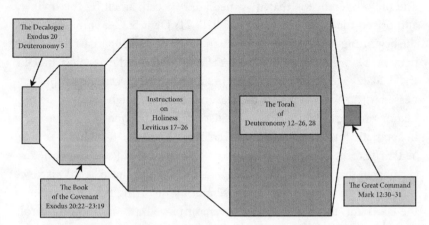

But did this mean that the Decalogue was elevated above and had greater authority than the rest of the law? Does this mean that, in contrast to the rest of the laws, which were temporally conditioned, the principles announced in the Decalogue were permanent and unalterable, as is commonly believed?[81] The weight of the evidence points in the opposite direction.[82] Simply because the Decalogue was special in its form, and in the manner of its revelation and preservation, does not mean it was more binding. This conclusion may be demonstrated both from within the Pentateuch and in the remainder of the Hebrew Bible.

1. The Pentateuchal Evidence

We have already noted that the Decalogue served as the foundational covenant document that would undergird all the subsequent revelation mediated through Moses and Moses' own exposition of the terms of the covenant in Deuteronomy. Evidence that each of these was regarded as authoritative and as permanently binding as the Decalogue is clear.

The Book of the Covenant (Exod 20:22—23:19). Several relevant features of this document stand out. First, the narrator prefaces the document with "And YHWH said to Moses: 'Thus you shall say to the Israelites,'" after which the contents of the speech are given. The Book of

---

81. See Lohfink, "Kennt das Alte Testament einen Unterschied von 'Gebot' und 'Gesetz'?" 63–89.

82. So also Crüsemann, *The Torah*, 351–57.

the Covenant represents the speech of God as much as the Decalogue. The only difference is that it is mediated speech, albeit by the divinely authorized mediator (Exod 19:9; 20:18–21; Deut 5:22–31). Second, like the beginning of the Decalogue, much of the document is cast in the first person, "I . . . you" form, that is, as YHWH's voice to the people.[83] Indeed, Exod 20:22b suggests this is a continuation of the speech the people witnessed (רָאָה) YHWH give from heaven. Third, although many of the regulations are cast in third person casuistic form,[84] an equal number are cast in apodictic form much like the Decalogue (Exod 22:18—23:19). Fourth, YHWH expressly urges the people to "Be on guard" (שָׁמַר, niphal) concerning all that he has said to them—assuming they have heard his voice (23:13). Fifth, if anything, in the ceremony involving the ratification of the covenant, the Book of the Covenant played a more important role than the Decalogue.[85]

The Instructions on Holiness (Lev 17–26). Similar features are found here. First, the entire section is cast as a series of divine speeches, each introduced with the divine speech formula, וַיְדַבֵּר יְהוָה אֶל־מֹשֶׁה לֵּאמֹר, "And YHWH spoke to Moses saying."[86] Second, the entire section is cast in the "I . . . you" form, as direct divine speech. Third, like the Decalogue, much of this material is apodictic rather than casuistic in form.[87] Fourth, the code is punctuated by divine exhortations to keep all the statutes and judgments as preconditions for the people's well-being,[88] by declarations that these statutes are timeless,[89] and by YHWH's self-identification, "I am YHWH [your God]" (almost fifty times), as if to remind the people whose voice is behind what they hear Moses relay to them.[90] Fifth, the

83. Exod 20:22–26; 21:13–14; 22:23–25, 27, 29–31; 23:13–15, 18.

84. Exod 21:1—22:17. Exodus 22:25–27 is in second person casuistic form.

85. While both the Decalogue and the Book of the Covenant were recounted and written down by Moses prior to the sacrifices and the sprinkling of the blood on the altar, prior to the sprinkling of the blood on the people Moses apparently read only the Book of the Covenant (24:1–8).

86. Lev 17:1; 18:1; 19:1; 20:1; 21:16; 22:1, 17, 26; 23:1, 9, 23, 26, 33; 24:1, 13; cf. also 25:1.

87. Lev 18, 19; 20:22—21:24; etc.

88. Lev 18:4–5, 26; 19:19, 37; 20:8, 22; 25:18; 26:3.

89. Lev 17:7; 23:14, 21, 31, 41; 24:3; cf. also Num 15:15; 18:23; 19:10; 21; cf. Lev 24:8–9, 34.

90. Lev 18:2, 4–6, 21, 30; 19:3–4, 10, 12, 14, 16, 18, 25, 28, 30–32, 34, 36–37; 20:7, 8, 24; 21:12, 15, 23; 22:2–3, 8–9, 16, 30–33; 23:22, 43; 24:22; 25:17, 55; 26:1–2, 13, 44–45.

Holiness Code concludes with a lengthy list of blessings and curses that Israel will experience in the future, depending on their fidelity or infidelity to his revealed will (Lev 26).

The deuteronomic Torah (Deut 4:1–40; 5:1–26:19; 28:1–69). If one's disposition regarding the relative authority of these laws is to be determined by the texts themselves, then surely the authority of the deuteronomic Torah exceeds them all. First, Moses expressly charged the people not to add to or delete any of the words that he commanded them (4:2). Second, the narrator declares that Moses' final pastoral instructions are entirely in accord with YHWH's command to him (1:3; 34:9). Third, the instructions are punctuated by notices of their timeless relevance.[91] Fourth, Moses declares that the people's well-being and their very life depend upon fidelity to the Torah (6:24–25; 32:44–47); indeed in setting the Torah before them he gives them the choice of blessing or curse (11:26–28; 30:15–20). Fifth, by prefacing the exposition of the Sinai revelation with the Decalogue, Moses declares the fundamental unity of his present utterances with the original covenant document. Sixth, both Moses (29:8, 18 [Eng 9, 19] and the narrator (28:69 [Eng 29:1]) explicitly elevate the Torah that Moses has proclaimed to the level of the original covenant made at Sinai. Finally, the narrator attaches the following colophonic interpretation to Moses' lengthy second address: "These are the words of the covenant that YHWH commanded Moses to make (כָּרַת) with the people of Israel in the land of Moab, in addition to [the words of] the covenant that he had made with them at Horeb" (28:69 [Eng 29:1]).

The terms of this covenant were revealed in stages.[92] Comparable to the amendments of the U.S. Constitution, already at Sinai, and then in later installments given during Israel's journey to the Promised Land, YHWH revealed his will in ever-greater detail. Moses' speeches in Deuteronomy represent the culmination of that revelatory process; and the covenant renewal ceremony that underlies the entire book represents the occasion when the Israelites committed themselves to the entire package—text and interpretation. The Decalogue was indeed a very special document, but it was no more or less binding on the people of Israel than any of the other

---

91. Deut 5:29; 6:24; 11:1; 12:1, 28; 14:23; 18:5; 19:9; 23:3, 6.

92. Despite the absence of any record of the detailed revelation, in Gen 26:5 YHWH describes Abraham as having kept "My charge (מִשְׁמֶרֶת), my commands (מִצְוֹת), my statutes (חֻקּוֹת) and my instructions (תּוֹרֹת)." These expressions echo those found in Num 18 and Deuteronomy, though it is unclear how specific Abraham's knowledge of the will of God was.

constitutional documents. It symbolized the covenantal relationship that YHWH had established with his people and laid the foundations for the way in which the people were to think about that relationship both horizontally and vertically.

2. The Evidence of the Rest of the Hebrew Bible

What evidence does the rest of the Hebrew Bible provide for an elevated status of the Decalogue? The total absence of citations of and allusions to the Decalogue is striking.[93]

Moshe Weinfeld has discussed the links between the Decalogue and the rest of the Hebrew Bible in detail in two essays.[94] He begins by citing supposed allusions within the other law collections. He notes that Lev 19 opens with references to the fifth, fourth, and first commands [sic; read fourth, third, and first]: "You shall each revere your mother and father, and you shall keep my sabbaths: I am YHWH your God" (Lev 19:3–4).[95] However, it is difficult to prove that this text borrows from the Decalogue; it may just as well have been based upon a general awareness of the importance of these three commands for maintaining a covenantal culture. If these commands are based on the Decalogue, why are they rearranged? Why does the first command use יְרָא, rather than כַּבֵּד, for "honor"? Why does it reverse the order of "mother and father"? Why does it speak of "sabbaths," which regularly refers to the high holy days of the cultic calendar, rather than "the Sabbath," that is, the last day of the week? Why does the prohibition on idolatry skip the first part of the command, and then employ language totally different from the decalogic statement? Indeed the language suggests it is influenced more by the golden calf incident than the Decalogue.[96] Weinfeld also points to the list of curses of Deut 27:15–26, but he himself recognizes that although references to idolatry, incest, murder, and dishonoring parents link the text curses to the Decalogue, the content, form, and style are quite different.

93. So also Rodd, "The Ten Commandments," 82–85.

94. Weinfeld, "The Decalogue: Its Significance, Uniqueness, and Place in Israel's Tradition," 18–26; Weinfeld, "The Uniqueness of the Decalogue and Its Place in Jewish Tradition," 15–21.

95. These links are also cited by Wenham, *The Book of Leviticus*, 264; and Kaiser, "Leviticus," 1131.

96. The word מַסֵּכָה, "cast image," is regularly used of this calf. Cf. Exod 32:4, 8; 34:17; Deut 9:12, 16; Neh 9:18; Hos 13:2.

David Noel Freedman has proposed that the structure of the narratives from Exodus to 2 Kings reflects serially the violation of each of the first nine commands.[97] However, to make this work, he works with the data extremely selectively, and is forced to rearrange the commands on stealing (Josh 7), murder (Judg 19), and adultery (2 Sam 11–12) on the basis of Jer 7:9. One could just as easily find illustrations of the violations of most of the other commands in each of these narratives.[98] Indeed, the aim of the Deuteronomistic historians in particular was to demonstrate that the fundamental problem with Israel was the abandonment of the spirit of the covenant, especially the demand for exclusive devotion to YHWH, not just violations of specific commands.

Series of commands are found in several other places in the Hebrew Bible. In Job 31 the venerable primary character presents his own code of honor before God, declaring his innocence (vv. 1–4) and averring that he has not cheated in his economic dealings (vv. 5–8); lusted after his neighbor's wife (vv. 9–12); abused his servants (vv. 13–15); withheld charity from the poor, the widow, and the fatherless (vv. 16–23); put his confidence in wealth or other gods instead of in God (vv. 24–28); been heartless toward his enemy or toward those outside his own household (vv. 29–34); or abused his land (vv. 38–40). We can find several thematic links with the Decalogue in Job's confession, and we recognize that he has caught its spirit, but again the tone is more deuteronomic than decalogic.

Lists of requirements also occur in Pss 15 and 24, both of which are often interpreted as entrance liturgies. The latter seems to assume three commands. Those whose worship is acceptable to YHWH "have clean hands and pure hearts," they "do not lift up their souls to what is false," and they "do not swear deceitfully." But these statements are extremely vague and bear no verbal links whatsoever to the Decalogue. Psalm 15 is more concrete, and apart from the fact that it contains ten qualifications for acceptable worship, specific links with the Decalogue are lacking. At best, the listing of commands in the Decalogue inspires other lists.

Although the Psalter deals with virtually all the spiritual and ethical issues raised in the commands of the Decalogue (except perhaps the Sabbath),[99] to say that the Psalter "supports the principles of the

---

97. Freedman, *The Nine Commandments.*

98. See also Rodd's critique, *Glimpses of a Strange Land*, 82.

99. Cf. Wenham, "The Ethics of the Psalms," 183.

Decalogue"[100] is a far cry from establishing that the Decalogue itself uniquely inspired the psalmists. In most instances the links that have been cited as allusive to the Decalogue are closer to the Torah of Deuteronomy or the Instructions on Holiness than to the Decalogue. Weinfeld argues that the tone of Pss 50 and 81 resembles the admonitions in Jeremiah and Hosea, and that both psalms hint at festive covenant ceremonies, which he takes to be Shabuoth.[101] He suggests that prophets (Jeremiah and Hosea) and psalmists deliberately remonstrated the people on the festival celebrating the theophany on Sinai and the revelation of the law. The thematic link between the theophany on Zion described in Ps 50:1–7, climaxing in the declaration, "I am God, your God," and the Sinai theophany seems obvious. Supposedly the Ten Words would be read at these festivals, but the psalmists and prophets seized the opportunity to expose the hypocrisy of those who led in these recitations but refused to live by the principles of the covenant.[102] However, Weinfeld overstates the case when he asserts that Ps 50:7 quotes the opening of the Decalogue. The differences between the divine self-introductions are obvious when they are juxtaposed:

| Exod 20:2 | אָנֹכִי יְהוָה אֱלֹהֶיךָ | I am YHWH your God. |
| Ps 50:7 | אֱלֹהִים אֱלֹהֶיךָ אָנֹכִי | God your God I am. |

Verses 16–19 may allude to the Decalogue, though they seem also to be influenced by other constitutional documents:

> [16]But to the wicked God says:
> "What right have you to recite my statutes,
> or take my covenant on your lips?
> [17]For you hate discipline,
> and you cast my words behind you.
> [18]You make friends with a thief when you see one,
> and you keep company with adulterers.
> [19]You give your mouth free rein for evil,
> and your tongue frames deceit" (NRSV).

---

100. Thus, ibid., 187.

101. Weinfeld, "The Uniqueness of the Decalogue," 21–27; Weinfeld, "The Decalogue in Israel's Tradition," 28–32.

102. Weinfeld, "The Uniqueness of the Decalogue," 23.

The references to theft, adultery, and falsehood in verses 18–20 *may* derive from the Decalogue, but the vocabulary and style mute specific memory of the document.

Psalm 81 offers a more likely candidate for direct decalogic influence, especially verse 11 [ET 10], which seems to echo the preamble to the Decalogue:[103]

Exod 20:2	מִבֵּית עֲבָדִים	מֵאֶרֶץ מִצְרַיִם	אֲשֶׁר הוֹצֵאתִיךָ	אֱלֹהֶיךָ	יְהוָה אָנֹכִי
Ps 81:11 [ET 10]		מֵאֶרֶץ מִצְרַיִם	הַמַּעַלְךָ	אֱלֹהֶיךָ	יְהוָה אָנֹכִי
Lev 11:45		מֵאֶרֶץ מִצְרַיִם	הַמַּעֲלֶה אֶתְכֶם		כִּי אֲנִי יְהוָה
Deut 20:1		מֵאֶרֶץ מִצְרַיִם	הַמַּעַלְךָ	אֱלֹהֶיךָ עִמָּךְ	כִּי־ יְהוָה

Exod 20:2	I am YHWH your God	who brought you out from the land of Egypt.
Ps 81:11 [ET 10]	I am YHWH your God	who brought you up from the land of Egypt.
Lev 11:45	For I am YHWH	who brought you up from the land of Egypt.
Deut 20:1	For YHWH your God is with you, who brought you out from the land of Egypt.	

But the link with the Decalogue is not as sure as it appears on first sight. The change of verb from הוֹצִיא, "to take out," to הֶעֱלָה, "to bring up," is striking. Furthermore, apart from the form of the initial personal pronoun, the psalmist's statement bears a closer resemblance to Lev 11:45 than to Exod 20:2. It also recalls the third person version of the divine introduction formula in Deut 20:1. Indeed the Shemaʿ in verse 9 [ET 8],[104] and the vocabulary around this verse link this psalm much more tightly to the deuteronomic Torah than the Decalogue.[105]

As for the Decalogue in the prophets, some have found analogues to the list of commands in the Decalogue in the three catalogues of actions that distinguish righteous people from the wicked that Ezekiel provides in chapter 18 (vv. 5–9, 10–13, 14–18).[106] Although the references to idolatry, adultery, and theft appear to link this list to the Decalogue, the sharp differences in language render direct inspiration unlikely. The lists in this

---

103. According to Schmidt (*Die Zehn Gebote*, 33) this echo demonstrates that the Decalogue was a fixture in Israel's worship.

104. Ps 81:9[Eng 8]: שְׁמַע עַמִּי וְאָעִידָה בָּךְ יִשְׂרָאֵל אִם־תִּשְׁמַע־לִי, "Hear, O my people, while I admonish you! O Israel, if you would but listen to me!"

105. Note the following "deuteronomic" expressions: "to testify against" (בְּ + הֵעִיד, v. 9[Eng 8]; cf. Deut 31:28); "strange god" (אֵל זָר, v. 10[Eng 9]; cf. זָרִים, Deut 32:16); "foreign god" (אֵל נֵכָר, v. 10[Eng 9]; cf. Deut 31:16); et passim in vv. 12–17[Eng 11–16].

106. For translation and discussion, see Block, *The Book of Ezekiel Chapters 1–24*, 564–79.

chapter display a pronounced priestly stamp, but I have argued elsewhere that some features may also have been inspired by what some call the royal "code of honor,"[107] perhaps a generally recognized if not codified standard of royal/administrative conduct.

Similar observations apply to Isaiah's version of the "entrance liturgy" in Isa 33:14b–16.

פָּחֲדוּ בְצִיּוֹן חַטָּאִים	[14]The sinners in Zion are afraid;
אָחֲזָה רְעָדָה חֲנֵפִים	trembling has seized the godless:
מִי יָגוּר לָנוּ אֵשׁ אוֹכֵלָה	"Who among us can dwell with 'Esh 'Okelah?
מִי־יָגוּר לָנוּ מוֹקְדֵי עוֹלָם:	Who among us can dwell with everlasting burnings?"
הֹלֵךְ צְדָקוֹת	[15]He who walks righteously
וְדֹבֵר מֵישָׁרִים	and speaks uprightly,
מֹאֵס בְּבֶצַע מַעֲשַׁקּוֹת	who despises the gain of oppressions,
נֹעֵר כַּפָּיו מִתְּמֹךְ בַּשֹּׁחַד	who shakes his hands, lest they hold a bribe,
אֹטֵם אָזְנוֹ מִשְּׁמֹעַ דָּמִים	who stops his ears from hearing of bloodshed
וְעֹצֵם עֵינָיו מֵרְאוֹת בְּרָע:	and shuts his eyes from looking on evil,
הוּא מְרוֹמִים יִשְׁכֹּן	[16]he will dwell on the heights;
מְצָדוֹת סְלָעִים מִשְׂגַּבּוֹ	his place of defense will be the fortresses of rocks;
לַחְמוֹ נִתָּן	his bread will be given him;
מֵימָיו נֶאֱמָנִים:	his water will be sure.

The opening question, מִי־יָגוּר, "Who may sojourn?" גוּר, "to sojourn, abide," recalls the questions in Ps 15:1 (24:3). In Isaiah's use of אֵשׁ אוֹכֵלָה (translated attributively "the devouring fire," by virtually all translations) as an epithet of YHWH,[108] we hear an allusion to the original revelatory event at Sinai and the people's fearful response,[109] but the combination of motifs is more deuteronomic than decalogic. As in Pss 15 and 24, Isaiah follows up this question with a series of six ethical responses, but these bear no relationship whatsoever to the Decalogue.

---

107. Block, *Ezekiel Chapters 1–24*, 568–69. See also Pohlmann, *Ezechiel Studien*, 225–31.

108. As in Deut 4:24; 9:3. Like most translations, the NIV treats both predicates אֵל קַנָּא and אֵשׁ אֹכְלָה as adjectives. However the pattern of verbless clauses in the Pentateuch suggests that the second element in both clauses functions as a proper noun. See Andersen, *The Hebrew Verbless Clause in the Pentateuch*. Elsewhere אֵל קַנָּא may mean, "a jealous/passionate God" (Exod 34:14b; Deut 6:15; 9:3; Josh 24:19; Nah 1:2), but Exod 34:14a explicitly identifies Qanna' as a proper name for God (so also Hoftijzer, "Nominal Clause," 494).

109. Deut 4:9–14, 36; 5:4, 22–27; 9:10, 15; 10:4; 18:16.

Hosea 4:2 is a more likely candidate for direct decalogic inspiration. Here Hosea summarizes YHWH's case against Israel in the eighth century BCE:

> ¹YHWH has a case against the inhabitants of the land.
> There is no faithfulness (אֱמֶת) or loyalty (חֶסֶד),
> and no knowledge (דַּעַת) of God in the land.
> ²There is cursing and lying,
> murder, and stealing, and adultery break out;
> bloodshed follows bloodshed.
> ³Therefore the land mourns,
> and all who live in it languish;
> together with the wild animals and the birds of the air,
> even the fish of the sea are perishing.

Admittedly, the vocabulary for murder (רָצַח), theft (גָּנַב), and adultery (נָאַף) is the same as in the Decalogue, but the order of the latter two is reversed.[110] Furthermore, the rest of the indictment has no connection at all to the Decalogue, suggesting these are three crimes drawn from common experience or from the constitutional documents in general.

In Jer 7:9–10 the prophet asks a telling question: "Will you steal, murder, commit adultery, swear falsely, make offerings to Baal, and go after other gods that you have not known, and then come and stand before me in this house, which is called by my name?" Again the vocabulary for theft, murder, and adultery is the same as in the Decalogue, but the order (theft, murder, adultery) differs from both Exod 20 and Deut 5 (murder, adultery, theft),[111] and the reference to "walking after other gods that you have not known" is thoroughly deuteronomic (Deut 6:14; 8:19; 11:28; 13:4 [Eng 3]; 28:14). More significantly, the context seems especially concerned with injustice against one's neighbors and exploitation of the poor, issues that in the Decalogue are latent at best. These charges may reflect the spirit of the Decalogue, rather than specific commands, but those features may be more easily attributed to deuteronomic rather

110. Weiss ("The Decalogue in Prophetic Literature," 71) argues that since these three crimes constitute a chiastic inversion of the arrangement in LXX^B to Exod 20, the prophet alludes to a variant tradition of "the Second Table" of the Decalogue. It seems more likely that Hosea influenced LXX^B.

111. Weiss (ibid., 70–71) argues that Jeremiah's order chiastically inverts the decalogic tradition that underlies Jesus' statement in Luke 18:20, Paul's in Rom 13:9, the Nash Papyrus, and LXX^B. But the influence may have been in the opposite direction. His claim that Amos 3:1–2 is based on the Decalogue (ibid., 72–81) is even less convincing.

than decalogic influence. Even though the Old Testament provides no evidence that the Decalogue was elevated above the other constitutional documents or that it had greater authority than the Book of the Covenant, Instructions on Holiness, or the Torah of Deuteronomy, it seems to have gained a special place in Jewish liturgical tradition in the Second Temple period. The Mishnah (*m. Tamid* 5:1) suggests that the morning ritual included priestly recitation of the Decalogue (Deut 5:6–21 [or Exod 20:2–17]), the Shema' (Deut 6:4–9), Deut 11:13–21, and Num 15:37–41. Based on the discovery of numerous phylacteries in the caves of Qumran, as well as the Nash Papyrus,[112] it seems that even away from the temple Jews would recite the Decalogue daily.[113] Whereas the phylacteries tend to cite the version of Deuteronomy, and although the Papyrus exhibits heavy influence from Deuteronomy, the latter follows Exod 20:8–11 in grounding the Sabbath in the divine creation week. Both Babylonian and Palestinian Talmuds note that the recitation of the Decalogue in daily prayers was later forbidden by the rabbis, because sectarians asserted that the Decalogue was the only part of the Bible revealed directly by God to Moses at Sinai.[114] This accords with early second century CE phylacteries found in the Wadi Muraba'at, which cited only the four traditional texts: Exod 13:1–10; 13:11–16; Deut 6:4–9; 11:13–21.[115] The omission of the Decalogue seems to have been a reaction to Christians' claim to its unique status above Israel's other constitutional documents. Judaism has refused to isolate it from the larger corpus of biblical law.[116]

The notion of the Decalogue's unique status among Christians has a long history, going back to Origen and the other church fathers,[117] despite

112. For an early discussion of the Decalogue in the Nash Papyrus, see Burkitt, "The Hebrew Papyrus of the Ten Commandments," 392–408. For a readily accessible photograph of the document, see Würthwein, *The Text of the Old Testament*, 144.

113. Fragments of the Decalogue occur on 4QPhyl^a and 4QPhyl^b. For discussion of the Phylacteries from Qumran and their liturgical significance, see Vermes, "Pre-Mishnaic Jewish Worship and the Phylacteries," 65–72.

114. *Berakhoth* 3c (P.T.) and *Berakhoth* (B.T.). See Vermes, "Pre-Mishnaic Jewish Worship," 69; Schiffmann, "Phylacteries and Mezuzot," 676.

115. *Menahoth* 3:7; *Kelim* 18:8; *Sanhedrin* 11:3.

116. For further discussion of the use of the Decalogue in early Judaism, see Vokes, "The Ten Commandments in the New Testament and in First Century Judaism," 146–54. Vokes observes that early Judaism exhibited an urge to sum up the law in one phrase, but insisted on the equality of every command in the Torah" (ibid., 150).

117. See Salvesen, "Early Syriac, Greek and Latin Views of the Decalogue."

the lack of support from the New Testament, which never formally cites the Decalogue as a cultic or liturgical document. Jesus and the apostles were obviously familiar with the Decalogue and grounded some of their teaching on it. The antitheses in the Sermon on the Mount (Matt 5:21–37) feature terms found in the Decalogue, but elsewhere Jesus reduces the principles of covenant relationship to two commands: "You shall love the Lord your God with all your heart and your neighbor as yourself" (Matt 19:16–30; Mark 10:17–31; Luke 18:18–30). This statement captures precisely the two dimensions of covenant relationship spelled out in the Decalogue, but these two dimensions are not unique to this document. Explicit citation of statements found in the Decalogue are found in both James (2:8–13) and Paul (Rom 8:7–13; 13:8–10; Eph 6:1–4).[118] Paul may have been alluding to the stone tablets in 2 Cor 3, where he emphasizes that the law engraved on stone letter by letter dispenses only death, whereas the law written on the heart by the Spirit dispenses life. This externalism often associated with the first covenant but really a problem of Judaism finally gives way in the new.[119] Paul's ready use of the document reflects longstanding Jewish catechetical tradition and the importance of the Decalogue in early Christian paraenesis.

Conclusion

Apart from Moses citation of the Decalogue at the beginning of his second valedictory address in Deut 5, there is no evidence that the Decalogue was deemed to have exceptional authority in Israel. The absence of unequivocal citations and the paucity of allusions to document in the Hebrew Bible present a striking contrast to pervasive influence by the Book of the Covenant and the Instructions on Holiness, but especially the Torah of Deuteronomy. If we find traces of the Decalogue, its wording and perspective appear refracted through the lenses of these documents, particularly the latter, so much so that when we spot apparent allusions we must ask whether they derive from the Decalogue itself or familiarity with the deuteronomic instruction.

118. Vokes ("The Ten Commandments in the New Testament and in First Century Judaism," 153) observes that for Paul, "The Law as law passes away, but as an ethical norm it still remains."

119. In this he agrees with Jer 31:31–34. But this internal aspect of the new covenant is not new absolutely. Every element of the new covenant cited by Jeremiah was operative in the hearts of true believers under the first covenant.

Indeed, if any single document incorporated into the Pentateuch was elevated above the rest in the thinking of Israel's spiritual leaders or the authors of Scripture, it had to be the deuteronomic Torah of Moses.[120] According to the internal evidence of Deuteronomy, the instructions he proclaimed as Torah rise to the level of the commands and statutes (30:8–11; cf. 1:3) that came directly from YHWH. YHWH himself authorized and directed Moses' utterances in the book. That is why they are canonical by definition (4:2): those who keep them will be declared righteous (6:25); obedience to them is the key to life and well-being for the people generally (11:1–32), but especially for the king, who was to embody covenant righteousness as described in the Torah of Moses (17:14–20); they were transcribed by Moses' own hand (31:9); they were handed to the Levitical priests as the guardians of the Torah (31:9; 33:10); the written copy was placed beside the ark of the covenant as a witness to their commitments, and equal in authority to that of the Decalogue (31:24–26); and only this document figures in the instructions for liturgical gatherings of the people. At the end of every seventh year, at the festival of Sukkoth, the entire Torah was to be read before all the people.[121] No such instructions have been given for the Decalogue. The importance of the liturgy involving the deuteronomic Torah is reflected in the formula for success in 31:12–13: "Read, that you may hear, that you may fear [YHWH], that you may obey, that you may live."

120. Note the frequency of references to obedience to YHWH "as I command you." Variations occur in Deut 1:43; 4:2, 40; 6:2, 6; 7:11; 8:1, 11; 11:8, 13, 22, 27; 12:11, 28, 32; 15:5, 11, 15; 18:18; 19:7, 9; 24:18, 22; 27:1, 4, 10; 28:1, 13, 14, 15; 30:2, 8, 11, 16; 32:46.

121. The Scriptures have a variety of names for the deuteronomic Torah. סֵפֶר תּוֹרַת מֹשֶׁה, "the book of the Torah of Moses" (Josh 8:31, 32; 23:6; 2 Kgs 14:6; Neh 8:1); סֵפֶר תּוֹרַת מֹשֶׁה, "the book of Moses" (Neh 13:1; 2 Chr 25:4; 35:12); תּוֹרַת מֹשֶׁה, "the Torah of Moses" (1 Kgs 2:3; 2 Kgs 23:25; 1 Chr 23:18; 30:16; Ezra 3:2; 7:6; Dan 9:11, 13; Mal 3:22); סֵפֶר תּוֹרַת־יְהוָה בְּיַד־מֹשֶׁה, "the book of the Torah of YHWH by the hand of Moses" (2 Chr 34:14, 15); and דְּבַר־יְהוָה בְּיַד־מֹשֶׁה, "the words of YHWH by the hand of Moses" (2 Chr 35:6). Compare the New Testament references to "the νόμος of Moses" (Luke 2:22; 24:44; John 7:23; Acts 13:39; 15:5 [cf. "the manner of Moses" in v. 1]; 28:23; 1 Cor 9:9; Heb 10:28); "Moses" used as a substitute for ὁ νόμος, (Luke 16:29, 31; 24:27; John 5:45, 46; Acts 6:11; 21:21; 26:22; 2 Cor 3:15); "the book of Moses" (Mark 12:26); Moses' "writings" (John 5:47); vaguer references to laws that Moses commanded (Matt 8:4; 19:7, 8; 22:24; Mark 1:44; 7:10; 10:3, 4; Luke 5:14; John 8:5; Acts 6:14); statements like "Moses wrote" (Luke 20:28, referring to Deut 25:5); "Moses says" (Rom 10:5, 19); "customs that Moses delivered to us" (Acts 6:14). In the Gospels Jesus himself frequently refers to Moses as a recognized authority in Jewish tradition and as an authority behind his own teachings.

Read ⇨ Hear ⇨ Fear ⇨ Obey ⇨ Live.

This extraordinary status of the deuteronomic Torah is evident throughout the Hebrew Bible. This book is the heart of the Torah, which priests were to teach, and model,[122] which psalmists praised,[123] to which the prophets appealed,[124] by which faithful kings ruled[125] and righteous citizens lived (Ps 1). And herein lies the profound significance of the Decalogue, for in the Torah of Moses the covenantal seed that was planted by YHWH himself has come to full flower. In the Torah he expounds on the grace of God demonstrated in his election and redemption of Israel, as summarized in the preamble to the Decalogue, and demonstrated in the revelation of his will, as summarized in the ten commands of the Decalogue. And herein we discover how multicolored and multifaceted is the decalogic call to love YHWH with all one's inner being, one's entire person, and all one's resources, and to love one's neighbor as oneself.

---

122. Deut 33:10; 2 Chr 15:3; 19:8; Mal 2:6, 9; cf. Jer 18:18; Ezek 7:26; Ezra 7:10.

123. Pss 19:7–14; 119; etc.

124. Isa 1:10; 5:24; 8:20; 30:9; 51:7.

125. 1 Kgs 2:2–4; 2 Kgs 14:6; 22:11; 23:25.

Excursus A:
How Shall We Number the Ten Commands?
The Deuteronomy Version (5:1–21)

Table 3: Two Approaches to Numbering the Decalogue

The Reformed Tradition	The Catholic and Lutheran Tradition
[6]I am YHWH your God, who brought you out of the land of Egypt, out of the house of slavery.	[6]I am YHWH your God, who brought you out of the land of Egypt, out of the house of slavery.
[7]You shall have no other gods before me.	[7]You shall have no other gods before me. [8]You shall not make for yourself a carved image, or any likeness of anything that is in heaven above, or that is on the earth beneath, or that is in the water under the earth. [9]You shall not bow down to them or serve them; for I YHWH your God am a jealous God, visiting the iniquity of the fathers on the children to the third and fourth generation of those who hate me, [10] but showing ḥesed to thousands of those who love me and keep my commands.
[8]You shall not make for yourself a carved image, or any likeness of anything that is in heaven above, or that is on the earth beneath, or that is in the water under the earth. [9]You shall not bow down to them or serve them; for I YHWH your God am a jealous God, visiting the iniquity of the fathers on the children to the third and fourth generation of those who hate me, [10] but showing ḥesed to thousands of those who love me and keep my commands.	
[11]You shall not bear the name of YHWH your God in vain, for YHWH will not hold him guiltless who takes his name in vain.	[11]You shall not bear the name of YHWH your God in vain, for YHWH will not hold him guiltless who takes his name in vain.

The Reformed Tradition	The Catholic and Lutheran Tradition
[12]Observe the Sabbath day, by keeping it holy, as YHWH your God commanded you. [13]Six days you shall labor and do all your work, [14]but the seventh day is a Sabbath to YHWH your God. On it you shall not do any work, you or your son or your daughter or your male servant or your female servant, or your ox or your donkey or any of your livestock, or the sojourner who is within your gates, that your male servant and your female servant may rest as well as you. [15]You shall remember that you were a slave in the land of Egypt, and YHWH your God brought you out from there with a mighty hand and an outstretched arm. Therefore YHWH your God commanded you to keep the Sabbath day.	[12]Observe the Sabbath day, by keeping it holy, as YHWH your God commanded you. [13]Six days you shall labor and do all your work, [14]but the seventh day is a Sabbath to YHWH your God. On it you shall not do any work, you or your son or your daughter or your male servant or your female servant, or your ox or your donkey or any of your livestock, or the sojourner who is within your gates, that your male servant and your female servant may rest as well as you. [15]You shall remember that you were a slave in the land of Egypt, and YHWH your God brought you out from there with a mighty hand and an outstretched arm. Therefore YHWH your God commanded you to keep the Sabbath day.
[16]Honor your father and your mother, as YHWH your God commanded you, that your days may be long, and that it may go well with you in the land that YHWH your God is giving you.	[16]Honor your father and your mother, as YHWH your God commanded you, that your days may be long, and that it may go well with you in the land that YHWH your God is giving you.
[17]You shall not murder.	[17]You shall not murder.
[18]And you shall not commit adultery.	[18]And you shall not commit adultery.
[19]And you shall not steal.	[19]And you shall not steal.
[20]And you shall not bear false witness against your neighbor.	[20]And you shall not bear false witness against your neighbor.

The Reformed Tradition	The Catholic and Lutheran Tradition
[21] And you shall not covet (חָמַד) your neighbor's wife. And you shall not desire (הִתְאַוָּה) your neighbor's house, his field, or his male servant, or his female servant, his ox, or his donkey, or anything that is your neighbor's.	[21] And you shall not covet (חָמַד) your neighbor's wife.
	And you shall not desire (הִתְאַוָּה) your neighbor's house, his field, or his male servant, or his female servant, his ox, or his donkey, or anything that is your neighbor's.

Considerations in Enumerating the Terms of the Decalogue[126]

1. The ambiguity of Exodus 20:17 in MT. The text is obviously cast as two independent clause commands. However, whereas the previous commands are marked as separate paragraphs by *sĕtûmôt* (סְתוּמוֹת, nine spaces) in the *Leningrad Codex* these two clauses are separated by only two spaces. The repetition of the verb חָמַד, "to covet," and the meaning of בַּיִת as "household," may suggest that the second command is intended to be interpreted as an expansion/clarification of the first. Nevertheless, the way the second clause opens (לֹא + imperfect) is identical to the previous four commands, which scribes and scholars unanimously separate as separate commands.

2. The modifications to these commands in Deuteronomy. Deuteronomy 5:17 removes the potential ambiguity by:

(a)   adding a *waw* conjunction to the second command exactly as it had done with the preceding four commands;

(b)   changing the verb of the second command from חָמַד, "to covet," to אוה (hithpael), "to crave for";

---

126. Discussions of the issue in Jewish tradition tend to focus on the relationship between the narrative opening statement and the commands. See Breuer, "Dividing the Decalogue into Verses and Commands," 291–330. Breuer also recognizes the syntactical and substantive differences between the Exodus and Deuteronomy versions of the Decalogue (ibid., 313–14). For a discourse analysis of the Decalogue yielding similar results, see DeRouchie, *A Call to Covenant Love*, 115–17, 127–32.

(c)   transposing בַּיִת, "house, household," and אֵשֶׁת רֵעֶךָ, "wife of your
        neighbor," thereby forestalling the treatment of one's wife merely as
        property like the rest of the household;

(d)   isolating the command not to covet one's neighbor's wife and treat-
        ing it as a separate "line-item";

(e)   adding "his field" as a complement to "his house," and creating a
        third pair of entities.

*3. The grammar, syntax, and content of Exod 20:3–6, which is identical to
Deut 5:7–10 (except for the addition of two* waw *conjunctions):*

Figure 3: A Comparison of Exodus 20:3–6 and Deuteronomy 5:7–10

Exodus 20:3–6	Deuteronomy 5:7–10
לֹא יִהְיֶה־לְךָ אֱלֹהִים אֲחֵרִים עַל־פָּנָי:	לֹא יִהְיֶה־לְךָ אֱלֹהִים אֲחֵרִים עַל־פָּנָי:
לֹא־תַעֲשֶׂה־לְךָ פֶסֶל וְכָל־תְּמוּנָה	לֹא־תַעֲשֶׂה־לְךָ פֶסֶל כָּל־תְּמוּנָה
אֲשֶׁר בַּשָּׁמַיִם מִמַּעַל וַאֲשֶׁר בָּאָרֶץ מִתָּחַת	אֲשֶׁר בַּשָּׁמַיִם מִמַּעַל וַאֲשֶׁר בָּאָרֶץ מִתָּחַת
וַאֲשֶׁר בַּמַּיִם מִתַּחַת לָאָרֶץ:	וַאֲשֶׁר בַּמַּיִם מִתַּחַת לָאָרֶץ:
לֹא־תִשְׁתַּחֲוֶה לָהֶם וְלֹא תָעָבְדֵם	לֹא־תִשְׁתַּחֲוֶה לָהֶם וְלֹא תָעָבְדֵם
כִּי אָנֹכִי יְהוָה אֱלֹהֶיךָ אֵל קַנָּא	כִּי אָנֹכִי יְהוָה אֱלֹהֶיךָ אֵל קַנָּא
פֹּקֵד עֲוֹן אָבֹת עַל־בָּנִים	פֹּקֵד עֲוֹן אָבוֹת עַל־בָּנִים
עַל־שִׁלֵּשִׁים וְעַל־רִבֵּעִים לְשֹׂנְאָי:	וְעַל־שִׁלֵּשִׁים וְעַל־רִבֵּעִים לְשֹׂנְאָי:
וְעֹשֶׂה חֶסֶד לַאֲלָפִים לְאֹהֲבַי	וְעֹשֶׂה חֶסֶד לַאֲלָפִים לְאֹהֲבַי
וּלְשֹׁמְרֵי מִצְוֹתָי:	וּלְשֹׁמְרֵי מִצְוֹתָי:

(a)   The commands regarding exclusive devotion to YHWH and the
        manufacture of images are held together by references to YHWH
        in the first person (like the preamble). Thereafter he is referred to
        in the third person.

(b)   The first imperative statement concerns the prohibition of rivals
        to YHWH. The second is best interpreted as a clarification of the
        first, that is, a prohibition of the manufacture of images that may
        be treated as rivals to YHWH and erected next to the ark of the
        covenant in the Tabernacle/Temple (cf. 1 Sam 5).

(c)   Following the presentation of YHWH as formless in 4:12–14, in
        4:15–19 the issue is clearly not the reduction of YHWH to plastic

image, but the manufacture of images that, alongside the heavenly objects, might vie for Israel's allegiance.

(d) The identification/characterization of YHWH in these statements as אֵל קַנָּא, "impassioned El," points to the manufacture of rival deities, not the manufacture of physical representations of YHWH. Elsewhere this expression occurs only in contexts involving the worship of idols, never in contexts involving the portrayal of YHWH in physical form.

(e) If these two imperatives are separated and treated as two different commands, then the plural suffixes on לָהֶם, "to *them*," and לֹא תָעָבְדֵם, "you shall not serve *them*," in Deut 5:9 lack an antecedent. Since all the nouns preceding these forms in verse 8 are singular, the nearest antecedent is אֱלֹהִים אֲחֵרִים, "other gods," in the first command.

(f) The Massoretes treated these as a single entity, running the prohibition on images immediately after the prohibition on other gods. In fact, in both Exodus and Deuteronomy, MT treats the declarative statement that functions as the preamble to this document as a part of this long paragraph.

3

Bearing the Name of the LORD with Honor[1]

THE DECALOGUE'S COMMAND CONCERNING the name of the LORD has been variously interpreted. I grew up thinking that the command "You shall not take the name of the LORD your God in vain" (Exod 20:7, KJV) was concerned primarily with the flippant use of epithets for God in profanities and swear words. And so to this day I am appalled when Christians use expletives like "Oh, my Lord!" and "Oh, my God!" for surely this is taking the name of the Lord in vain.

Traditional Jewish understanding of the second command of the Decalogue[2] is reflected in the NJPSV translation, "You shall not swear falsely by the name of the LORD your God; for the LORD will not clear one who swears falsely by his name." By this interpretation this command bans the use of the divine name in false oaths to back up assertions in court or otherwise.[3] But another Jewish tradition, dating to the Second

---

1. This essay was previously published in *Bibliotheca Sacra* 168 (2011) 20–31.

2. Following the Roman Catholic and Lutheran traditions of numbering the commands, this reflects the discourse structure of the document better than the Reformed numbering, which views this command as third, not second. See Block, "'You Shall Not Covet Your Neighbor's Wife,'" chapter 5 in Block, *The Gospel according to Moses*.

3. Possibly "to swear falsely" in Jer 7:9 provides early evidence for interpreting the second command of the Decalogue as a prohibition on false oaths. See Jepsen, "Beiträge zur Auslegung und Geschichte des Dekalogs," 291–92. However, it uses different terms than Exod 20:7 and Deut 5:11, and in any case it says nothing about the name. Where the name is significant in false oaths, "in my name" is added to the idiom (Lev 19:12; Zech 5:4). It is not difficult to see how the present expression could have been interpreted this

Temple period, based the avoidance of *pronouncing* the name of YHWH on this command. "You shall not take the name of the LORD in vain" then means either "You shall not mispronounce it" or "You shall not pronounce it in a wrong context (outside the temple),"[4] thereby bringing on a person the curse of God.[5] The fact that יהוה continued to be used in names found in extrabiblical texts until the Exile[6] and in biblical texts well after the Exile[7] suggests that the name was regularly pronounced with its vowels well into the fifth century BCE. However, by the time the Septuagint was translated in the third century BCE, Jews had developed such fear of misusing God's name that they stopped speaking the name aloud, for fear of death should they mispronounce it (cf. Lev 24:16).[8] Therefore they replaced it with אֲדֹנָי. This meant that when the translators encountered the tetragrammaton (YHWH) they rendered it as Κύριος,[9] which carries over into New Testament citations of Old Testament texts involving the divine name,[10] and into English translations of the name as

---

way. If one bears the name of Yahweh as a brand borne by a vassal, then it is natural in oaths to invoke one's suzerain as guarantor of the oath. In Deut 6:13 and 10:20 swearing by the name of Yahweh (alone) is one dimension of exclusive covenant commitment (cf. 1 Kgs 22:16; 2 Chr 18:15; Isa 48:1; Jer 12:16). To swear falsely by the name of Yahweh is one application of falsely bearing the name of Yahweh. The same would be true of blessing people in the name of Yahweh (Ps 129:8; cf. Deut 10:8; 21:5), or coming in the name of Yahweh (Ps 118:26), or prophesying in his name without having been authorized to do so. So swearing falsely involves the fraudulent use of the name, but it should not be limited to this.

4. Cf. *m. Tamid* 7:2, "In the sanctuary one says the Name as it is written, but in the provinces, with a euphemism." See also Josephus, *The Antiquities of the Jews* 2.12.4; 1QS 6:27b–7:2a; *m. Sotah* 7:6; *b. Sotah* 38b; *m. Tamid* 7:2; *m. Sanhedrin* 10:1; *m. Berakhot* 9:5; *b. Pesahim* 50a.

5. Cf. Hartman and Sperling, "God, Names of," 675.

6. For example, see Lachish 2:2 in the Lachish Letters.

7. Many Yahwistic names occur in the list of returnees in Neh 12:1–37.

8. The *Tanakh* reads, "If he also pronounces the name LORD, he shall be put to death" (NJPSV).

9. However, some early Septuagintal manuscripts render the name with the tetragrammaton in archaic script or as Greek Ἰαω. See Rösel, "Names of God," 600–602. This practice of rendering יהוה as κύριος creates an interesting problem in Ezekiel, where אֲדֹנָי יהוה "the Lord Yahweh," occurs more than two hundred times. Usually one word is dropped, but in more than fifty instances the Greek reads κύριος κύριος (e.g., Ezek 12:10).

10. This is often unsignaled in English translations of New Testament citations of Old Testament texts (e.g., Rom 10:13, "Everyone who calls on the name of the Lord shall be saved," NRSV).

"LORD." To this day orthodox Jews refer to YHWH by saying, "*Ha-Shem*" or "the [Ineffable] Name."[11]

Based on extrabiblical analogues some scholars today understand this command as a taboo on the *magical use* of the name to manipulate deity and to exploit divine power in self-interested pursuits.[12]

These interpretations are all very interesting—certainly more interesting than the bland renderings in the New International Version ("You shall not misuse the name of the LORD your God, for the LORD will not hold anyone guiltless who misuses his name"), the New Revised Standard Version ("You shall not make wrongful use of the name of the LORD your God, for the LORD will not acquit anyone who misuses his name"), or the misleading traditional rendering of the King James Version ("Thou shalt not take the name of the LORD thy God in vain, for the LORD will not hold him guiltless that taketh his name in vain").

Given the prominence of "name theology" in the Scriptures, all these interpretations may actually miss the central issue, namely, that of *wearing the name of YHWH as a badge or a brand of ownership.* The key to this injunction may well be the verb נָשָׂא which does not mean "to take," "to misuse," or "to pronounce,"[13] all of which call for different idioms.[14] Here it bears its normal sense of "to bear, to carry." The present collocation of "bearing a name" occurs elsewhere only in Exod 28:12 and 29, the first of which speaks of the names of the sons of Israel inscribed on the two onyx stones of remembrance on the shoulder pieces of the ephod. The high priest thus "bears" (נָשָׂא) these names on the breastpiece of judgment on his heart (v. 29), whenever he goes into the holy place representing the Israelites before God. Aaron literally and physically bore the names of the Israelite tribes on his body, reminding YHWH of his covenant with them. Also on the front of the high priest's turban was a

---

11. Joel M. Hoffman argues that the tetragrammaton (which is made up entirely of consonants that are often used as vowel letters) was never pronounced (*In the Beginning*, 44–47).

12. See Walton, "Interpreting the Bible as an Ancient Near Eastern Document," 313–18.

13. Contra *HALOT* 1:725–26.

14. In addition, "they carry in vain" is elliptical for "they carry your name in vain." So also Briggs, *Psalms*, 499. "To lift on one's lips" (Ps 50:16), or "to lift [the names of the gods] on my lips" (16:4; author's translation), means "to pronounce." This sense is reflected in Exod 23:13, "and make no mention of the names of other gods, nor let it be heard on your lips" (author's translation).

medallion engraved with קֹדֶשׁ לַיהוה, "holy belonging to YHWH" (28:36, lit. translation). According to Num 6:27, in the future the Aaronic priests would "put" YHWH's name on the Israelites by declaring for them what came to be known as "the Aaronic blessing." And because they bore the stamp of his name they were objects of his blessing. In Deuteronomy the expression קֹדֶשׁ לַיהוה, "holy belonging to YHWH," is applied to Israel as a whole (Deut 26:19; cf. 7:6; 14:2, 21). Like the Shema', which was to be inscribed on houses and gates and on phylacteries on the forehead, to bear the name of God means to have his name branded on one's person as a mark of divine ownership.

Others carried or bore the name of YHWH in a slightly different sense. When YHWH commissioned prophets, he authorized them to use professional formulas like the citation formula, "Thus has the Lord YHWH declared" (Ezek 2:4), or the summons formula, "Hear the word of the LORD" (Amos 3:1). The prophetic expression "the declaration of the Lord YHWH" (נְאֻם אֲדֹנָי יהוה) functioned as an oral signatory formula. It is like the stamp of a king's official bearing the name of the king. With such a stamp, authorized personnel would mark official documents on the king's behalf (e.g., "Belonging to Shama, servant of Jeroboam" [Megiddo Seal]; "Belonging to Jaazaniah servant of the King" [Tel-en-Nasbeh Seal]; or more directly, "Belonging to Hezekiah [son of] Ahaz King of Judah"). In Ezek 13:3–9 YHWH complained about false prophets.

> Thus has the Lord Yahweh declared:

> Woe to the foolish prophets, who follow their own impulse, even though they have not seen a thing. Your prophets, O Israel, have lived like jackals among ruins. You have not gone up into the breaches, nor repaired the wall around the house of Israel, that it might stand in the battle, on the day of Yahweh.

> Those who say, "The declaration of Yahweh" have envisioned emptiness and deceptive divination. Even though Yahweh has not commissioned them, they expect him to fulfill the pronouncement! Surely you have envisioned an empty vision and declared a deceptive divination—you, who say, "The declaration of Yahweh," when I have not even spoken.

> Therefore thus has the Lord Yahweh declared: "Because you have made empty pronouncements, and have envisioned lies— therefore, I am challenging you!"—the declaration of the Lord Yahweh. My hand will come upon those prophets who envision emptiness and who divine lies.

> In the company of my people, they will not be found, and in
> the register of the house of Israel, they will not be recorded; and to
> the land of Israel, they will not come back. Then you will know that
> I am the Lord Yahweh.[15]

Everything about these prophets was false: their message, their tone, their claim to speak for the Lord, their use of the signatory formula when they were never authorized to do so.[16]

Strictly speaking, however, the metaphor involved in the Decalogic command derives from the practice of branding or marking slaves like animals with the name of their owner. This custom was widespread in the ancient world, being attested in Egypt from the New Kingdom (sixteenth to eleventh centuries) to the fifth century BCE, as well as in Assyria and Babylonia.[17] Especially interesting is the marking of temple slaves in ancient Mesopotamia. Slaves of the Eanna temple in Uruk were branded on the wrist with the star of Ishtar; in Borsippa slaves belonging to Marduk and Nabu were branded on the wrists with images of the spade and reed stylus, the symbols of these gods respectively.[18]

Some such practice seems to underlie Isa 44:5: "This one will say, 'I am YHWH's,' another will be called by the name of Jacob, still another will inscribe his hand, 'belonging to YHWH [ליהוה],' and claim the name of Israel" (author's translation). The custom of inscribing *lamed* + a name is well known from Israelite and Judahite stamp seal inscriptions on bullae and pottery sherds identifying the owners of vessels or documents.[19] In Isa 44:5 the five letters ליהוה function as a brand on the hand identifying the bearer as the property of YHWH.[20] This is what Israel had become at Mount Sinai. Through the covenant ratification proceedings, the beneficiaries of YHWH's great acts of deliverance—the people who had only recently been the enslaved property of Pharaoh but had been

---

15. As translated by Block, *Ezekiel Chapters 1–24*, 396–97.

16. See also the reference to swearing and blessing falsely in the name of Yahweh in note 2 above.

17. See Dandamaev, *Slavery in Babylonia*, 229–35.

18. Ibid., 488–89.

19. See also "Belonging to Berekiah son of Neriah the scribe" (Avigad, "Jerahmeel and Baruch," 114–18).

20. For a related notion, see Jer 15:16, where, in the context of being totally under the control and protection of Yahweh, Jeremiah declared that Yahweh's name "was read/called" on him, that is, he bore it as a brand.

freed to become the vassals of YHWH—were stamped with his name. But in this case the stamp not only claimed Israel as the people belonging to YHWH; it also meant that everywhere the people went they represented him and declared to the world the privilege of being his. As Christopher Wright has often noted, Israel is hereby identified as the agent chosen to declare to the world YHWH's glory and grace.[21] Her missional function as God's covenant people is declared in Deut 26:16–19, where Moses announced that YHWH had set Israel, his covenant people, high above all the nations for praise, fame, and glory. Speaking of advertising the Lord's gracious generosity, in Deut 28:9–10 Moses was even more direct. "The Lord will establish you as his holy people, as he has sworn to you, if you keep the commandments of the Lord your God and walk in his ways. All the peoples of the earth shall see that you are called by the name of the Lord, and they shall be afraid of you" (NRSV).

Verse 10 reads literally, "All the peoples of the earth will see that YHWH's name is read/called on you" (cf. NJPSV). The New Jerusalem Bible interprets the clause correctly, "The peoples of the earth, seeing that you bear Yahweh's name, will all be afraid of you." Wherever they went, the Israelites represented Him, and like baseball caps and football jerseys with the logos of one's favorite school or sports team they advertised his name.

In the prohibition in the Decalogue, "You shall not bear the name of the LORD your God in vain," the expression "in vain" (לַשָּׁוְא) means "for nothing, worthlessly, futilely," that is, being branded by YHWH's name and claiming to belong to Him, while doing homage to and serving other gods and so acting as if one belongs to some other god.

If the Israelites would claim YHWH as their God and claim to be his people, then they must live according to his revealed will, which is variously expressed as "walking in the ways of YHWH," "serving Him," "observing his commands and the stipulations of the covenant." If the Israelites would do this, the nations would see how blessed they were to have such righteous laws by which to live (Deut 4:6–8), and YHWH's fame would spread to all the earth (26:19). But if, having been stamped by YHWH's name, they behaved like the nations, as if they belonged to Baal or some other god, and committed abominable crimes, then his name would be profaned (Lev 18:21), defiled (Ezek 43:8), and blasphemed (Lev

21. C. J. H. Wright, *The Mission of God*, 224–25, 329–33.

24:11, 16). Instead of advertising YHWH's glory and grace, those he chose to be his handpicked treasure to declare his praises among the nations misrepresented him and brought shame to his name. And then when judgment came, God's reputation would be further smudged, because the nations would not see in this the divine response to human infidelity. On the contrary they would draw all the wrong conclusions about God: either he had changed his mind about Israel as his people and had abandoned them, or he was unable to stand up for them in the face of challenges by other gods (Exod 32:12; Num 14:13–16). Since both conclusions are wrong, Israel's infidelity soiled God's reputation on two counts. First, when the Israelites behaved like the nations, they misrepresented the character of their God who called them to be holy as he is holy (Lev 19:2) and to be compassionate as he is compassionate (Deut 10:17–18). Second, when they went into exile they not only spread this poison to the lands of their captivity, but they also caused people to draw the wrong conclusions about God. Ezekiel captured this issue perfectly in 36:17–23.

> Human, concerning the house of Israel, at the time they were oc-
> cupying their land, they defiled it with their conduct and their
> unrestrained behavior. So I poured out my fury upon them, on
> account of the blood they had poured out on the land and for their
> pellets of dung with which they had defiled it. I scattered them
> among the nations, and they were dispersed among the countries.
> I punished them in accordance with their conduct and their un-
> restrained behavior. But when they arrived among those nations,
> they caused *my holy name to be desecrated*, inasmuch as it was said
> of them, "These are the people of Yahweh? How is it then that they
> have had to leave his land?" Then I was concerned about *my holy
> name which the house of Israel had desecrated* among the nations
> to which they had come.
>
> Therefore, say to the house of Israel, "Thus has the Lord Yahweh
> declared: It is not for your sake that I will act, O house of Israel, but
> *for the sake of my holy name*, which you have desecrated among
> the nations wherever you have gone. I will sanctify my great name,
> which has been desecrated among the nations—which you have
> desecrated in their midst. And the nations will know that I am
> Yahweh—the declaration of Yahweh—when I manifest my holi-
> ness through you before their very eyes."[22]

---

22. As translated by Block, *Ezekiel Chapters 25–48*, 343–44, 349 (italics added).

This is followed by the fabulous declaration of Israel's transformation and renewal for the sake of God's name. This sheds light on Daniel's prayer in Dan 9, particularly verses 16–19.

> O Lord, in view of all your righteous acts, let your anger and wrath, we pray, turn away from your city Jerusalem, your holy mountain; because of our sins and the iniquities of our ancestors, Jerusalem and your people have become a disgrace among all our neighbors. Now therefore, O our God, listen to the prayer of your servant and to his supplication, and for your own sake, Lord, let your face shine upon your desolated sanctuary.
>
> Incline your ear, O my God, and hear. Open your eyes and look at our desolation *and the city that bears your name*. We do not present our supplication before you on the ground of our righteousness, but on the ground of your great mercies.
>
> O Lord, hear; O Lord, forgive; O Lord, listen and act and do not delay! For your own sake, O my God, *because your city and your people bear your name!* (author's translation).[23]

The sentences in verses 18 and 19 involve variations of a clause meaning literally, "For your name is read/proclaimed on your city and on your people." Daniel pleaded with God to restore his people and his city, not for their sakes *but for the honor of his name.* The Lord's reputation is linked directly to the people who bear the brand of his name.

Of course this is not a distinctly Old Testament notion; it carries over into the New Testament, beginning with the Sermon on the Mount. Like Israel, Jesus' disciples are to let their lights shine through their good works, which will cause observers to glorify their Father in heaven (Matt 5:16). The same concept is reflected in the opening to the Lord's Prayer: "Our Father in heaven; hallowed be your name. Your kingdom come. Your will be done on earth as it is in heaven" (6:9–10). In contrast to the Gentiles, Jesus' followers are to avoid empty repetitions. Having set the agenda, Jesus then elaborated in verses 11–13, "Give us today the bread that we need—because your reputation is at stake; and forgive us our transgressions as we forgive those who transgress against us—because your reputation is at stake; and lead us not into temptation but deliver us

---

23. Isa 43:7 speaks of "everyone who is called by my name, whom I created for my glory" (NRSV). See also Isa 63:19; Jer 14:9; 15:16; 25:29; and Amos 9:12. In the temple Yahweh's name was inscribed over the entrance or on the foundation stone (1 Kgs 8:43; 2 Chr 6:33; Jer 7:10–11, 14, 30), and on the ark of the covenant (2 Sam 6:2; 1 Chr 13:6).

from the evil—because your reputation is at stake. For yours is the king-dom and the power and the glory forever. Amen" (author's translation).

Paul expressed keen awareness of what this means, for in Rom 2:17–29 he referred to some who hypocritically claimed the name "Jew." As declared in Isa 44:5, to be a true Israelite is to be branded by the name of YHWH. So here Paul declared that to "bear the name" (ἐπονομάζῃ, Rom 2:17) and to behave immorally, that is, to violate the Torah, is to dishonor God and cause his name to be blasphemed (vv. 23–24). Physical circumci-sion is not the distinguishing brand of a true Jew; rather the "brand" is the inward circumcision of the heart, by the Spirit not the letter (γράμματι, v. 29). This may not win the praise of people, but it is guaranteed to bring praise from God. While γράμμα/γράμματος is generally understood as the literally correct form of the Law, it might actually mean the brand, the very letters of God's name. In any case, those who are circumcised inwardly receive the praise of God and are affirmed, for they represent him with honor. Elsewhere Paul seemed to allude more directly to the practice of branding slaves: "From now on, let no one make trouble for me; for I carry the marks [στίγματα] of Jesus branded on my body" (Gal 6:17, NRSV).[24]

The fullest adaptation of this idea is found in 1 Pet 4:14–19: "If you are reviled for the name of Christ, you are blessed, because the spirit of glory, which is the Spirit of God, is resting on you. But let none of you suffer as a murderer, a thief, a criminal, or even as a mischief maker. Yet if any of you suffers as a Christian, do not consider it a disgrace, but glorify God because you bear this name [ἐν τῷ ὀνόματι τούτῳ, lit., "in that name"]. For the time has come for judgment to begin with the household of God; if it begins with us, what will be the end for those who do not obey the gospel of God? And 'If it is hard for the righteous to be saved, what will become of the ungodly and the sinners?' Therefore, let those suffering in accordance with God's will entrust themselves to a faithful Creator, while continuing to do good" (NRSV).

To suffer for the name of Christ is the highest honor imaginable. Those who bear his name share in his suffering. However, Peter distin-guished between suffering caused by bearing his name and suffering caused by being morally reprehensible. Those who are immoral (mur-derers, thieves, criminals, and meddlers), and those who do not obey the

24. On στίγμα or στίγματος as a "tattoo-mark" or mark of a slave, including a person devoted to temple service, see LSJ 1645; and Betz, "στίγμα," 657–64.

gospel deserve the suffering they get, for they have not only violated the standards of righteousness of the One whose name they claim to bear, but they have also brought shame on the name itself. But those who suffer in accord with God's will—rather than their own—trust in their faithful Creator for vindication.

James 2:7 is an equally striking reference, with even clearer echoes of Lev 24:11 and 16, on the one hand, and Deut 28:10 and Dan 9:18–19, on the other. "Are they not the ones who blaspheme the honorable name by which you were called [lit., 'the honorable name that is called/read on you']?" (author's translation). Some such custom may also underlie the expression "to be baptized in the name of Jesus Christ" (Acts 2:38; 10:48), because after baptism new believers were recognized as bearers of the Name.[25]

Conclusion

What relevance has all this for believers today? At academic conferences attendees wear name tags, and most name tags have more than a person's name on them. They also have the names of the institutions being represented. The public draws conclusions about a school from the way its representatives do their work and the way they conduct themselves. Through their conduct, they can be either a credit or a liability to the institutions that sent them.

Christian believers have an identity marker that is far more important than temporal institutional labels. They bear the brand of Christ, which means that everywhere they go they represent Him. Outsiders draw conclusions about the Savior from the way believers conduct themselves and the way they perform their professional responsibilities. To borrow from the words of the Lord Himself, those who are "branded" with his name are characterized as poor in spirit; they grieve with those who grieve; they are meek; they hunger and thirst after righteousness; they are pure in heart; they are peacemakers; they accept persecution and ridicule for righteousness' sake. Will those who bear the brand of Christ be salt and light in a dark world, and when others view their lives, will they glorify God in heaven, whose name they bear (Matt 5:1–16)? Or will they be like parasites sucking glory for themselves?

25. Martin, *James*, 67.

Biblical scholars can be as insensitive toward cabdrivers and as impatient with hotel management and staff as those in the general population. And they can also be as ruthless with their detractors, as arrogant and egotistical in their demeanor, as jealous of personal accomplishments, as unkind and cutting toward others even within their own discipline, as people in other branches of ministry. These temptations are not foreign to those who bear the brand of Christ.

Some time ago at a scholarly conference a panel of seasoned scholars was asked by a young student in the audience what advice they would give him and others as they entered the competitive world. One of the panelists, who was retired at the time, gave terse, wise counsel when he said, "Be good at what you do, and be good, period."

This counsel touches on two critical dimensions of bearing the name of Christ with honor. First, those who bear the brand of Christ must pursue good scholarship. There is no place for shoddy and irresponsible work. If any are careless with the data, if they misrepresent the opposition in a debate, or if their style of communication is insensitive to the issues that characterize public discourse, no matter how polished their work, those inside and outside will not take such scholars and teachers seriously, and they should not. A cue may be taken from the noble woman of Prov 31:31: may an individual's good works praise him or her "in the city gates" (NRSV).

And this leads to the other dimension of responsible Christian scholarship: being good people. Some scholars, it is true, are rejected simply because of the institution whose name they bear on their name tags. Some, however, are superb scholars, but others have difficulty respecting their work because they are known personally. Some individuals complain that their work is not taken seriously because they are conservative, or evangelical. They may even wear this kind of rejection as a badge of honor, thinking they are suffering for the name of Christ, when in fact they are rejected because they are unpleasant people: they are closed-minded in their thinking; they are dismissive of people who think differently; their arguments are often ad hominem rather than addressing the issues; they are overly impressed with their own work; they are more focused on defending their own understanding of truth than in engaging in the search for truth; they are more concerned about making a name for themselves than about healthy conversation, let alone making a name for Christ.

These are temptations for people in every field of work: schoolteachers, medical doctors, building contractors, bus drivers, farmers, flight attendants, salespersons, dock workers, engineers, lawyers, professional athletes, students. No one is exempt, either by task or by time. Wherever believers go, they bear the name of Christ. While engaging with colleagues, business associates, and friends, it is well to remember the words of Heb 10:24, "Let us consider how to provoke one another to love and good deeds" (NRSV). Paul's advice to young Titus is perpetually and universally relevant: "Show yourself in all respects a model of good works, and in your teaching [or whatever else your calling] show integrity, gravity, and sound speech that cannot be censured; then any opponent will be put to shame, having nothing evil to say of us" (Titus 2:7–8, NRSV).

Believers are branded with the name of the King of kings, the Lord of lords, the great, mighty, and awesome God! But with this high honor comes a high challenge: to do one's work and to conduct one's life in ways that bring honor to the Lord. As Paul wrote to the Colossian Christians, "Let the word of Christ dwell in you richly; teach and admonish one another in all wisdom; and with gratitude in your hearts sing psalms, hymns, and spiritual songs to God. And whatever you do, in word or deed, do everything in the name of the Lord Jesus, giving thanks to God the Father through him" (Col 3:16–17, NRSV). May every Christian worker determine to build others up in the faith and in the work to which he or she has been called, to give radiant testimony to the grace of Christ, for the advance of truth, the health of the church, and the honor of the One whose name believers humbly but boldly bear.

4

How Many Is God?

An Investigation into the Meaning
of Deuteronomy 6:4–5 [1]

I. Introduction

IN DEUT 6:4 MOSES commences the second major section of his second address. The limits of this segment are marked by his call, "Listen, O Israel!" at the beginning, and the warning of Israel's certain doom at the end, "because you would not listen to the voice of YHWH your God" (8:20). This demarcation is confirmed by 9:1, which signals the beginning of a new subsection with a third call to "Hear!" (cf. 5:1). Between these two markers, Moses offers a profound exposition of the essence of Israel's covenant relationship with YHWH. Moses announces the grand theme of this section in emphatic but eloquent style with the Shemaʻ in 6:4–5: a call for exclusive covenant commitment to YHWH.

Moses maintains his covenantal focus throughout this section particularly through the repetition of the phrase "YHWH your God," which occurs thirty-one times, and "YHWH our God," which occurs an additional four times, yielding a total of thirty-five occurrences in sixty-eight verses. The covenant mediator describes this relationship from both sides. On the one hand, he notes YHWH's love for Israel (7:7, 8, 13), his faithfulness to his covenant (6:10, 18, 23; 7:8, 9, 12; 8:18), and his providential care for them (8:2–16). On the other hand, he emphasizes the response that YHWH expects from his people: love (6:5); fear (6:13, 24; 8:6); trust

---

1. This essay was previously published in *Journal of the Evangelical Theological Society* 47 (2004) 193–212.

(7:17–24); and remembrance (6:12; 8:11, 18, 19); to say nothing of obedience, which is a constant theme.

Deuteronomy 6:4–9 represents the thematic introduction to this extended segment of Moses' second address. This paragraph is probably more familiar to us than any other part of Deuteronomy. The NIV translates it as follows:

> Hear, O Israel: The Lord our God, the Lord is one. Love the Lord your God with all your heart and with all your soul and with all your strength. These commandments that I give you today are to be upon your hearts. Impress them on your children. Talk about them when you sit at home and when you walk along the road, when you lie down and when you get up. Tie them as symbols on your hands and bind them on your foreheads. Write them on the doorframes of your houses and on your gates.

This first subsection of 6:4—8:20 may be the shortest, but it is the most eloquent, and in many ways the most profound. Readers tend to fix their attention on the opening "Hear, O Israel," but we need to realize that this שְׁמַע is just the first of a series of six imperatives that dominate the paragraph consisting of verses 4–9: "Hear," "Love," "Impress," "Speak," "Bind," and "Write." The two exceptions to this pattern (vv. 6, 8b) are cast in the third person, with inanimate objects as their subject. However, since the words cannot find their place "upon your hearts" (v. 6), nor appear as phylacteries "between your eyes," by themselves (v. 8b), even these statements have imperatival import.

Moses' challenge in Deut 6:4 is known as the Shema', a designation that derives from the first word in Hebrew.[2] The Shema' represents one of the most important symbols of Judaism. In most Hebrew manuscripts the last letters of the first and last words are exceptionally large, presumably to warn the reader that at this point the reading is to be especially pre-

---

2. Although this paper is concerned primarily with verse 4, verse 5 is often treated as part of the Shema'. This is taken for granted in Paul Foster's most recent discussion of the forms and use of the Shema' in the Gospels in "Why did Matthew get the *Shema* wrong?" 309–33.

cise.[3] The LXX prefaces the Shemaʿ with a long introduction, apparently an adaptation of 4:45:[4]

> Καὶ ταῦτα τὰ δικαιώματα καὶ τὰ κρίματα, ὅσα ἐνετείλατο κύριος
> τοῖς υἱοῖς Ισραηλ ἐν τῇ ἐρήμῳ ἐξελθόντων αὐτῶν ἐκ γῆς Αἰγύπτου
> . . .

> And these are the judgments that *the Lord* commanded the sons of Israel in the desert when they went out of the land of Egypt . . .

The catechetical/liturgical significance of the Shemaʿ in ancient Judaism is reflected by the fact that it appears immediately after the Decalogue in the Nash Papyrus, a second-century BCE liturgical text,[5] and in a first-century CE phylactery text from Cave 8 at Qumran, where the Shemaʿ is written in a rectangle and surrounded by other texts.[6] To this day, Orthodox Jews recite the Shemaʿ twice daily as part of their prayers: in the morning when they wake up, and at night before they fall asleep (cf. the instruction in v. 7).[7] In so doing they take "the yoke of the kingdom," which is to say that they place themselves under the sover-

3. Thus Yeivin, *Introduction to the Tiberian Masorah*, 48. To read the final *daledh* as a *resh* (the two letters were often confused) would create a blasphemous אַחֵר, "another, other." Alternatively the combination of the two last letters, *ʿayin* and *daledh,* spells עֵד, "witness," suggesting either that the Shemaʿ is a witness to the unity of Yahweh (Tigay, *Deuteronomy*, 441), or that the Shema is a witness against Israel, in which case it functions like the Song of Moses in 31:19–21. Cf. Ps 50:7, "Hear, O my people, and I will speak; O Israel I will testify against you; I am God your God."

4. So also Wevers, *Notes on the Greek Text of Deuteronomy*, 114.

5. The papyrus includes a Hebrew version of the long introduction found in the LXX. See Tov, *Textual Criticism of the Hebrew Bible*, 118; Würthwein, *The Text of the Old Testament*, 34, 144–45. For a discussion of the nature and liturgical significance of the Shemaʿ in the Nash Papyrus, see Foster, "Why did Matthew get the *Shema* Wrong?" 327–28.

6. 8QPhyl; published by Baillet, *Les "Petites Grottes" de Qumrân*, 149–51. For discussion of these texts, see VanderKam, *The Dead Sea Scrolls Today*, 33; Schiffman, "Phylacteries and Mezuzot," 2:675–77; Foster, "Why did Matthew get the *Shema* Wrong?" 329–30.

7. The tradition goes back a long time. See Josephus, *Antiquities* 4.8, 13; *m. Ber.* 1,2,3. There may also be an allusion to the practice in 1QS 10:10, "At the onset of day and night I shall enter the covenant of God, and when evening and morning depart I shall repeat his precepts; and by their existence I shall set my limit without turning away" (as translated by Martínez and Tigchelaar, *The Dead Sea Scrolls Study Edition*, 1:95). For discussion, see Leaney, *The Rule of Qumran and its Meaning*, 239–41, 245.

eignty and kingship of YHWH.[8] The Shemaʿ is as close as early Judaism came to the formulation of a creed.

The importance of the Shemaʿ in Jewish tradition is also reflected in the Gospels. One day, apparently seeking to change the subject away from the issue of the resurrection, over which the Pharisees and Sadducees were arguing, one of the scribes asked Jesus, "Which commandment is the most important of all?" To which Jesus replied, "The most important is, 'Hear, O Israel: The Lord our God, the Lord is one. And you shall love the Lord your God with all your heart and with all your soul and with all your mind and with all your strength.' The second is this: 'You shall love your neighbor as yourself.' There is no other commandment greater than these" (Mark 12:29–31 ESV).[9]

II. The Problem of the Shemaʿ

Despite the importance of the Shemaʿ in Jewish and Christian tradition, it is in fact quite enigmatic, and has fueled scholarly discussion out of all proportion to these six small words.[10] The style and meaning of the first two words are clear—a vocative addressing Israel (cf. 4:1; 5:1; 9:1; 27:9)[11]—and accord with the oral rhetorical style of the book as a whole. But the construction of the remainder is difficult and without parallel in

---

8. According to the Talmud (*Ber.* 15b), "Gehenna is cooled for whoever pronounces the Shema correctly." For discussions of the Shemaʿ in early Judaism, see Jacobs, "Shema, Reading of," 14:1370–74; McBride, "The Yoke of the Kingdom," 273–306, esp. 275–79; Vokes, "Creeds in the New Testament," 582–84.

9. Neither Matthew (22:37–40) nor Luke (10:26–27) includes the first clause of the Shemaʿ in the citation. For analysis of the synoptic issues, especially the variations in the forms of the call for unreserved love for God, see Foster, "Why did Matthew get the *Shema* Wrong?" 309–33.

10. See most recently Bord and Hamidović, "Écoute Israël," 13–29.

11. A rabbinic tradition reflected in *Sifre Deuteronomy* §31 and Targum Pseudo-Jonathan understands "Israel" as an individual appellation, that is, the patriarch Jacob. This is evident in the latter's very expansive reading of verses 4–5:

> And it was, *when the time was reached for our father Jacob to be gathered from the midst of the world*, he was afraid lest there be a defect among his sons. He called them and asked them: is there any guile in your hearts? All of them replied as one and said to him: "Hear, Israel, our father, 'the Lord our God, the Lord is one.'" Jacob answered and said: "Blessed be his glorious Name for ever and ever. Moses, the prophet, said to the people, the Israelites: follow the true worship of your fathers and love the Lord your God *following your hearts' inclination even if he take your lives along with all your wealth.*"

As translated by Clarke, *Targum Pseudo-Jonathan: Deuteronomy*, 24–25.

the entire Old Testament, leading to wide variation in the way translations and commentators render the statement. The following represent
the main possibilities that have been proposed:

> "Hear, O Israel, YHWH our God, YHWH is one."[12]
> "Hear, O Israel, YHWH our God is one YHWH."[13]
> "Hear, O Israel, YHWH is our God; YHWH is one."[14]
> "Hear, O Israel, YHWH is our God; YHWH is One/Unique."[15]
> "Hear, O Israel, YHWH is our God; YHWH alone."[16]

While the merits of each reading vary, the wide range of interpretations
offered by scholars cautions us to deem provisional all solutions to the
problem, especially our own.

Following the vocative of address, the Shemaʿ consists of four nominal elements: the divine personal name YHWH, which occurs twice; a
common noun with the first person plural suffix; and a numeral. On the
surface, the four words appear to be arranged in an ABAB parallel order:

> יהוה אֱלֹהֵינוּ   YHWH our God
>
> יהוה אֶחָד   YHWH one

Although a verb is absent, most scholars agree that this should be interpreted as one or two verbless clauses in the present tense. But this is
where the agreement ends. While many today interpret the first colon as
a clause, "YHWH is our God,"[17] the NIV follows a longstanding tradition
of reading the clause appositionally: "The Lord our God." This accords

12. Moberly, "Yahweh is One," 209–15; McConville, *Deuteronomy*, 137, 141.

13. AV, ASV, RSV n., NIV n., JB; Lohfink, "אֶחָד *echādh*," 1:196; Weinfeld, *Deuteronomy 1–11*, 330, 337–38; Craigie, *The Book of Deuteronomy*, 168–69.

14. NAS, NIV, RSV; Janzen, "On the Most Important Word in the Shema," 280–300; Merrill, *Deuteronomy*, 162–63.

15. Gordon, "His Name is 'One,'" 198–99; cf. Dahood, "Yahweh our God is the Unique," 361.

16. Ibn Ezra, NRSV, NJPSV; Mayes, *Deuteronomy*, 175–77; Veijola, "Höre Israel!" 528–41; Tigay, *Deuteronomy*, 76. These are not the only possibilities. Nielsen ("Weil Jahwe unser Gott ein Jahwe ist," 106–18) proposes, "Because Yahweh our God is one Yahweh . . . you shall love Yahweh your God with all your heart." For surveys of the most impor-tant interpretations of the Shemaʿ, see Miller, "Pivotal Issues in Analyzing the Verbless Clause," 4–6; Loretz, "Die *Einzigkeit* Jahwes (Dtn 6,4) im Licht der ugaritischen Ball-Mythos," 26–47; Bord and Hamidović, "Écoute Israël," 14–15.

17. Thus NRSV, NAS, NJPSV.

with the general pattern by which the name YHWH (יהוה) and the divine epithet God (אֱלֹהִים) are juxtaposed in Deuteronomy. R. W. L. Moberly notes that יהוה and אֱלֹהִים are juxtaposed 312 times in this book. He argues that since the terms always occur in apposition elsewhere, the same must be true here.[18] Furthermore, as Lohfink observes, "when *'ĕlohîm* is used predicatively after *yhvh*, it is always preceded by *hû'* (Deut 4:34; 7:9; Josh 24:18; 1 Kgs 8:60),"[19] to which Bord and Hamidović add that the designation for deity always adds the article, *viz.*, הָאֱלֹהִים.[20]

However, this appeal to the appositional use of "our/your God" is not as convincing as it appears on first sight. First, in response to Bord and Hamidović, inasmuch as the suffixed form אֱלֹהֵינוּ, "our God," is already definite, the addition of the article is morphologically impossible. Second, the overwhelming number of occurrences of "YHWH our God," etc., are found in verbal clauses, with this phrase serving either as the subject of action performed or the object of Israel's action. Here we have a verbless clause. Third, all recognize the uniqueness of the syntax of the Shemaʿ,[21] so that even if the construction יהוה אֱלֹהֵינוּ functions appositionally in 100 percent of the other cases, usage elsewhere may not override the requirements of the present syntax or context; nor should we disregard the evidence of a potentially single possible exception.

The second colon is more problematic. While a variety of interpretations have been offered, the two main alternatives are "The Lord is one" (as in NIV), or "The Lord alone" (as in NRSV). The primary arguments in favor of the former are two. First, this interpretation of אֶחָד, "one," follows the normal use of this cardinal number. If "alone" had been intended, the author would have been expected to say יהוה לְבַדּוֹ, "YHWH by himself." Second, this is clearly the interpretation of these words in (1) the Nash Papyrus,[22] which adds a pleonastic הוּא after אֶחָד, that is, הוא אחד יהוה; (2) the Septuagint, which reads, ἄκουε, Ισραηλ, κύριος ὁ θεὸς ἡμῶν κύριος

18. Moberly, "Yahweh is One" 209–15.

19. *TDOT* 1.197.

20. Bord and Hamidović, "Écoute Israël" 19.

21. Even Janzen, "On the Most Important Word in the Shema," 296.

22. According to Andersen's Rule #4 for verbless clauses, this yields an unequivocal reading "Yahweh is one." See Andersen, *The Hebrew Verbless Clause in the Pentateuch*, 45.

εἷς ἐστιν, and should be translated, "Hear, O Israel! The Lord our God is one Lord";[23] and the New Testament, which follows the LXX precisely.[24]

But if this reading is correct, what does the statement mean? Three interpretations are possible. First, this is a reminder that YHWH the God of Abraham, YHWH the God of Isaac, and YHWH the God of Jacob all represented a single deity (cf. Exod 3:6, 15; 4:5). Second, this is a polemical mono-Yahwistic declaration combating the potential poly-Yahwism reflected in names such as "YHWH of Sinai" (Deut 33:2; cf. Judg 5:5; Ps 68:9), "YHWH of Mount Paran" (Deut 33:2; Hab 3:3), "YHWH of Edom" (Judg 5:5), and "YHWH of Teman" (Hab 3:3).[25] Third, this is a declaration

23. Wevers (*Notes on the Greek Text of Deuteronomy*, 114) treats κύριος ὁ θεὸς ἡμῶν as a "pendant nominative, whose chief purpose is to identify *Kurios* as Israel's covenant God." LXX follows MT in rendering the charge "Hear" as singular, but the plural response reflects a communal voice. Wevers translates the Greek, "As for the Lord our God, the Lord is one." He continues, "By adding the linking verb the translator excluded the possibility of understanding b) as the predicate of a)." According to Herrmann ("Jahwe und des Menschen Liebe zu ihm zu Dtn. VI 4," 47), the LXX reads the Hebrew as a verb7 less clause in which, linked with the numeral "one," the second element functions as predicate for the proper divine name.

24. On the other hand, it must be noted that in Mark 12:32, in the scribe's response to Jesus' citation of the Shema‛, after he has said, "You are right in saying that God is one," he adds, "and there is none other besides him" (καὶ οὐκ ἔστιν ἄλλος πλὴν αὐτοῦ).

25. One might also imagine "Yahweh Sebaoth of Jerusalem," "Yahweh of Bethel," "Yahweh of Hebron," "Yahweh of Samaria," etc. This declaration then accords with the repeated references to Yahweh choosing a single place for his name to dwell (Deut 12). This kind of theological perspective seems to be reflected in four ninth–eighth-century BCE Hebrew Inscriptions from Kuntillet 'Ajrud (as translated by McCarter in *COS*, 2:171–72):

Utterance of 'Ashyaw the king: "Say to Yehallel and to Yaw'asah and to [. . .]: 'I bless you by Yahweh of Samaria and his asherah!'"

[. . .] to Yahweh of the Teman and his asherah. And may he grant (?) everything that he asks from the compassionate god [. . .] and may he grant according to his needs all that he asks!

Utterance of 'Amaryaw, "Say to my lord 'Is it well with you? I bless you by Yahweh of Teman and his asherah. May he bless and keep you, and may he be with my lord!'"

[. . . May] he prolong (their) days, and be satisfied [. . .] Yahweh of Teman has dealt favorably [with . . .]

For discussion of these texts, see Smith, *The Early History of God*, 118–25; Albertz, *The History of Israelite Religion in the Old Testament Period*, 1:206. This perception of Yahweh compares with Mesopotamian references to Ishtar of Arbela, Ishtar of Nineveh, Ishtar of Akkad (*ANET* 205); Egyptian references to Amon-Re in Thebes, Amon-Re in Heliopolis, etc.; and biblical references to Baal of Peor, Baal of Gad, Baal of Tamar, Baal of Maon, Baal of Hermon, Baal of Hazor, etc. These gods were worshiped in many different places, perhaps as local manifestations of the one deity.

of the integrity of YHWH, a cryptic reference to his internal consistency and fidelity, that is, morally and spiritually he is one.[26] According to J. G. Janzen, "God's 'oneness' is the unity between desire and action, between intention and execution."[27]

III. Significant Factors in the Interpretation of the Shema'

However, the arguments for the unitary interpretation are weak. Moving centrifugally from the word, to the syntax of the sentence, the immediate context, the broader literary context, and finally to the canonical context, at each level we observe features that raise questions about the traditional interpretation.

1. *The meaning of* אֶחָד. In response to those who argue that if "alone" had been the intended sense, the statement would have read, יהוה לְבַדּוֹ, Weinfeld rightly points out that לְבַדּוֹ is an adverb. Since the Shema' consists of nominal clauses (or a nominal clause), this word is inappropriate in this context.[28] At the same time, we note that although the dictionary definition of the word אֶחָד is indeed "one," to read something like "alone" here is not as exceptional as many imagine. Scholars have identified a variety of texts scattered throughout the Old Testament in which this word functions as a semantic equivalent to לְבַדּוֹ, "unique, only, alone":[29]

26. Lohfink (*TDOT* 1:197) rightly dismisses C. J. Labuschagne's contention that Yahweh is being described here as "the One Detached," that is, God lacks both a female consort and a household. Cf. Labuschagne, *The Incomparability of Yahweh in the Old Testament*, 137–38.

27. In the second part of the Shema', Israel is called upon to reflect God's spiritual and moral "oneness." See Janzen's "On the Most Important Word in the Shema," 287; cf. also Janzen, "The Claim of the Shema," 244.

28. Weinfeld, *Deuteronomy 1–11*, 338, with acknowledged indebtedness to A. B. Ehrlich.

29. 2 Kings 19:19: "That the earth may know that you alone (לְבַדּוֹ) O Yahweh are God"; Isa 2:11, 17: "Yahweh alone (לְבַדּוֹ) will be exalted on that day." The ambiguity of the Hebrew text of the Shema appears to be eliminated in a recently published Samaritan inscription containing the Shema. This inscription, dated by the publisher G. Davies some time after the fourth century CE, seeks to clarify the meaning of אחד, "one," by adding an appositional לבדו, "he alone." See Davies, "A Samaritan Inscription," 3–19, for full discussion. Less likely is the interpretation of H.-G. von Mutius ("Sprachliche und religionsgeschichtliche Anmerkungen zu einer neu publizierten samaritanischen Textfassung von Deuteronomium 6,4," 23–26), who proposes that the Samaritan reading either affirms that Yahweh is different from all other gods on the basis of his unique inner unity or in the fact that he alone has no wife/consort.

Josh 22:20: With respect to Achan, the Israelites say, "Now that man did not perish alone (אֶחָד) for his iniquity."

2 Sam 7:23 (= 1 Chr 17:21): David recognizes that as the privileged recipient of YHWH's saving grace, Israel is "a unique nation" (גּוֹי אֶחָד).

1 Chr 29:1: David refers to Solomon as "My son Solomon, the only one (אֶחָד) whom God has chosen."

Job 23:13: Job says of God, "But he is unique (אֶחָד) and who can turn him."

Job 31:15: Again Job says of God, "And he alone (אֶחָד) fashioned us in the womb."

Song 6:9: "But my dove, my perfect one, is the only one (אַחַת הִיא); the only one (אַחַת הִיא) of her mother."

Zech 14:9: "For YHWH will be king over all the earth; in that day YHWH will be אֶחָד, and his name אֶחָד."[30]

Some of these examples are admittedly more convincing than others. However, even if they were all rejected (which is unlikely), this would still not rule out the possibility of an exceptional significance in this case. Janzen's claim that the Shemaʿ refers to YHWH's internal integrity is forced, and to render יהוה אֶחָד as "YHWH is one," in almost any sense is illogical. H. C. Brichto has rightly observed,

> A translation affirming that a person known by a proper name "is one" is as meaningless of a deity as it would be of a human being. A discrete entity is not normally in danger of being taken for more

30. Counterparts to exclusive use of אֶחָד may be found in other Near Eastern languages and texts as well. Although the vocabulary is obviously different, attestation of Enlil's aloneness, uniqueness, and exclusivity is reflected in a Sumerian text: "Enlil is the lord of heaven and earth; he is king alone" (cf. Weinfeld, *Deuteronomy 1–11*, 338). But nearer home geographically and linguistically, we note the Phoenician statement, *'nk lhdy*, "I only," or "Only I" (*DNWSL* 34), and especially Baal's quotation of Mot in the Ugaritic text, *KTU* 1.4 vii50–52:

> I am the only one who rules over the gods, (*ahidy dymlk ʿl ilm*)
> who fattens gods and men,
> Who satiates the hordes of the earth.

As translated by Pardee, "The Baʿlu Myth," in *COS* 2:263; cf. the translation by Wyatt, *Religious Texts from Ugarit*, 111. For the Ugaritic text and a similar translation, see Smith, "The Baal Cycle," 137.

than one or less than one. The assumption that the Hebrew word אֶחָד means "one" in its every appearance is an example of the folly of literalness. This folly would appear obvious to every speaker of English were he to remember that *only* is "one-ly" and *alone* is "all-one." The endurance of this mistaken rendering is a tribute to the mischief that has been done to biblical meanings by the substitution of a common noun *lord*, rendered as a proper noun *the Lord*, for the ineffable name YHWH and also to an anachronistic assumption by theists of the biblical persuasion that Moses anticipated the unitarian-versus-trinitarian division.[31]

2. *The syntax of the Shema*: With reference to the syntax of the sentence, if the last clause had intended to say "YHWH is one," as a verbless clause it should have read either יהוה אֶחָד הוּא or אֶחָד יהוה, but not יהוה אֶחָד.[32] Furthermore, if Moses had intended to communicate the "integrous" character of YHWH, he had several clear and natural expressions at his disposal, including the pattern he follows in Deut 7:9, יהוה אֱלֹהֶיךָ הוּא הָאֱלֹהִים הָאֵל הַנֶּאֱמָן, "YHWH your God is God, the faithful El." Based on this model, the Shemaʿ should read, יהוה אֱלֹהֶיךָ הוּא הָאֱלֹהִים יהוה הָאֶחָד, "YHWH your God is God, the ʿintegrousʾ YHWH."

On lexical and syntactical grounds, therefore, we conclude that two or three English renderings of the Shemaʿ capture the required sense. First, if one insists on reading the first element, יהוה אֱלֹהֵינוּ, in accord with the appositional usage everywhere else in Deuteronomy, the Shemaʿ may be interpreted as a cryptic utterance, "YHWH our God! YHWH alone!" If one argues for a nominal sentence in the first element, then "Our God is YHWH, YHWH alone!" is possible. F. I. Andersen compares the syntax of the first element of Shemaʿ with Isa 33:22, which he translates as in the second column:

---

31. In Brichto, *Toward a Grammar of Biblical Poetics*, 232–33. I am indebted to Joe Sprinkle for drawing Brichto's discussion to my attention.

32. As [apparently] in Sir 42:21: אֶחָד הוּא מֵעוֹלָם, "He is one from eternity" (or "one and the same," according to NRSV, and Skehan and Di Lella, *The Wisdom of Ben Sira*, 484). Cf. Andersen's Rule #3 (*Hebrew Verbless Clause*, 42–45). Cf. חֲלוֹם אֶחָד הוּא, "the dream is one," in Gen 41:26. The Nash Papyrus and Septuagintal readings made the required adjustments to secure the sense of "Yahweh is one." However, no one argues that these readings are preferable to MT. Those responsible for the Nash Papyrus obviously treasured the Shemaʿ for its liturgical value, but in adding the pleonastic pronoun to secure the sense of LXX they had to violate Deut 4:2.

כִּי יהוה שֹׁפְטֵנוּ   For our judge is Yahweh,

יהוה מְחֹקְקֵנוּ   our legislator is Yahweh,

יהוה מַלְכֵּנוּ   our king is Yahweh;

הוּא יוֹשִׁיעֵנוּ   He will save us![33]

Third, if one insists on rendering the second element as a nominal sentence, then "YHWH our God, YHWH is the only one," or "YHWH our God, YHWH is the one and only," represent the correct interpretation, even if they express it awkwardly. All accord with the pervasive and fundamental demand of Deuteronomy in general and the first commandment of the Decalogue that Israel worship only YHWH, and absolutely avoid all other spiritual allegiances.

3. *The immediate literary context of the Shema῾.* This interpretation is reinforced in the immediate context by verses 5–9, where Moses explains explicitly what he means by total and exclusive allegiance to YHWH. The determinative word here is "love" for YHWH. As demonstrated in 4:37, Hebrew אָהֵב denotes the fundamental disposition of commitment within a covenant relationship that seeks the well-being and the pleasure of one's covenant partner, often without regard for oneself. Although passion is obviously not absent from the word אָהֵב, as used in Deuteronomy, this is not primarily an emotional term, but an expression of covenant commitment demonstrated in action.[34] Moses will have a great deal more to say about this matter later, but for the moment, in order to grasp his understanding of the concept, a look at the expressions he correlates with the word is revealing. Israel is to demonstrate her love for God by holding fast (דָּבַק) to him (11:22; 30:20), listening to/obeying his voice (30:20),[35] fearing him (10:12), walking in his ways (10:12; 11:22; 19:9; 30:16), and serving him (10:12; 11:13).

In Deuteronomy, YHWH himself provides the model of covenant love. Because YHWH loved Israel's ancestors, he chose their descendants to be his covenant partners (4:37; 10:15); because YHWH loves Israel, he

33. Andersen, *The Hebrew Verbless Clause in the Pentateuch,* 47.

34. See the excellent presentation of this issue by Malamat, "'You Shall Love Your Neighbor As Yourself': A Case of Misinterpretation?" 111–15; cf. his more popular treatment in "'Love Your Neighbor as Yourself': What it Really Means," 50–51. This study is carried further by Ackerman, "The Personal is Political," 437–58.

35. The correlation of שָׁמַע, "to hear, obey," and אָהֵב, "to love," also occurs in Ugaritic. Cf. UT 67V:17–18, on which see Dahood, *Ras Shamra Parallels,* 1:566.

delivered them from the bondage of Egypt (7:8); because YHWH loves Israel, he will bless them and cause their families, crops, and herds to multiply (7:13); because YHWH loves the sojourner, he gives him food and clothing (10:18); because YHWH loved Israel, he turned Balaam's curse into a blessing for them (23:6[Eng 6]). He had demonstrated his love for the ancestors by choosing their descendants and rescuing them from their slavery in Egypt (4:37). The word אָהֵב belongs to the covenant-al semantic field, along with words like חֶסֶד, "steadfast love, loyalty," and אֱמוּנָה, "fidelity, faithfulness."

In verses 5–9 Moses calls on his people to answer the gracious love of YHWH and to confirm their verbal commitment expressed in the Shemaʿ with unreserved and unqualified love for him. He begins in v. 5b by describing the intensity of the love for YHWH that a covenant relationship with him demands: with all one's heart and with all one's soul and with all one's strength. Christian exegetes have tended to interpret these expressions as complementary attributes of the human personality, which together make up the inner person, and to marshal this text as evidence for a trichotomous biblical view of humanity, in contrast to a dichotomous view. Generally appealing to the Greek translations of the Hebrew expressions, proponents of the former argue that a human being consists essentially of mind/intellect (*dianoia/kardia*), a soul (*psychē*), and spiritual/moral power (*dynamis*). However, as S. D. McBride demonstrated thirty years ago,[36] this represents a fundamental misreading of the text. Verse 5 is not a Greek psychological statement, but an emphatic reinforcement of absolute singularity of devotion to YHWH as called for by the Shemaʿ. The contrast between the psychological and literary interpretations of verse 5 is reflected in Figures 4 and 5.

---

36. McBride, "The Yoke of the Kingdom," 273–306.

Figure 4: The Psychological Interpretation of Deuteronomy 6:5

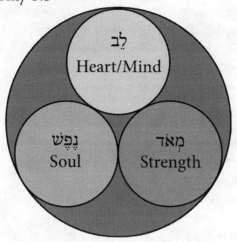

Figure 5: The Literary Interpretation of Deuteronomy 6:5

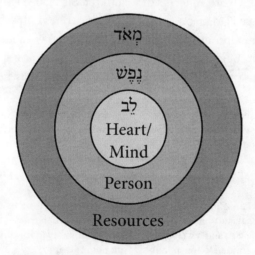

Each of the Hebrew expressions calls for brief comment. Literally, לֵב denotes "heart," but more often than not it is used metaphorically for either the seat of the emotions or the intellect or both. Biblical Hebrew has no separate word for "mind"; one's לֵב is both one's "feeler" and "thinker." In this context, we do not need to choose between the two, for both are in mind;[37] the word serves comprehensively for one's inner being.

The basic meaning of נֶפֶשׁ is "breath," though it can be used more concretely of the throat or neck (through which breath is inhaled; Jonah 2:5[6]; Ps 69:1[2]). However, the word is usually used in a series of derived metaphorical senses of appetite/desire (Prov 23:2; Eccl 6:7), life (Gen 9:5; 2 Sam 23:17),[38] and ultimately a person as a living being (Lev 21:11; Ezek 4; etc.), the whole self (Lev 26:11).[39] Here the word refers to one's entire being.

The common rendering of the last expression, מְאֹד, as "strength" follows the Septuagint, which reads δύναμις, "power" (rendered ἰσχύς in Mark 12:30), but again it flattens the nuanced reading of the Hebrew. This is one of only two places in the Old Testament (cf. 2 Kgs 23:25) where the word is used as a noun; elsewhere it always functions adverbially, meaning "greatly, exceedingly."[40] Although the Septuagint interprets the word in the sense of strength, it should be understood in the sense of economic or social strength, an interpretation confirmed by the Aramaic Targums, which render the word in terms of wealth (cf. Sir 7:30–31).[41] In this context the reference is to all one possesses, that is, one's entire household.

The progression and concentricity in Moses' vocabulary now becomes apparent. Beginning with the inner being, he moves to the whole person, and then to all that one claims as one's own, as he calls on all

37. This explains why, when Mark reports Jesus' quotation of this verse in 12:30, he actually cites four Greek words: καρδία (= Hebrew לֵב), ψυχή (= Hebrew נֶפֶשׁ), διάνοια (= Hebrew לֵב), and ἰσχύς (= Hebrew מְאֹד). Cf. Matt 22:27, which has only three elements, "heart, soul, and mind," drops Hebrew מְאֹד and retains two words for לֵב. Luke 10:27 flattens the sense of לֵב by representing it only with καρδία, and retains ἰσχύς for the third element.

38. Note especially Deut 12:23: "But be sure you do not eat the blood, because the blood is the life (נֶפֶשׁ), and you must not eat the life (נֶפֶשׁ) with the meat (בָּשָׂר)." Note also the merismic use of נֶפֶשׁ and בָּשָׂר ("body and soul") for totality in Isa 10:18. In Job 2:4–6, the adversary is permitted to touch Job's בָּשָׂר but not his נֶפֶשׁ.

39. How far removed the usage of נֶפֶשׁ may be from its basic meaning is indicated by Lev 21:11, where the word denotes a corpse, which by definition has no breath! On the usage of the word, see further Fredericks, NIDOTTE 3:133–34.

40. Cognate adjectival expressions occur in both Ugaritic (mad/mid, "great, strong, much"; Kirta 1.ii.35 [Parker, Ugaritic Narrative Poetry, 15]; Baal Cycle 10.v.15 [Ugaritic Narrative Poetry, 130]) and Akkadian (mādum, "many, numerous," ma'du, quantity, fullness," from the verb mâdum, "to become numerous" [AHw, 573]). Cf. HALOT 2:538.

41. Cf. Weinfeld, Deuteronomy 1–11, 232.

Israelites to "love" God without reservation or qualification. All that one is and has is to submit to "the yoke of the kingdom."[42] Covenant commitment must be rooted in the heart, but then extend to every level of one's being and existence.

In the remainder of this paragraph (vv. 6–9) Moses describes how this kind of unreserved commitment is to permeate all of life. In his presentation of the dimensions of covenant commitment Moses continues his centrifugal rhetorical pattern, beginning again on the inside and working his way out, the concentric circles of existence becoming ever larger.

First, the commitment expressed in the Shema' and the attendant call for unreserved love for YHWH must be indelibly written on one's heart/mind (v. 6), that is, be internalized, integrated, and incorporated in one's very being. This injunction reminds the reader that from the very beginning, Israelite faith and religion were to be internal matters of the heart, and not merely the possession of external symbols of covenant relationship or the performance of ritual acts.[43] Second, this covenant commitment was to be a family matter, demonstrated through the intentional indoctrination of the children and the spontaneous discussion of the issue with the members of one's household at every possible opportunity (v. 7).[44] Third, this covenant commitment was to be a public matter. Moses continues his pattern of triadic expression by charging his people to bind these words on their hands, apply them as phylacteries on their foreheads (literally between their eyes), and inscribe them on the doorposts of their buildings.

Verse 5 confirms that the fundamental issue in the Shema' is exclusive and total devotion to YHWH, a sense scarcely reflected in the traditional translation of the verse.

---

42. The serial use of three expressions may also be interpreted as a way of expressing the superlative degree. Just as "iniquity, rebellion, and sin" in Exod 34:7 refers to "every conceivable sin," so "heart, life, and property" refers to every part of a person.

43. For later references to actual internalization of the will of God in the hearts of believers, see Pss 37:31; 40:8, 119:11; Isa 51:7.

44. To express the former, Moses employs a verb that occurs nowhere else in the OT: שָׁנַן, "to repeat, to inculcate by repetition." Traditionally the term has been viewed as deriving from a root שָׁנַן, "to whet, sharpen." Thus BDB 1042; but so also Weinfeld, *Deuteronomy 1–11*, 332–33. However, in the light of the Ugaritic usage of the cognate *tnn*, "to repeat, to do twice," the word is better interpreted as a denominative of the numeral שְׁנַיִם/שְׁנֵי, "two." Cf. Craigie, *Deuteronomy*, 170 n. 17. The sense of the word is clarified by the parallel passage, 11:19, which uses לָמַד, "to teach."

4. *The broader literary context of the Shemaʻ*. Throughout 6:4—8:20 Moses' gaze is cast forward beyond the day when Israel will cross the Jordan to the time of occupation and settlement (6:10, 20; 7:1, 2; 8:10, 12). In this portion of the second address he repeatedly challenges his audience to keep alive the memory of YHWH's past actions. He will declare that the greatest threat to their relationship with YHWH is not posed by the enemies who live in the land, but by their own hearts and minds, which are prone to forget the grace of God.

Verses 10–25 perform a double rhetorical and literary function. In the first instance these verses look back to 6:4–9, unpacking the foregoing by deepening, concretizing, and intensifying the statements made there. Karin Finsterbusch seems to be on the right track when she recognizes the thematic and structural links between these two parts.[45] The relationship between these two texts may be illustrated synoptically as in Table 4 below.

Of special significance for our study is the correlation between verse 4b and verses 14–15. To translate Finsterbusch, "The prohibition of the worship of the gods of the peoples surrounding Israel is the logical consequence of v. 4bb, as well as a concretization of this declaration. V. 15 advances v. 14 by warning of the specific effects of worshiping foreign gods (the annihilation of Israel by YHWH). With this warning attention is drawn to the actual meaning of the declaration, 'YHWH alone.'"[46]

---

45. Finsterbusch, "Bezüge zwischen Aussagen von Dtn 6,4–9 und 6,10–25," 433–37.

46. "Das Verbot, Götter der Völker in Israels Umgebung zu verehren, ist die logische Konsequenz von V. 4b und konkretisiert diese Aussage überdies. V. 15 führt V. 14 fort, wobei V. 15b warnend die Folge der Fremdgötter-verehrung (Vernichtung Israels durch Jhwh) nennt. Mit dieser Warnung wird auf die existentielle Bedeutung der Aussage 'Jhwh ist einzig' (V. 4bb) aufmerksam gemacht" (ibid., 434).

Table 4: The Relationship between Deuteronomy 6:4–9 and 6:10–25

6:4–9	6:10–25
	10 And when YHWH your God brings you into the land that he swore to your fathers, to Abraham, to Isaac, and to Jacob, to give you—
	11 with great and good cities that you did not build, and houses full of all good things that you did not fill, and cisterns that you did not dig,
4a Hear, O Israel: Our God is YHWH,	and vineyards and olive trees that you did not plant— and when you eat and are full,
	12 then take care lest you forget YHWH, who brought you out of the land of Egypt, out of the house of slavery.
	13 It is YHWH your God you shall fear. Him you shall serve, and by his name you shall swear.
	14 You shall not go after other gods, the gods of the peoples who are around you,
	15 for YHWH your God in your midst
4b YHWH alone!	is an impassioned God, lest the anger of YHWH your God be kindled against you, and he destroy you from off the face of the earth.
5 You shall love YHWH your God with all your heart and with all your soul and with all your might.	16 You shall not put YHWH your God to the test, as you tested him at Massah.
	17 You shall diligently keep the commandments of YHWH your God, and his testimonies and his statutes, which he has commanded you.
6 And these words that I command you today shall be on your heart.	18 And you shall do what is right and good in the sight of YHWH, that it may go well with you, and that you may go in and take possession of the good land that YHWH swore to give to your fathers
	19 by thrusting out all your enemies from before you, as YHWH has promised.

6:4–9	6:10–25
	20 When your son asks you in time to come, "What is the meaning of the testimonies and the statutes and the rules that YHWH our God has commanded you?"
	21 Then you shall say to your son,
7 You shall teach them diligently to your children,	"We were Pharaoh's slaves in Egypt. And YHWH brought us out of Egypt with a mighty hand.
and shall talk of them when you sit in your house,	22 And YHWH showed signs and wonders, great and grievous, against Egypt and against Pharaoh
and when you walk by the way,	and all his household, before our eyes.
and when you lie down,	23 And he brought us out from there,
and when you rise.	that he might bring us in and give us the land that he swore to give to our fathers.
	24 And YHWH commanded us to do all these statutes, to fear YHWH our God, for our good always, that he might preserve us alive, as we are this day.
	25 And it will be righteousness for us, if we are careful to do all this commandment before YHWH our God, as he has commanded us."

8   You shall bind them
as a sign on your hand,
and they shall be
as frontlets between your eyes.

9   You shall write them
on the doorposts
of your house
and on your gates.

Moses has actually begun his role as authoritative interpreter and expositor of the covenant. In the second instance, verses 10–25 look forward. Here Moses lays the groundwork for what follows in the next two chapters. His rhetorical strategy is evident in the structure of 6:4—8:20, which may be portrayed diagrammatically as follows in Figure 6 below.

Moses' flow of thought in the respective sections is not always smooth or logical by modern definitions, and occasionally a modern reader may get bogged down with the repetition. But each section consists of three discrete parts: (1) Moses' announcement of the nature of the test of exclusive devotion; (2) Moses' introduction of a hypothetical interlocutor who responds verbally to the test; and (3) Moses' answer to the hypothetical interlocutor.

Moses' primary aim in this entire section is to explain to his people what he means by unreserved "love" for YHWH. He does so by preparing the Israelites for a series of "tests" of their devotion that life in the Promised Land will present. The Israelites will pass the test if they demonstrate conformity to *das Hauptgebot* (to love YHWH exclusively and totally) by obedience to his graciously revealed will.[47]

Figure 6: The Structure of Deuteronomy 6:4—8:20

Hear, O Israel! Our God is YHWH! YHWH alone! And you shall love YHWH your God with all your heart, and with all your being, and with all you possess.			
Structural Feature	**6:10–25**	**7:1–26**	**8:1–20**
Rhetorical Presentation of the Test	The Internal and External Tests of Love for YHWH (10–19)	The External Test of Love for YHWH (1–16)	The Internal Test of Love for YHWH (1–16)
Audience Response	*Question from Child:* What is the meaning of these commandments? (20)	*Question from Audience:* How can I dispossess these nations? (17)	*Conclusion by Audience:* I have achieved this myself. (17)
Rhetorical Answer	Moses' Catechetical Answer (21–25)	Moses' Promise and Warning (18–26)	Moses' Reminder and Warning (18–20)

47. This motif keeps resurfacing at critical junctures: 6:17–18; 7:11–12; 8:1, 6, 11.

In 6:10–19 Moses presents the heart of the matter. Verses 13–17 represent the center of gravity here as Moses unpacks what he had meant in the Shemaʿ: exclusive devotion to YHWH demonstrated in the repudiation of all other gods, and scrupulous adherence to his will. The motif of testing is highlighted in verse 16. In accordance with normal suzerainty treaty relationships, Moses forbids Israel the vassal from testing YHWH the suzerain. But these verses are framed by advance notices of two kinds of tests of covenantal fidelity the divine Suzerain presents before his vassal in the Promised Land: the challenge of prosperity (vv. 10–12), and the challenge of the people they will face (6:18–19).[48] Adopting a rhetorical strategy I have elsewhere called "resumptive exposition," in chapters 7 and 8 Moses will develop these two tests in detail, albeit in reverse order.

Although the character of YHWH's devotees is a concern in chapter 6 (cf. v. 5), the primary issue with respect to YHWH in the broader context is neither his unitary character nor worship devoted to him in a single form/manifestation of the deity, the God of Israel. The question addressed here by Moses is not, "How many is YHWH?" or "What is YHWH like?" but "Whom will the Israelites worship?" It may have seemed legitimate in some circles to ask, "How many YHWHs are there?" but we must distinguish between popular religion and official orthodox Yahwism.[49] In any case, this is not the question raised by Deut 6 or 6:4—8:26, or any other text in Deuteronomy, for that matter. The issue facing the Israelites who were about to cross the Jordan was not how many YHWHs there were, nor which YHWH they should serve (God is one!), nor even how many

---

48. They had faced this test earlier and failed miserably (1:19–32).

49. The Kuntillet ʿAjrud inscriptions represent exceptions that prove the rule, pointing precisely to the kind of syncretism in popular religion in ancient Israel against which Moses inveighs in Deuteronomy and that eventually led to the fall of both Samaria and Jerusalem. Support for a polemic against competing or alternative Yahwehs here and elsewhere in the OT has been overestimated. References to Yahweh the God of Abraham, the God of Isaac, and the God of Jacob all occur in Exodus, the narratives of which are emphatic about the identity of the God of the patriarchs and the God of the exodus (cf. 3:6, 14–16; 6:2–3). Exodus 32:1–6 provides no evidence for interpreting the golden calf as representing a different Yahweh than the Yahweh of the exodus. Aaron displays some consciousness of Yahweh (v. 5), but strictly interpreted, the Israelites requested the calf as a replacement for Moses, "who had brought us up from the land of Egypt" (v. 2). The same applies to Jeroboam's calf cult, which he establishes as an alternative to the Yahweh cult in Jerusalem (1 Kgs 12:25–33). The interpretation of the Yahwehs of Teman and Paran as separate manifestations of Yahweh, analogous to Baal Peor, etc., represents unwarranted literalism.

is YHWH. The question that concerned Moses was whether they would remain exclusively devoted to YHWH who had rescued them from Egypt and called them to covenant relationship with himself, or be seduced by and commit spiritual harlotry with the gods of the land of Canaan. The Israelites were not to bow down to gods of their own making (cf. 4:16–18) nor worship the astral deities (4:19), for YHWH their God in their midst was a passionate God (6:15). In the face of the threat posed by other gods, the Shemaʿ served as the obverse of the first principle of covenant relationship in the Decalogue, "You shall have no other gods beside/besides me." As a declaration of Israel's complete, undivided, unqualified, and undistracted devotion to YHWH, "Our God is YHWH, YHWH alone," represents the required verbal response to the *Hauptgebot*. To YHWH alone they shall cling; him alone shall they serve; and by his name alone they shall swear (Deut 6:13; 10:20).

2. *The scriptural afterlife of the Shemaʿ*. Given the theological and confessional weight of the Shemaʿ it is remarkable how faint are its echoes in the Old Testament. And when it is finally sounded, it breaks out of the parochial and ethnocentric box of Moses' original utterance with a supranational boom. After almost a thousand years of history in which the Shemaʿ proved to be "more honored in the breach than in the observance," after the horrors of destruction and exile had signaled the suspension of the covenant blessings (586 BCE), and after YHWH had revisited his people only "in small measure,"[50] we hear the only certain OT echo in Zech 14:9, though here the enigmatic verbless clause is transformed into a verbal declaration:

> YHWH will be king over the whole earth.
> On that day YHWH will be [the only] one,
> and his name the only name.[51]

---

50. The postexilic period did indeed represent fulfillment of Yahweh's ancient promises to Israel, specifically the vision of the prophets as in Ezek 37:15–28, but only מְעַט, "in small measure" (Ezek 11:16): (1) from Israel's vast population only a few returned (ca. 40,000, cf. Ezra 2:64), and they represented primarily the tribe of Judah; (2) from the breadth of the Promised Land, only a small portion in and around Jerusalem was occupied; (3) in contrast to the glory of the Davidic/Solomonic Temple, only a small building served as the house of Yahweh (Hag 2:1–9), and even here the glory apparently never returned; (4) a Davidide (Zerubbabel) was indeed installed with political authority, but he was only a governor on behalf of the Persians; he was no King David.

51. Cf. NJPSV, footnote, "I.e., the LORD alone shall be worshiped and shall be in-

The issue here is obviously not the unification of God in one deity, but expanding the boundaries of those who claim only YHWH as their God to the ends of the earth. The ideal that Moses had hoped for Israel will be realized not only in Israel, but throughout the earth. The God of Israel will command the allegiance of all humanity, and he will be addressed by the only name he has revealed to his people.

Since New Testament writers tend to appeal to the Septuagint when they cite OT texts, we should not be surprised if Jesus' quotation of the Shema' in Mark 12:32–33 follows the Septuagintal reading. However, we should not make more of Jesus' statement than the present context demands. When Jesus begins his identification of *das Hauptgebot* in Mark 12:29 with "Hear, O Israel, the Lord our God is one Lord" (which is the unambiguous meaning of the Greek), his debate with the scribe does not concern the nature of God or his unity/multiplicity. The issue is which commandment is the most important of all (v. 28). In citing the Shema' Jesus is in perfect accord with Moses, the rest of the Old Testament, and orthodox Jewish tradition. In fact, even though he absolutizes the statement beyond the immediate context of Deut 6 (where the Shema', concerns the identity of the God of Israel), in Mark 12:32 the scribe who had asked the question of Jesus affirms and clarifies the linkage of the Shema' with Deut 4:32,[52] confirming our interpretation of יהוה אֶחָד as a declaration of YHWH's exclusivity. After declaring, "You are right in saying that God is one," he adds, "and there is none other besides him" (καὶ οὐκ ἔστιν ἄλλος πλὴν αὐτοῦ).[53]

While Jesus cites the Shema' as a sort of creedal statement linked with the great commandment, it falls to Paul to draw out its christological significance. The apostle seems to allude to the Shema' in Rom 3:29–34, where he announces that God is the God of the Gentiles as well as the Jews, since the one who justifies the circumcised by faith and the un-

voked by his true name." The Hebrew reads, בַּיּוֹם הַהוּא יהיה יְהוָה אֶחָד.

52. The Greek reads καὶ οὐκ ἔστιν ἄλλος πλὴν αὐτοῦ, "and there is none other besides him."

53. This represents an adaptation of LXX's reading of Deut 4:35, the only change being the replacement of ἔτι, "exception, what is left over," with ἄλλος, "other." A similar concern for the exclusivity of Yahweh, specifically as the object of worship is evident in Jesus' response to Satan, "You shall worship the Lord your God, and serve him alone" (μόνος, Matt 4:10; Luke 4:8). This statement is based on Deut 6:13 (though here προσκυνέω, "to prostrate oneself before, worship," replaces LXX's φοβέω, "to fear"), which clearly involves Yahweh's claim to Israel's exclusive devotion.

circumcised through faith is one and the same.[54] Here Paul draws the Gentiles into the covenant community of faith, asserting that in Christ this most-favored creedal statement of the Jews also applies to the Gentiles. In perfect accord with Moses, Paul's comment has less to do with the unity of God than with the universalization of his claim to be the God of all (in fulfillment of Zech 14:9).

However, Paul establishes the christological significance of the Shema' most pointedly in 1 Cor 8:1–6. His polemic against idolatry in this text is obviously rooted in Deut 6:4–5 and beyond.[55] The first hint of a connection surfaces in verse 3, where Paul, who has a lot to say about God's love for people, inserts a relatively rare reference to people loving God. On first sight, in verse 4 Paul appears to appeal to the Shema',[56] but a more direct antecedent for, "There is no God but one,"[57] had come at the end of Moses' first address, in Deut 4:35, 39, with his explicit declaration, "YHWH, he is God, there is no other."[58] Firmly in the tradition of Moses, Paul hereby declares the uniqueness and exclusive existence of YHWH in contrast to the nothingness of idols, which is a very deuteronomistic theme.

His comments in verses 5–6 reflect a thorough understanding of the Shema' in its original context. For the sake of argument, he declares hypothetically that even if one concedes the existence of other gods (which, in the light of verse 4, he is obviously not actually willing to do), "*but for us* (ἀλλ' ἡμῖν) there is but one God (εἷς θεός), the Father, from whom all things came (cf. Deut 32:6, 18) and for whom we live (cf. Deut 14:1); and there is but one Lord (εἷς κύριος), Jesus Christ, through whom all things came and through whom we live." Translated into its original context on the plains of Moab, this is precisely the sort of thing that Moses could have said: "Even if one concedes the existence of other gods (which in

54. So also Schreiner, *Romans*, 205.

55. For studies of Paul's reformulation of the Shema' in 1 Cor 8, see Dunn, *Christology in the Making*, 179–83; Wright, "Monotheism, Christology and Ethics," 120–36; Hurtado, *One God, One Lord*, 97–100.

56. Thus Moberly, "Toward an Interpretation of the Shema," 141.

57. A stricter adherence to the Shema' would have said, "There is no Lord [i.e., Yahweh] but one," referring to the God of Israel, rather than, "There is no God but one" (καὶ ὅτι οὐδεὶς θεὸς εἰ μὴ εἷς).

58. This impression is reinforced by Paul's reference in verse 5 to so-called gods, whether "in heaven or on earth," which seems to echo, "He is God in heaven above and on the earth below, there is no other," in Deut 4:39.

the light of Deut 4:35, 39 he is obviously unwilling to do), *but for us* there is but one God, our Father (cf. Deut 1:31; 14:1; 32:6, 18), from whom all things came (cf. Gen 1:1—2:4a) and for whom we live (cf. Exod 19:5–6); his name is YHWH, through whom all things came (Exod 20:11; 31:17), and through whom we live (Exod 20:2; Deut 5:6)." What is remarkable in Paul, however, is his insertion of the name "Jesus Christ" after κύριος, which, on first sight, reflects Hebrew "Yahweh" of the Shemaʿ. However, in view of his reference to "many gods" and "many lords" in verse 5, here he appears to have in mind the title אֲדֹנָי rather than the personal name YHWH.[59] But the christological effect is extraordinary. In the words of N. T. Wright, "Paul has placed Jesus *within* an explicit statement of the doctrine that Israel's God is the one and only God, the creator of the world. The *Shema* was already, at this stage of Judaism, in widespread use as *the* Jewish daily prayer. Paul has redefined it christologically, producing what we can only call a sort of christological monotheism."[60]

On the one hand, YHWH, the one and only God to whom the Israelites declared allegiance is hereby identified unequivocally with Jesus. What the Old Testament has said about YHWH may now be said about the Christ. On the other hand, in and through Jesus Christ one encounters the one and only God.[61] Inasmuch as Paul is writing to the Corinthians, representatives of the kingdoms of the earth, in the conversion of the Gentiles one witnesses the beginning of the fulfillment of Zechariah's prophecy as well.

III. Conclusion

The Shemaʿ should not be taken out of context and interpreted as a great monotheistic confession. Moses had made that point in 4:35, 39: "For YHWH (alone) is God; there is none beside(s) him." Nor is the issue in the broader context the nature of God in general or his integrity in particular—though the nature and integrity of his people is a very important concern. This is a cry of allegiance, an affirmation of covenant commitment in response to the question, "Who is the God of Israel?" The language of the Shemaʿ is "sloganesque" rather than prosaic: "YHWH our

---

59. Cf. Deut 10:17, where Yahweh is referred to as "God of gods and Lord of lords" (אֲדֹנֵי הָאֲדֹנִים). The latter title is explicitly applied to the Lamb in Rev 17:14.

60. Wright, "Monotheism, Christology and Ethics," 129.

61. Similarly Moberly, "Toward an Interpretation of the Shema," 142.

God! YHWH alone!" or "Our God is YHWH, YHWH alone!" This was to be the distinguishing mark of the Israelite people; they are those (and only those) who claim YHWH alone as their God.

This interpretation of the Shemaʿ raises the question of how it should be rendered in translation. In his 1990 article, R. W. L. Moberly argued for the translation, "Yahweh our God, Yahweh is one."[62] But in his 1999 interpretation of the Shemaʿ he declares, "What 'YHWH is one' means must be something that makes appropriate the total and unreserved response of 'love' that is immediately specified [in v. 5]." He goes on to write, "To say that YHWH is 'one' is not to say something about God that is separable from its human counterpart of 'love,' but rather designates YHWH as the appropriate recipient of unreserved 'love.'"[63] The way theologians use this verse demonstrates that this is precisely what is *not* communicated when יהוה אֶחָד is translated "YHWH is one." While this may represent a literally formal translation of the words of the Shemaʿ, it actually misleads the reader. The statements in Scripture should be translated according to their meaning *in context*, not according to dictionary definitions of the words.

Our interpretation of the Shemaʿ is confirmed by verses 5–8, in which Moses declares that within the context of covenant relationship, Israel's love for YHWH is to be absolute, total, internal, communal, public, and transmitted from generation to generation. "YHWH our God! YHWH alone": these are the words to be imprinted on the heart, to be worn on one's hands and forehead, and to be inscribed above the doors and gates— that all the world may know that in this place YHWH alone is served. This is what makes an Israelite a true Israelite. Whether they are descended from Abraham or not, the true covenant community consists of all and only those who make this their cry of allegiance, and who demonstrate this commitment with uncompromising covenant love.

62. Moberly, "Yahweh is One," 209–15.
63. Moberly, "Toward an Interpretation of the Shema," 132, 133.

5

The Joy of Worship

The Mosaic Invitation to the Presence of God (Deut 12:1–14)[1]

True worship involves reverential human acts of submission and homage before God, the divine Sovereign, in response to his gracious revelation of himself, and in accordance with his will.

Introduction

WHEN SOMEONE ANNOUNCES A series of studies on worship, people's ears perk up. This is not surprising, since evangelical churches in America are presently engaged in what many are calling "worship wars." In the past, churches have fought and divided over doctrinal issues, such as Calvinism versus Arminianism, modes of baptism, speaking in tongues, and head coverings. Today the battle is over worship styles. In fact some are arguing that commitments to certain styles of worship (contemporary versus traditional and informal versus liturgical) are more important than devotional styles. In many churches the tensions over these issues are sharp.

One reason many churches split over forms of communal worship may be the relative paucity of direct guidance from the New Testament. Nowhere does the New Testament say Christians should build churches, meet on Sundays, have morning worship services, open with song and a prayer, have a long sermon, and close with a benediction. About the only custom it prescribes as a regular occurrence is participation in the

1. This essay was previously published in *Bibliotheca Sacra* 162 (2005) 131–49.

Lord's Supper (1 Cor 11:23–34), in remembrance of Christ's saving work and in anticipation of the great eschatological meal in the presence of God himself. Remarkably, the one liturgical rite that the New Testament prescribes has been denigrated as optional, while believers squabble over other elements.

The crisis in the contemporary evangelical church arises from the woeful absence of a biblical theology of worship. If true worship actually involves reverential acts of submission and homage before the divine Sovereign, in response to his gracious revelation of himself, and in accordance with his will, then it is important to know what his will is with regard to reverential acts of submission and homage. Deuteronomy 12:1–14 may help in this matter.

This literary unit represents the first in a long series that extends to 26:19, which scholars generally refer to (though unhelpfully) as the Deuteronomic Law Code. Together with chapters 5–11, chapters 12–26 make up the bulk of Moses' second address delivered to the Israelites on the plains of Moab. Despite the obvious links to the Decalogue and the Book of the Covenant, in tone and style much of Deut 12–26 bears a closer resemblance to chapters 6–11 than it does to the Sinai documents[2] on which many of Moses' instructions were based. In fact there is no appreciable shift in style and tone as one moves from chapter 11 to chapter 12 and beyond. While scholars recognize in the speeches of the book of Deuteronomy the voice of a prophet or a scribe or even a priest,[3] the concerns and style of the speaker are better understood as those of a pastor. These are the final addresses of a man who knew that his tenure as shepherd of God's sheep was about to end (cf. Num 27:15–17). In his preaching Moses was concerned not only with civil and liturgical matters, but especially the future spiritual and physical well-being of the people. He was particularly passionate about the people's relationship with God, a relationship that was to be treasured as an incredible gift and demonstrated in a life of grateful obedience to their divine Redeemer and Lord. Deuteronomy 12:1–14 represents the introduction to Moses' specific instructions on the life of faith and godliness for his people.

2. These are the Book of the Covenant (Exod 20:22—23:33), the so-called Holiness Code (Lev 17–26).

3. For a helpful discussion of the prophetic and scribal voices, see Watts, *Reading Law*, 112–21. On the priestly voice, see von Rad, *Deuteronomy*, 23–27.

While this covenant relationship has its roots in God's election and call of Abraham (cf. 4:37; 7:6–8), it was formalized with Abraham's descendants at Sinai (Exod 19–24; cf. Gen 17:7). In an incredible and unprecedented moment of self-revelation, YHWH had descended on "the mountain of God" (Exod 3:1; 4:27; 18:5; 24:13), transforming it into a temporary terrestrial divine "palace," to which the people were invited for an audience with himself, the Lord of all the earth and Redeemer of his people. Later he charged the Israelites to construct the Tabernacle, which would serve, in a sense, as his palace.[4] This structure provided a graciously designed and revealed means for Israel to relate personally with their God, and the rituals performed therein provided a way to maintain their covenant relationship with YHWH.

The design and decoration of the Tabernacle were determined by two considerations. First, like all temples in the ancient world it was designed to reflect the glory and majesty of its divine Resident—hence the gold and silver, the scarlet and purple, and the luxury goatskin leather. Second, since the Israelites had a long journey ahead of them, the divine palace needed to be portable, easily dismantled and re-erected at the order of its Resident. At the time Moses preached the sermons found in the book of Deuteronomy, the Israelites' travels were over, and they were looking forward to a settled life in the Promised Land. In 12:1–14 Moses announced for the first time that the travels of the tabernacle would not go on indefinitely. At the appropriate time YHWH would identify a particular place where his name would dwell.

The Style and Structure of Deuteronomy 12:1–14

Sandwiched between the opening call for obedience to the statutes and laws (v. 1) and an appeal to obey all the commands of Moses and thus do what is good and right in the sight of God (v. 28), verses 2–27 divide into two panels, virtually identical in length.[5] The first calls for singularity of sacrificial slaughter (vv. 2–14), and the second authorizes the free distribution of profane slaughter (vv. 15–27). These two parts are held together by the sixfold repetition of the formula by which God called for

4. The tabernacle is referred to as his "sanctuary" (מִקְדָּשׁ), "residence" (מִשְׁכָּן), or "tent of appointments" (אֹהֶל מוֹעֵד).

5. Counting אֵת, the sign of the definite direct object, with the following substantive, verses 2–14 consist of 199 words, and verses 15–27 have 200 words.

worship at the shrine he would choose. These six are evenly distributed, three occurring in the first panel (vv. 5, 11, 14) and three in the second (vv. 18, 21, 26).

Commentators tend to refer to verses 2–12 as the "Deuteronomic Altar Law."[6] However, such a label is misleading. On the one hand the focus of attention is not the altar. Indeed the altar is not even mentioned until verse 27. On the other hand, classifying this passage as "law" obscures its pastoral tone and drowns out a remarkable grace that is hereby declared. Instead this text should be seen as a glorious invitation to worship YHWH in his presence. It represents a wonderful provision for the perpetuation of the extraordinary event that happened at Mount Sinai, where YHWH had personally called his people into his presence and invited them to rejoice there.

Grammatically and syntactically this text divides into three parts: Moses' invitation to worship (vv. 2–7), Moses' description of the nature of true worship (vv. 8–12), and Moses' concluding exhortation (vv. 13–14). The symmetry observed earlier in the division of 12:2–27 into two segments virtually identical in length is evident here as well, inasmuch as the first two subsections (vv. 2–7 and 8–12) consist of eighty-five and eighty-nine Hebrew words respectively. The final exhortation is shorter (twenty-five words). The purpose of this article is to explore the substance of this passage by noting the contrasts between true and false worship, in answer to questions related to the following chart (Table 5).

Table 5: Wrong and Right Worship according to Deuteronomy 12:1–14

Feature	The Nature of False Worship	The Nature of True Worship
Object of Worship	The gods of the nations (vv. 2–3)	YHWH (v. 1, and ten other times) The God of your ancestors (v. 1) Your God (v. 2, and seven other times)
Subjects of Worship	The nations (v. 2)	Everyone: you, your household, your sons, your daughters, your male servants, your female servants, the Levites in your gates (vv. 7, 12)

6. Many see here a late adaptation and revision of the original altar law in the Book of the Covenant (Exod 20:24–26). See for example Levinson, *Deuteronomy and the Hermeneutics of Legal Innovation*, 23–53.

Feature	The Nature of False Worship	The Nature of True Worship
Place of Worship	Multiple locations (v. 2) Where the nations served their gods (v. 2) On the high mountains (v. 2) On the hills (v. 2) Under every green tree (v. 2) Where the god's name is put (v. 3) Wherever one chooses (v. 13)	Singular location (vv. 5, 11, 14) Chosen by YHWH (vv. 5, 11, 14) Where YHWH's name is established (vv. 5, 11) Where YHWH dwells (v. 11)
Focus of Worship	Accoutrements: altars, sacred pillars, asherim, carved images (v. 3)	The personal presence of YHWH (vv. 7, 12)
Motivation for Worship	(None stated)	Response to YHWH's grace: in giving the land (vv. 1, 10) in blessing the people (v. 7) in giving rest (v. 9) in giving a grant (vv. 9–10, 12) in providing security (v. 10)
Norm for Worship	The practice of the nations (v. 2) What is right in one's own eyes (v. 8)	Moses' command (vv. 1, 11, 14)
Activities in Worship	Whatever is right in one's own eyes (v. 8) (Care and feeding of the gods)	Not like the nations (v. 4) Whatever Moses commanded (v. 14) Come (vv. 5, 9) Bringing your offerings and gifts (vv. 6, 11): whole burnt offerings, sacrifices, tithes, contributions, votive offerings, freewill offerings, firstborn offerings Eat before YHWH (v. 7) Rejoice (vv. 7, 12) Offer burnt offerings (vv. 13–14)

Who Is the Object of True Worship?

Moses answered the question regarding the object of false worship with the barest of details. He spoke of the gods of the nations whom the Israelites were to dispossess, without identifying the gods by name.[7] Of course, these divinities did not deserve naming, for they were the products of the futile imaginations of depraved human minds. They were

7. The expression "gods of the nations" appears in Deuteronomy only in 29:19[Eng 18].

nothing but physical objects made of wood and stone, and decorated with silver and gold. As Moses had declared earlier in 4:28, they were the work of human hands, and they do not see, hear, eat, or smell. In 29:16[Eng 17] Moses referred to these lifeless idols as שִׁקֻּצִים and גִּלֻּלִים, a hendiadys for "disgusting excrement pellets."[8] These expressions declare what God thinks about all expressions of religious devotion that displace him as the object of worship with humanly inspired or man-made substitutes.

By contrast, the Israelites are called to worship YHWH, "the living God" (5:26), who had not only revealed to his people his eternal name (Exod 3:15), but who had personally established himself as "the God of your ancestors" (12:1). This is the God who had graciously revealed his will to his people (4:1–8), and who in fulfillment of Gen 17:7 graciously invited Israel to covenant relationship with himself (4:9–31). Because he loved the ancestors, he chose their descendants and graciously redeemed Israel from the bondage of Egypt (vv. 32–40), and thus he demonstrated that he is the one and only God—there is no other (4:35, 39). Not only had YHWH become the personal God of this people;[9] as Moses declared in 14:1–2, he had also adopted them as his sons, set them apart as his holy people, and chosen them to be his royal treasure (סְגֻלָּה). A starker contrast between Israel's God and the gods of the nations can scarcely be imagined.

Who Are the Subjects of True Worship?

Here I use the word "subjects" not in the sense of "about whom is worship?" but in the grammatical sense of "who may worship acceptably?" Deuteronomy 12 speaks of two kinds of worshipers. On the one hand, it speaks of "the nations whom you shall dispossess" (v. 2): the Hittites, Girgashites, Amorites, Canaanites, Perizzites, Hivites, and Jebusites, seven nations greater and stronger than Israel (7:1). These are the nations whose worship was an abomination, with whom the Israelites were to make no covenants and show no favor, with whom they were forbidden to inter-

8. שִׁקֻּצִים derives from a root meaning "to detest, abhor" (cf. 7:26), and גִּלֻּלִים seems to be an artificial construct derived from the verb, גָּלַל "to roll," but vocalized after the pattern of שִׁקֻּצִים. The adoption of this word as a designation for idols may have been prompted by the natural pellet-like shape of sheep feces, or less likely, the cylindrical shape of human excrement. The word "dung" would be an appropriate translation.

9. The expression "YHWH, your God" appears eight times in this text: six with the plural pronoun (vv. 4–5, 7a, 10, 11, 12), and twice with the singular (vv. 7b, 9).

marry, "for they will turn your children away from following me to serve other gods" (v. 4). These are people whose worship YHWH abhors.

Whereas the persons whose worship is rejected are lumped together in one generic expression הַגּוֹיִם, "the nations," the persons who are invited to worship are specifically identified. Moses was obviously addressing the heads of the households in verse 7 when he referred to the worshipers as "you." But he immediately made it clear that acceptable worship is not restricted to adult males, for he added "and your households." In so doing Moses democratized what had been the experience of only a privileged few at Horeb: Moses and Aaron and the elders/nobles (Exod 24:1, 11). In Deut 12:12 and 18 he clarified what he meant by "households," specifying "your sons and daughters, your male and female servants, and the Levite in your gates."[10] Whereas 16:18 requires only males to participate in the pilgrimage festivals, 12:12 and 18 suggest that in fact the worship of YHWH was open to all. Throughout his addresses, Moses perceived Israel as a community of faith that was to gather regularly for worship in God's presence: a chosen people in a chosen land gathered at the chosen place for worship of the One who had graciously chosen them.

This is a remarkable statement, declaring that in the presence of God all believers are equal and that all have equal access to him. When more than a thousand years later Paul would write that "there is neither Jew nor Greek, slave nor free person, male nor female, for you are all one in Christ Jesus" (Gal 3:28), he was not fixing an Old Testament problem. Instead he was correcting the misogynistic social developments reflected in rabbinic writings[11] and institutionalized in the design of Herod's Temple, with its separate courts of the women and Gentiles respectively.[12] But this kind of social stratification in the assembly of worshipers is foreign to the Old Testament. Moses envisioned all the members of the community of faith having equal access to God's presence.

---

10. In 31:10–12 Moses spoke of men and women, children and aliens.

11. Hear, for example, the famous declaration of Rabbi Judah: "Three benedictions a man must bless every day: Blessed [are you, Lord,] who did not make me a Gentile. Blessed [are you, Lord,] who did not make me a woman. Blessed [are you, Lord,] who did not make me an uncultured person" (Chapman, "Marriage and Family in Second Temple Judaism," 208). This perspective is also reflected in Sir (Ecclesiasticus) 25:13—26:12. For discussion of and bibliography on this issue, see further ibid., 206–10.

12. For a diagram, see *EncJud²*, 15:962. For a schematic presentation of this social world, see Murphy, *Early Judaism*, 45–46.

Where Is the Place of True Worship?

The contrasts between acceptable and unacceptable worship continue when one considers the location of the respective patterns. Moses set the stage for his restriction of the worship of YHWH to "the place" (singular) that YHWH would choose to place his name, by condemning the plurality of pagan cult centers: "all the places where the nations . . . serve their gods" (v. 2). He elaborated on the significance of the plural by adding "on the high mountains and on the hills and under every green [lit., 'spreading' or 'luxuriant'] tree." The use of three expressions reflected both the intensity of the threat the Canaanite religious system would be to the Israelites once they crossed the Jordan and the emptiness and vanity of the Canaanite system. People who are frustrated by gods who do not see or hear or smell (cf. 4:28) feel obligated to claim for liturgical purposes every potential place where a god might be contacted. Moses' emphasis on the plethora of places served as an important foil against which to interpret YHWH's claim to a single place in 12:5 and 11.

Verse 5 is one of the most important verses in the chapter and in Deuteronomy as a whole for understanding the history of Israelite religion. "The place that YHWH your God will choose from among all your tribes to establish his name there for his dwelling" is the first of twenty-one occurrences of "the place formula" in Deuteronomy.[13] The formula occurs in a variety of forms, ranging from the most elemental, "the place that he chooses" (16:16; 31:11), to the most complex, as in 12:5. In setting the stage for all that follows, this declaration makes four fundamental statements about "the place."

First, it speaks of a place that YHWH, the God of Israel, would choose. The verb בָּחַר, "to choose," represents the most explicit term for "election" in Deuteronomy. Except for 23:17 [Eng 16] and 30:19, this verb in Deuteronomy always has YHWH as the subject. He fulfilled the patriarchal covenant by choosing Israel out of all the peoples on earth (4:37; 7:6–7; 10:15; 14:2); he chose the Levites as priests from all the tribes (18:5; 21:5); and he would choose a king from the people of Israel to govern for him (17:15). He would also "choose" the place for his name. In keeping with longstanding ancient Near Eastern tradition, the gods selected the

13. Deut 12:5, 11, 14, 18, 21, 26; 14:23, 24, 25; 15:20; 16:2, 6, 7, 11, 15, 16; 17:8, 10; 18:6; 26:2; 31:11. All occurrences are found in Moses' speeches. Variations or echoes of the formula appear in later writings as well (Josh 9:27; 2 Kgs 21:7; 23:27; Jer 7:12; Ezra 6:12; Neh 1:9).

place where their devotees were to worship them.[14] Here YHWH, the God of Israel, announced in advance that he would choose his "place."

Second, the place was to be chosen "from all your [plural] tribes." This comment is rendered only slightly more concrete in verse 14, "in one of your [singular] tribes." Obviously this expression excludes Mount Sinai as the place of YHWH's permanent dwelling and the destination of future pilgrimages. Here Moses envisioned some location within the territorial tribal allotments promised in Num 34 and fulfilled by Joshua in Josh 14–19. Although Gen 49:10 had predicted that the future monarchy would come from the tribe of Judah, neither the preceding material in the Pentateuch nor the book of Deuteronomy itself provides any hint about which place God had in mind. This seems intentional; by not naming the place, Moses kept the focus on the Person rather than the place.[15] However, in due time Judah was recognized both as the tribe from which the king would come and as the tribal territory in which YHWH's place (Jerusalem/Zion) would be located. The psalmist captured both dimensions in Ps 78:69–71 and linked the election of Judah/Zion as YHWH's eternal dwelling place with the election of David as king:

He also rejected the tent of Joseph,
and did not choose the tribe of Ephraim;
but chose the tribe of Judah, Mount Zion, which he loved.[16]
And he built his sanctuary like the heights,
like the earth which he has founded forever.
He also chose David his servant
and took him from the sheepfolds;
from the care of the ewes with suckling lambs.
He brought him to shepherd Jacob his people
and Israel his inheritance.[17]

14. On the initiative of deities in ancient Near Eastern accounts of temple construction, see Hurowitz, "I Have Built You an Exalted House," 135–67.

15. Jeremiah applied the formula to Shiloh at an early stage in the nation's history (Jer 7:12–14).

16. For citations of extra-biblical texts that speak of deities "loving" their favored city or mountain, see Hurowitz, "I Have Built You an Exalted House," 155–57.

17. For additional explicit references to the election of Jerusalem/Zion "out of all the tribes of Israel," see 1 Kgs 8:16, 11:32; 14:21; 2 Kgs 21:7; 2 Chr 6:5; 12:13; 33:7. For references to the election of Jerusalem without mention of Israel's tribes, see 1 Kgs 8:44, 48; 11:13, 36; 2 Kgs 23:27.

Although it would be a mistake to read later, highly developed Zion theology into Moses' vague reference to the place that YHWH would choose, there can be no doubt that the One who inspired Moses in this address, ultimately had Jerusalem in mind, even as he had David in mind in Deut 17:15.

Third, the place would have YHWH's name on it. Here and on two other occasions (12:21; 14:24) Moses expressed this notion with the phrase "to put/place his name there."[18] The expression speaks of divine ownership. Just as a person who bears the name of YHWH is recognized as belonging to him,[19] so the place bearing the imprint of his name is recognized as his possession.[20] In this context the expression serves as the equivalent of "the place where I [YHWH] cause my name to be remembered" (Exod 20:24), or "the place on which my name is called/read." This seems to refer to an inscription on the foundation stone of the building. Such inscriptions validated the site as chosen by the one whose name was inscribed. In this case it would declare the place a cult locale where God could be worshiped and confidently invoked.

Fourth, the place will be a dwelling place for YHWH. "For his dwelling" (לְשִׁכְנוֹ)[21] is a unique expression. Like other temples in the ancient world the place of worship was to be viewed as the personal residence of YHWH in the midst of his people.

However, YHWH's dwelling place would be different from the pagan shrines. Echoing statements made earlier in Deut 7:2–5, Moses provided helpful clues in 12:3 about the nature of the cult shrines on the hilltops and under trees. In keeping with idolatry in general, which sought to translate abstract religious ideas into concrete images, Moses emphasized

18. The expression occurs elsewhere in 1 Kgs 9:3; 11:36; 14:21; 2 Kgs 21:4, 7; 2 Chr 6:20; 12:13. Cf. the related clause, "for his name to be there," in 1 Kgs 8:16, 29 (= 2 Chr 6:20) and 2 Kgs 23:27.

19. See Deut 5:11 and Isa 44:5. Isaiah called Mount Zion "the place of the name of the Lord of hosts" (18:7). Several texts refer to building a house for the name of YHWH (2 Sam 7:13; 1 Kgs 3:2; 5:17–19; 8:17–20, 44, 48).

20. Equivalent expressions also occur in Akkadian and Egyptian texts. For the former, see EA 287:60–63, "Behold the king has set his name (*ša-ka-an šum-šu*) in the land of Jerusalem forever; so he cannot abandon the lands of Jerusalem!" (*ANET,* 488; cf. EA 288:5 in ibid.). For the latter, see Rameses III's reference to building a temple for Amon "as the vested property of your name" (ibid., 261). For detailed discussion of these matters, see Richter, *The Deuteronomistic History and the Name Theology.*

21. The expression seems to presuppose an otherwise unattested noun, שֶׁכֶן, "dwelling."

the physical aspects of pagan cult centers. Altars were viewed as the tables of the gods (cf. Ezek 39:17–20; 41:22; 44:16; Mal 1:7, 12), on which the worshipers presented offerings of food and beverage. These altars could consist of hilltop rock outcrops or be built of earth, or metal, or wood and plated with precious metal; but usually they were built of stones. In pagan cultic contexts pillars were upright stones, either natural or cut, and often engraved with religious symbols, symbolic of the male deity. "Asherim" refers to objects representing the female principle in these pagan religions. Whereas the King James Version renders the term "Asherim" as "groves," in the light of Ugaritic and other ancient textual evidence Asherah is now known to have been a prominent goddess in the Canaanite mythology, the wife of the high god El and mother of seventy gods. In this instance the object was probably a standing wooden image, carved in the form of a woman with exaggerated sexual features. The word פְּסִילִים, "images," is a generic term for images, usually carved from wood and plated with silver or gold.

Moses' disposition toward these objects is reflected in the verbs he used to describe how they were to be treated. These altars were to be "torn down," the sacred pillars smashed, the Asherim burned with fire, and the images of their gods chopped down (Deut 12:3). The violence of these actions served a double purpose: to demonstrate the futility of idolatry (the gods cannot even defend themselves; cf. Judg 6:31–32) and to expunge the land of any evidence of the pagan practices of the Canaanites. Like the names of the gods themselves (Deut 12:3), the symbols of their worship were to be totally eradicated.

This emphasis on the concrete symbols of divinity at pagan shrines contrasts with the way Moses portrayed the place where YHWH was to be worshiped. Moses said nothing of buildings or images or cultic appurtenances. Instead he focused on the presence of YHWH himself. If the place YHWH chose to establish his name is the place where he dwells, then it is natural for him to describe the location of worship as "before YHWH," which Moses does twice (vv. 7, 12). Elsewhere he recognized the special status of the Levites and their role in worship.[22] However, for the

---

22. The Levites' responsibilities and privileges are summarized in Deut 10:8 (cf. 18:5; 21:7): to carry the ark of the covenant, to stand before YHWH, to serve him, and to bless in his name. But Moses recognized other roles for the Levites as well: to serve as judges (16:9; 19:17; 21:7); to oversee or witness the king's writing of the Torah for himself (17:18); to oversee the treatment of leprosy (24:8–9); to assist in covenant renewal rituals (27:9); to serve as custodians of sacred texts (31:9).

kind of worship envisioned here he declared that all members of the community could freely worship. Access to YHWH is not a privilege reserved for the few; it is for all.

What Is the Motivation for True Worship?

Neither in this context nor elsewhere in Deuteronomy did Moses spell out the motivation behind pagan worship. Based on explicit attributions of prosperity to YHWH (as in 7:12–16), one might surmise that the primary motivation behind the religion of pagan nations was an insatiable demand for security—security defined in terms of physical prosperity and numerous progeny. Moses did in fact speak of the seductive and deceptive power of idolatry (4:15–19; 11:16; 13:5–10 [Eng 6–11]), and he warned against curiosity about how the nations worshiped their gods (12:30). In 32:37–38 YHWH himself gave the clearest hint of the driving force behind idolatry:

> Where are their gods,
> the rock in which they took refuge,
> who ate the fat of their sacrifices,
> and drank the wine of their drink offering?
> Let them rise up and help you;
> Let them be your hiding place!

These statements suggests that while the ultimate aim of pagan religious exercises was security and protection from hostile external forces, this goal was achieved only through the care and feeding of the gods.

By contrast, Deut 12 provides an exciting series of reasons why future generations should be motivated to worship YHWH. Whereas Moses had repeatedly grounded Israel's ethical conduct in God's past actions of deliverance, covenant, revelation, and providential care (see Deut 4), here he highlighted YHWH's future actions on the nation's behalf as the grounds for worship. First, he would give them the land promised to their ancestors (vv. 1, 10). Second, he would bless the Israelites in all their economic activities (v. 7). Third, he would give them rest (v. 9). Fourth, he would give Israel the land of Canaan as her special grant (v. 9). Fifth, he would provide security for them (v. 10). By reminding the Israelites of these gracious actions, Moses illustrated the fundamental character of true worship: reverential human acts of submission and homage before the divine Sovereign, *in response to* his gracious revelation of himself and in accord with his will. Worship involves a glorious celebration of privilege and relationship, rather than fright and manipulation.

What Are the Characteristics of True Worship?

Deuteronomy 12 includes hints of both the right and the wrong ways to worship. First, true worship does not take its cues from the world. True worship is designed by the object of worship, not the worshiper or the world from which the worshiper comes. In this context Moses' portrayal of idolatrous worship is sketchy. On the one hand, he talked about the nations "serving" their gods (v. 2). In contexts of idolatry this expression envisages the elaborate rituals involved in the care of the gods, especially feeding and clothing them.[23] However, the semantic range of the word עָבַד, "to serve," is much broader, denoting any expressions or acts of servitude before a person whom one recognizes as one's superior. So to serve other gods is to acknowledge their lordship over oneself, which is a direct affront to YHWH, who has created all humankind (cf. 4:32).

On the other hand, Moses forbade the Israelites from worshiping any way they choose. He characterized the false worship of any fellow Israelite as doing "whatever is right in his own eyes" (v. 8). Earlier Moses had commended the Israelites who stood before him for being more committed to YHWH than their parents had been (4:4). But in chapter 9 he went to great lengths to demonstrate that far from being given the land of Canaan as a reward for their superior righteousness, the present generation was stiff-necked just like their predecessors (v. 6). In fact they had been rebellious and stiff-necked from the day he first knew them. Moses' admonition in 10:16 to circumcise their hearts and to stop stiffening their necks apparently addressed a current problem. Later God himself reinforced this conclusion in 31:16–18 by predicting that after Moses' death the Israelites will "play the harlot" with the gods of the land, forsake him and break his covenant with them. Moses expressed the same fear in 31:27–29. The present generation is far from perfect.

If worshiping other gods like the nations and doing what is right in one's own eyes are fundamentally objectionable to God, what does true worship look like? The short answer from the immediate context is that

---

23. For a discussion of the "care and feeding" of the gods in Mesopotamia, see Oppenheim, *Ancient Mesopotamia*, 183–98; Saggs, *The Greatness That was Babylon*, 351–54; Curtis, "Idol, Idolatry," 378; Rudman, "When Gods Go Hungry," 37–39.

true worship happens when the people follow what Moses commanded (12:1, 11, 14). A longer answer may be found by examining all the other contexts in which the "place formula" occurs in Deuteronomy and asking what types of activity were to transpire there. The following represents a summary of the answers. At the place YHWH chooses to establish his name his people may participate in the following worshipful activities:

(1)   "See the face of YHWH" (31:11; cf. 16:16).

(2)   Hear the reading of the Torah (31:11).

(3)   Learn to fear YHWH (14:23; 31:9–13).

(4)   Rejoice before YHWH (12:18; 14:26; 16:11–12, 14; 26:11).

(5)   Eat before YHWH (12:7, 18; 14:23, 26, 29; 15:20; 18:6–8).

(6)   Present their sacrifices, which would include "the holy things" they owned, votive offerings, and whole burnt offerings (12:26–27), tithes of grain, new wine, and oil, and the firstborn of the herds and flocks (14:22–27), and the consecrated firstborn of herds or flocks (15:19–23).

(7)   Celebrate the three great annual pilgrimage festivals: the Passover (16:1–8), the Festival of Weeks (Pentecost, 16:9–12), and the Festival of Booths (16:13–17; 31:9–13).

(8)   Settle legal disputes before the Levitical priest or the judge (17:8–13).

(9)   Observe Levites serving in the name of YHWH (18:6–8).

(10)   Present thanksgiving offerings and recall YHWH's saving and providential grace (26:1–11).

(11)   Demonstrate their covenant commitment to YHWH by gifts of charity to needy people (26:12; cf. 10:12–22).

(12)   Demonstrate communal solidarity by celebrating with one's children and servants, the Levites, and aliens (14:27–29; 16:11).

This is a remarkable list of worshipful activities to be performed or experienced in YHWH's presence at the place he would choose. But chapter 12 contains Moses' fullest statement of the purpose of the place to which the LORD invites them. His statement actually consists of two parts: verses 5–7 describe some general aspects of worship, and verses 11–12 give some clarifying elaboration.

Moses' instructions for worship in verses 5–7 are dominated by five verbs: "you shall *make a pilgrimage* to the place," and "you shall *come* there" (v. 5), "you shall *bring* your offerings" (v. 6), "you shall *eat*" (v. 7a), and "you shall *rejoice* in all activities" (v. 7b).[24] These five expressions reflect the five dimensions of Moses' paradigm for worship. Each has a profoundly positive sense and may be construed more as an invitation than as a command, yielding a picture of Old Testament worship that flies in the face of common perceptions.

First, Moses invited the Israelites to make regular pilgrimages to the place where YHWH would reside. Translated literally, Moses' first challenge reads, "On the contrary, to the place that YHWH your God will choose . . . you may seek/repair and there you may come." Contrary to most English translations, the Hebrew idiom, דְּרַשׁ אֶל־הַמָּקוֹם, does not mean either "to seek the place" (NIV, ESV, NRSV, RSV) or "to seek YHWH at the place" (NAS, NLT, NJB), as if the place needed to be found. The phrase "to seek to the place" (literal translation) idiomatically means "to make a pilgrimage to the place," or "to visit the place with spiritual intent."[25] Moses hereby invited the Israelites regularly to visit the place that YHWH would choose for his residence. Contrary to the usual designation of these verses as "the altar law," in reality they represent a gracious initiative by YHWH, who has provided a way whereby he would continue to relate to his people more or less as he had at Sinai. This is as much an invitation to continuous and repeated fellowship with him as it is a command to appear before him regularly.[26]

Second, Moses invited the Israelites to come to/enter the place where YHWH resides. New International Version and many other translations render the verb בּוֹא as "go," but this obscures the perspective of the statement. Speaking on behalf of YHWH, Moses said, "There you may

---

24. These are the author's translations.

25. Tigay, *Deuteronomy*, 120. The sense is captured by the rendering in the Revised English Bible, "Instead you are to resort to the place which the Lord your God will choose."

26. Exodus refers to Sinai as a place where Israel would "serve" YHWH (Exod 3:12; 4:23; 7:16, 26[Eng 8:1]; 8:16[Eng 20]; 9:1, 13; 10:3, 7–8, 11, 24, 26; 12:31), offer sacrifices to him (3:18; 5:3, 8, 17; 8:4, 21–25 [Eng 8, 25–29]; 10:25), and celebrate a festival in his honor (5:1; cf. 10:9). Also God said to Israel, "You yourselves have seen what I did to the Egyptians, and how I bore you on eagles' wings *and brought you to myself*" (19:4, italics added).

come/enter.”[27] The verb presents the movement of the Israelites from the perspective of the person at the destination rather than the perspective of the person sending them off on a journey: Israel was invited to come to YHWH and/or enter his presence.[28] This is the Old Testament equivalent to Jesus’ invitation, “Come to Me, all who are weary and heavy-laden” (Matt 11:28), and “If anyone is thirsty, let him come to Me and drink” (John 7:37). True worship occurs in God’s presence by his invitation.

Third, Moses invited the Israelites to bring all their offerings to YHWH at the place where he would establish his name (Deut 12:6, 11). The meaning of the previous two statements is reinforced by the use of the hiphil of בּוֹא, “to bring,” by which Moses maintains the perspective of the person at the destination rather than the source.[29] We recognize his enthusiasm at this point in his listing of seven types of offerings: whole burnt offerings, animal sacrifices, tithes, specially dedicated donations, votive offerings, freewill offerings, and the firstborn of herds and flocks. Moses’ concern here was not so much to give Israel a comprehensive manual for ritual worship, but rather to provide his people with a theology of worship. So his list is not exhaustive.[30] Like the list of Canaanite tribes in 7:1, this catalogue of seven types of gifts represents the full range of sacrifices prescribed elsewhere. Moses thus served as YHWH’s herald, inviting the Israelites to bring all their offerings to him at the place he would choose, knowing that he will accept them. The chosen people offering specially chosen gifts in the place chosen by YHWH—this is the key to maintaining in the land the covenant relationship established at Sinai.

Fourth, Moses invited the Israelites to eat there in the presence of YHWH their God. According to Exod 24:10–11, at Sinai the elders of Israel observed the glorious presence of YHWH as they ate and drank. Once in the land, YHWH would make provision for this experience to be repeated indefinitely in the future. Moses’ present statement is significant on at least four counts. (1) As elsewhere in ancient Near Eastern

27. “To go” would have been expressed with הָלַךְ.

28. The opposite of בּוֹא, “to come, enter,” is יָצָא, “to go out” (cf. Deut 28:6, 19).

29. So also verse 11. Taking or carrying the offering to a place might have been expressed with נָשָׂא, “to carry,” as in verse 26.

30. Many sacrifices are not included in Moses’ list: peace offerings, thanksgiving offerings, Passover sacrifices, ordination offerings, sin/purification offerings, reparation offerings, elevation offerings, cereal offerings, special gifts, and liquid libations.

and biblical contexts, eating together was a ritual act of fellowship and communion, often the culminating event of a covenant-making ritual (Gen 31:54; Exod 24:5–11). (2) Unlike the experience at Sinai, where only Moses, Aaron, and the elders had eaten in the presence of God, here the privilege was democratized—all are invited. (3) Unlike the emphasis in pagan contexts, where offerings were presented as food for the gods, here the focus was on the offerings as food for the worshipers. (4) The words "there in the presence of YHWH your God" reflect the true nature of this relationship. In keeping with the image of ancient custom the Israelites' God would host his vassals at this banquet table, but he would not eat with them.[31] This is an invitation to be guests at a banquet he prepares whenever they "come to the place he had chosen to reside." That place provided a way by which the communion Israel experienced with YHWH at Sinai may be experienced repeatedly in the Promised Land.

Fifth, the Israelites were invited to celebrate YHWH's blessing on their work. Later Moses would instruct worshipers to confess before the Levitical priest their awareness that the crops represent "the good" that YHWH had granted them and their households (26:10–11). As noted earlier, "your households" (12:7) are further defined in verse 12 to include not only children and servants but also the Levites who lived within the town, but who were at the mercy of the peoples' charity, since they had no grant of land in which to produce their own food.

Many Christians today think of Israelite worship as boring and repetitive rituals performed by priests on behalf of worshipers who stood by passively observing the proceedings. But the picture Moses painted here in Deuteronomy differs radically from this image.[32] This is not to say that Deuteronomy includes the full picture of Israelite worship. The book is silent on "sin/purification" or "guilt/reparation" offerings, as well as the solemn Day of Atonement. Moses was keenly aware of Israel's stubbornly

31. Moses, Aaron, and Israel's elders ate with Jethro "before God" (Exod 18:12). Uriah ate before David (2 Sam 11:13), Adonijah's supporters ate before him (1 Kgs 1:25), and Jehoiachin ate "before" his overlord, the king of Babylon (2 Kgs 25:29//Jer 52:33). In Ezek 44:3, the prince eats "before YHWH." This compares with the banquet Joseph prepared for his brothers, as described in Gen 43:26–34. The brothers sat "before" rather than "with" Joseph (v. 33).

32. On Israelite worship as joyful celebration, see Weinfeld, *Deuteronomy and the Deuteronomic School*, 210–24; Braulik, "The Joy of the Feast," 27–65; Weinfeld, "Commemoration of Passion and Feast of Joy," 67–85; Willis, "Eat and Rejoice Before the Lord," 276–94.

sinful side (9:6–24) and their propensity to ingratitude and pride (8:11–20; 9:4–5). However, when he contemplated worship in the Promised Land in his final addresses to the people, he muted the penitential and somber side of worship. Furthermore, whereas the Sinai revelation had high-lighted the mediatorial roles of the priests and Levites in the tabernacle ritual and the elders in the covenant ratification ritual, in Deuteronomy worship is presented as the spontaneous response of all members of the community who personally entered YHWH's presence. Furthermore, whereas verbs for joy and celebration occur only once in the Sinai legisla-tion (Lev 23:40), in Moses' second address he set the mood of worship in the presence of YHWH with the verb שָׂמַח, "to rejoice," which occurs in various forms seven times in connection with appearing before YHWH.[33]

Moses seems to have seized upon the phrase found in the legisla-tion concerning the Festival of Booths in Lev 23:40, "and you shall rejoice before YHWH your God," and made it normative for the regular worship that would transpire before YHWH at the presentation of tithes (Deut 14:21–27), the Festival of Weeks (16:9–12), the Festival of Booths (16:13–17), the presentation of the first fruits (26:1–11), and the celebration of entrance into the Promised Land (27:1–8). Obviously this rejoicing was to be a celebration of gratitude for YHWH's favor.

Although the privilege of access is extended to all individuals, this worship was not to be individualistic. On the contrary, true worship cel-ebrates the vertical relationship, but it also manifests itself in horizontal charity toward the marginalized and economically vulnerable. The bless-ings from God that the worshiper celebrates are to be shared in generosity to male and female servants, Levites, aliens, orphans, and widows (12:18; 16:11, 14; 26:11).

Concluding Reflections on Worship

Having explored the significance of Deut 12:1–14 for ancient Israelite worship, we may reflect on its implications for a Christian theology of worship. What lessons on worship can we learn from this passage that need to find expression in our worship today?

---

33. Deut 12:7, 12, 18; 14:26; 16:11, 14; 26:11. To this list should be added 27:7, the context of which sets the agenda for the first worship service of the type envisioned in this address in the Promised Land at Mount Ebal. The verb "to rejoice" also occurs in 24:5 and 33:18 in reference to rejoicing in other circumstances.

First, the only legitimate object of worship is YHWH, the creator of heaven and earth, the God of Israel, and Redeemer of humankind, who appeared as the divine incarnate Son, Jesus Christ. All other objects of worship are illegitimate and in fact abominable.

Second, the only persons who may worship God legitimately are the redeemed, those whom God has brought from bondage in the kingdom of darkness and ushered into the realm of his marvelous light. The only acceptable form of worship for unbelievers is prostration before the holy God and pleas for mercy (like the tax collector in Luke 18:33).

Third, true worship involves an audience with the divine King. Accordingly it transpires in God's place by his invitation on his terms. Ultimately it is not up to the worshipers, least of all the unregenerate or carnal, to determine the forms and standards of behavior in his presence. Entrance into the presence of God is an incredible privilege, to be accepted with humility and awe.

Fourth, in true worship the location is less important than the presence of the divine Host. Jesus' words to the Samaritan woman in John 4:21–24 about worshiping "in spirit and in truth" may not have been as radical or revolutionary as we think. True worship has always been driven and animated by the Spirit of God and in accord with the revealed will of God. For Israel this meant focusing on the divine Host rather than the building. As Stephen recognized, Israel's spiritual pilgrimage took a wrong turn when they lost sight of the divine Resident and became preoccupied with his earthly residence (Acts 7:47–50). According to Moses the object of worship has always been more important than the place—which probably explains why he spoke of the latter so vaguely.

Fifth, the redeemed anticipate worship with both delight and sobriety. On the one hand those who worship God in spirit and in truth realize the incredible grace he has lavished on them first in his redemption and second in his invitation to feast in his presence (cf. Ps 95:1–5). On the other hand those who worship God in spirit and in truth are to acknowledge their unworthiness to come before him and to recognize that in worship what he has to say is always more important than what worshipers have to say to him (cf. vv. 6–11). Worship is never to be entered into flippantly, casually, or lightly.

Sixth, true public worship is communal, rather than private. Of course, there is a place for private basking in the presence of God, but when God's people gather for corporate worship they gather to bring collective praise or petition to God. And true worship includes the marginal-ized as well. Those who are genuinely grateful will share their gifts with needy believers and will invite them to walk together into the presence of God. Unfortunately many worship services today have are segregated by race, age, maturity, and musical tastes. But people who are overwhelmed by their own unworthiness on the one hand and the grace of God on the other will be more concerned about worship that pleases him than about pleasing themselves. If God's people should be united about anything, it should be about the joy and privilege of worshiping him—together!

May the Lord renew in his church a passion to worship him in spirit and in truth. May those who have been redeemed answer his invitation to come and celebrate his grace for the glory of God.

6

The Burden of Leadership

The Mosaic Paradigm of Kingship (Deut 17:14–20)[1]

*Responsible godly leadership involves submission and homage
before God, the divine Sovereign,
and humble modeling of covenant righteousness before his people
in accord with his will
and for their good.*

Introduction

THE CHURCH IN AMERICA is experiencing a crisis of leadership, not only with respect to leadership style, but also with respect to definition. The Teal Trust, a British organization that aims to help develop effective Christian leaders, defines leadership as "enabling a group to engage together in the process of developing, sharing and moving into vision, and then living it out."[2] Warren Bennis, author of dozens of books and essays on leadership, defines leadership as "the process by which an agent induces a subordinate to behave in a desired manner."[3] Perhaps Peter Drucker has the simplest approach to leadership when he asserts, "The

---

1. This essay was previously published in *Bibliotheca Sacra* 162 (2005) 259–78.

2. Teal Trust introduction page at http://www.teal.org.uk/about.htm.

3. Bennis, "Leadership Theory and Administrative Behavior," quoted in Bass, ed., *Stogdill's Handbook of Leadership*, 9. L. Smircich and G. Morgan define leadership more subjectively as "the process whereby one or more individuals succeeds in attempting to frame and define the reality of others" ("Leadership: The Management of Meaning," 258).

only definition of a *leader* is someone who has *followers*" (italics his).[4] John C. Maxwell says that "leadership is influence—nothing more, nothing less."[5] He then cites his favorite leadership proverb, "He who thinks he leads, but has no followers, is only taking a walk."[6]

After Moses herded his father-in-law's sheep for about twenty years, this seems to have been the only kind of walk Moses was willing to take. His five responses to God's call to the leadership of his people are classic. "I am nobody" (Exod 3:11). "I have no authority" (3:13). "I have no credibility" (4:1). "I have no talents/gifts" (4:10). "I don't want to go" (4:13). Remarkably in responding to these protestations YHWH refused to answer according to modern definitions of leadership, which often sound slightly narcissistic.[7] Instead in each instance YHWH deflected Moses' focus away from his own inadequacies to God's absolute sufficiencies. In the mission to which Moses was called, the issue was not who Moses is, but who God is. It was not Moses' natural or derived authority, but God's. It was not Moses' credibility, but God's. It was not Moses' giftedness, but God's control over gifts. It was not Moses' own will, but God's.

The most eloquent presentation of servant leadership in the entire Old Testament is found in Moses' instructions in Deut 17:14–20 on the conduct of Israel's future kings. This passage is part of Moses' second address to his people, an address that runs from 4:44 through 26:19, is interrupted momentarily by chapter 27, and then resumes in 28:1–69[Eng 29:1]. More specifically, this text appears in the middle of five literary units concerned with institutions of leadership (16:18—18:22). These units exhibit a chiastic arrangement:

A   Instructions concerning communal judges as guardians of justice and orthodoxy (16:18—17:7)
   B   Instructions concerning the Levitical priests as the Supreme Court (17:8–13)
      C   Instructions concerning the king of Israel (17:14–20)

---

4. Drucker, "Forward: Not Enough Generals Were Killed," xii.

5. Maxwell, *The 21 Irrefutable Laws of Leadership*, 17.

6. Ibid., 20.

7. Bennis writes that "Leadership is a function of knowing yourself, having a vision that is well communicated, building trust among colleagues, and taking effective action to realize your own leadership potential" (http://www.teal.org.uk/about.htm).

B'   Instructions concerning the Levitical priests as cultic officials (18:1–8)

A'   Instructions concerning prophets as guardians of orthodoxy (18:9–22)

The present unit (C) subdivides into two parts, the first (vv. 14–15) being dominated by second person singular verbs and pronouns, and the second (vv. 16–20) by third person singular verbs and pronouns. Accordingly, these sections may be titled, "The Installation of a King over Israel Anticipated" and "The Conduct of the King of Israel Prescribed."

What Circumstances Call for This Paradigm of Leadership?

Moses began his instructions about kingship rather matter-of-factly with a lengthy temporal clause predicting the circumstances under which a monarchy might be contemplated in Israel. The opening clause, beginning with כִּי ("When"), anticipates a future historical situation that is noted by three verbs—when Israel *has entered* the land, when they *have taken possession* of it, and when they *have established their residence* in it. However, with respect to form, vv. 14–15 bear an even more striking resemblance to 12:20, as Table 6 demonstrates below.

Both texts divide into three principal parts, which set the context, announce the key issue, and declare the divine response. In both, the context is introduced temporally with a כִּי clause, anticipating the circumstances of the event. Both texts highlight the key issue by casting it in the form of direct speech, signaled by the verb, "and you say," followed by the declared desire, expressed with a cohortative verb: "I would like to eat meat"; "I would like to install a king over me."

Table 6: Synopsis of Deuteronomy 12:20 and 17:14–15

Text	Deuteronomy 12:20	Deuteronomy 17:14–15
Anticipated Context	When YHWH your God enlarges your territory, as he has promised you,	When you come to the land that YHWH your God is giving you, and you possess it and dwell in it,
Expression of Desire	and you say, "I would like to eat meat," because you crave meat,	and you say, "I would like to install a king over me, like all the nations that are around me,"
Divine Response	you may eat meat whenever you desire.	you may indeed set a king over you whom YHWH your God will choose. One from among your brothers you shall set as king over you. You may not put a foreigner over you, who is not your brother.

The present request catches the reader by surprise. Neither in the previous chapters of Deuteronomy nor in the narratives of Exodus and Numbers has anyone in Israel imagined the nation being constituted as a monarchy with a king other than YHWH their God.[8] Israel was a theocracy. However, this does not mean that the notion is entirely new. Included in God's covenant with the patriarchs was the promise that Abraham's descendants would become a multitude of nations (גּוֹיִם, Gen 17:4–6, 16; 25:23; 35:11; 48:19), which are by definition monarchies (cf. 1 Sam 8:5, 19–20).[9] More specifically, on three occasions God had expressly promised the ancestors, including Jacob, that kings would be among their descendants (Gen 17:6, 16; 35:11). Jacob expressly pronounced the tribe of Judah as the bearer of the royal scepter (49:10). Moses' generation of Israelites would undoubtedly have been familiar with the oracles of the pagan prophet Balaam, who reinforced this notion twice, predicting first that Israel as a kingdom and her king would be exalted (Num 24:7),

8. Explicit references to YHWH's kingship over Israel appear only in poetic texts (Exod 15:18; Num 23:21; Deut 33:5). Exodus 19:6 includes an implicit reference to YHWH's kingship, inasmuch as he refers to Israel as his "kingdom of priests."

9. So also Block, "Nations," 966–72.

and second that a star/royal scepter (שֵׁבֶט) would rise from Jacob/Israel (v. 17). However, since the Israelites had left Egypt, no one in Israel had raised the issue of a human monarchy.

Although the present text offers no clues why the Israelites would request a king, scholars recognize that ancient Near Eastern kings were expected to fulfill several roles.[10] First, as warrior, the king was to lead his nation in battle and protect the society from outside threats. With the imminent departure of Moses and the battles awaiting the Israelites on the other side of the Jordan, one might have expected the request to include a motive clause like the one presented to Samuel centuries later in which they said they wanted a king to fight their battles (1 Sam 8:20).[11] But in Deut 17 the people will request a king *after* they have dispossessed the enemy and have settled in the land.

Second, as chief judge, the king was to guarantee justice within the nation. However, in the immediately preceding paragraphs (Deut 16:18—17:13) Moses has just called for the appointment of judges and other officials to administer justice in the land, and assigned to the Levitical priests a judicial role, thereby taking the gavel of justice out of the hands of any future king.

Third, as patron of the cult, the king was to maintain places of worship and provide materials and personnel needed for the religious rituals. But this notion is foreign to the Book of Deuteronomy,[12] for YHWH himself would choose the place to establish his name and He himself established the form of worship without the involvement of a king.

In 17:16–20 Moses repudiated prevailing models of kingship for Israel, despite the people's request to have a king "like all the nations" around them (v. 14). Grammatically "like all the nations" could refer to the king, in which case the desire was to have "a king like all the nations [have]." However, it is more likely that the phrase refers to the rationale for and the process of installing a king as the nations do, in which case the request reflected a desire to *be* like the nations. This interpretation seems

10. Cf. Whitelam, "Israelite Kingship," 130.

11. Remarkably the people did not make Joshua a king. YHWH's command to Joshua to have the Torah on his lips continuously (Josh 1:7–8), seems to be based on the paradigm of kingship presented in Deut 17.

12. Knoppers, "The Deuteronomist and the Deuteronomic Law of the King," 330; Knoppers, "Rethinking the Relationship between Deuteronomy and the Deuteronomistic History," 404–5.

to be supported by the way the elders of Israel understood the statement when they demanded that Samuel give them a king (1 Sam 8: 5). They betrayed their true colors when they said, "No, but there shall be a king over us, *that we also may be like all the nations*, and that our king may judge us and go out before us and fight our battles" (vv. 19–20; italics added).

The present statement expresses Moses' realism concerning the spiritual future of his people. He had spoken repeatedly of the seductive attractions of the Canaanite religious ideas (4:15–19; 7:3–4; 11:16; 12:29–31; 13:3, 7, 14 [Eng 2, 6, 13]), and even suggested that Israel's spiritual demise was inevitable (5:29). But now he spoke of the seductive attractions of the Canaanite *politeia*, their political system. Despite having taken over the land of the Canaanites, and despite the nations' having recognized the righteous nature of Israel's constitution (cf. 4:8), the people were expected, amazingly, to want to follow the political system of those whom they displaced.

Although one might be suspicious of the motivation behind the request for a king, Moses' response was fundamentally positive: "You may indeed install a king over yourself" (17:15). Unlike the appointment of judges, which Moses prescribed in 16:18–20, this statement represents a granting of permission to act according to the people's desire. That Moses should approve the request demonstrates that the Israelite constitution was not opposed in principle to a monarchical system. But Moses narrowed the qualifications for candidates for kingship (17:15), and then set strict limits on the conduct of those who would be installed as king (vv. 16–20).

What Qualifies a Person for This Kind of Leadership?

Although Moses anticipated the idea for a king originating with the Israelites, he quickly restricted the people's freedom in the selection of the king. He identified two prerequisite qualifications for the future king. First, the king must be chosen by YHWH. The concept of divine election is familiar to readers of Deuteronomy. YHWH had chosen Israel as his people out of all the peoples on earth (4:37; 7:6, 7; 10:15; 14:2), he chose the Levites as priests out of all the tribes (18:5; 21:5), and in the future he will choose a place to establish his name (12:5, 14).[13] Here Moses spoke

13. The fact that YHWH would choose a place to establish for himself occurs an additional twenty times in Deuteronomy (12:11, 18, 21, 23; 14:23, 24, 25; 15:20; 16:2, 6, 7, 11, 15, 16; 17:8, 10; 18:6; 23:16; 26:2; 31:11).

of YHWH choosing (בָּחַר) a king from the people of Israel to govern the nation for him (17:15).

The notion of the gods choosing a person to serve as their royal representative was widespread in the ancient Near East. This is attested as early as the eighteenth century BCE in Mari on the Euphrates River[14] and in Babylon,[15] and as late as eighth century BCE Syria,[16] seventh century BCE Assyria,[17] and sixth century BCE Persia.[18] However, Moses envisioned a chosen ruler governing the chosen people on YHWH's behalf. But he gave no clue about who this person might be.[19]

14. The relevant texts are published in transliteration and translation by Nissinen, *Prophets and Prophecy in the Ancient Near East*. Prophecies from Mari speak of Adad raising up Zimri-Lim in his lap and establishing him on his ancestral throne (ibid., 18; 1:13–19), and Adad declaring, "I have given the whole country to Yah dun-Lim" (ibid., 21; 2:5–7).

15. In the prologue to the Law Code of Hammurabi, the Old Babylonian king characterizes himself as the one named by Anum and Enlil to promote the welfare of the people, to promote the cause of justice in the land, to destroy the wicked and defend the rights of the weak—in general to light up the land. He is the shepherd called by Enlil to ensure prosperity for the land (*ANET*, 164).

16. In the stela of Zakir, usurper of the thrones of Hamath and Luash, Zakir introduced himself as the one whom Ba'alshamayn made king over Hazrak (ibid., 655; and Nissinen, *Prophets and Prophecy*, 205).

17. Especially intriguing is the introduction of Esarhaddon in a text describing his rise to power: "Esarhaddon, the great king, legitimate king, king of the world, king of Assyria, regent of Babylonia, king of Sumer and Akkad, king of the four rims [of the earth], true shepherd, favorite of the great gods, whom Assur, Shamash, Bel, and Nebo, the Ištar of Nineveh, [and] the Ištar of Arbela, has chosen me—in due form and in the presence [lit., assembly] of all my brothers—saying: This is the son to (be elevated) to the position of a successor of mine" (*ANET* 289; see also Nissinen, *Prophets and Prophecy*, 137).

Elsewhere Neo-Assyrian prophecies speak of the divinely chosen kings, Esarhaddon and Ashurbanipal, as persons whom the gods called by name to kingship (ibid., 172), with whom the gods have established a covenant (ibid., 120), the "son" or "creation" of the gods, and "beloved of the gods." On these epithets and the relationship of Neo-Assyrian kings to the gods, see Parpola, "The King as God's Son and Chosen One," xxxvi–xliv.

18. According to the Cyrus Cylinder Inscription, "He [Marduk] surveyed and looked throughout all the lands, searching for a righteous king whom he would support. He called out his name: Cyrus, king of Anshan; he pronounced his name to be king over all (the world)." (*COS* 2:315).

19. According to 1 Sam 13:14, God had David in mind from the beginning, for he alone was the "the man after his own heart." While this statement says little if anything about any special quality of David, it does more than merely emphasize YHWH's free selection of the occupant of the throne (McCarter, *I Samuel*, 229). The verse points to David as the one whom YHWH had in mind when he promised Abraham that his seed

In verse 15b Moses added a second qualification for an Israelite king: he must be a fellow Israelite. He made this point emphatically, first, by declaring that the candidate must be one "from the midst of your brothers," and second, by stating that an outsider (אִישׁ נָכְרִי), one "who is not your brother,"[20] was not to be installed. Throughout the history of Israel this proscription appears to have been strictly observed, with Athaliah, the daughter of Ahab and Jezebel, representing the nearest the Israelites came to violating this requirement (2 Kgs 11). According to Moses the people were to be ruled by a viceroy of YHWH chosen from their own ranks, not brought in as an expert from outside.

How Does a True Leader Exercise Leadership?

Having expressed his fundamental support of the appointment of a king in Israel's future, Moses turned his attention to the manner in which the responsibilities of kingship are to be exercised (Deut 17:16–20). His instructions present a significant contrast between the royal office and the other administrative offices. Whereas Moses had commanded the Israelites to institute the office of judge (16:18–20; 17:9), described the office of priest as already instituted by YHWH (17:9; 18:1–8), and predicted the future institution of the prophetic by YHWH (18:9–22), he presented the office of king as optional, subject to the desire of the people. However, Moses' severe circumscription of the Israelite king's powers was more revolutionary than the optional nature of the office of king. He described the duties of the future king in two parts, first with a triad of proscriptions intended to prevent common abuses of the office (vv. 16–17) that could arise out of ambition and greed, and second with an extraordinary spiritual and ethical prescription for the king (vv. 18–20).

---

would possess the gate of his enemies (Gen 22:17; the verb "possess" is singular), and when he inspired Jacob to declare that the one who would wield the royal scepter would be from the tribe of Judah (Gen 49:10). The narrator of 1 Samuel never viewed Saul as a legitimate holder of this office. See also Block, "My Servant David," 38–40.

20. The word נָכְרִי occurs in Deut 14:21 and 15:3, and appears again in 23:21 and 29:22 [Heb 21], where he is defined as "one who comes from a distant land." On the status of the נָכְרִי, see Block, "Sojourner; Alien; Stranger," 562. Assuming Moses delivered the speeches in Deuteronomy in the second millennium, a recent illustration of foreign control over a nation would have been provided by the fifteenth and sixteenth dynasties of Egypt, lines of Asiatics, who controlled Egypt from their capital in Avaris for more than a century from 1650–1530 BCE, and whose name meant "ruler(s) of foreign land(s)." See Redford, "Hyksos," 341–44.

The Danger: Ambition (vv. 16–17)

Moses signaled his transition to a new phase of his instructions about kingship in Israel with the restrictive particle רַק, "only, except, by no means." The emphatic particle does quadruple duty, applying to all four of the following negative commands. Although the proscriptions consist of four main statements, they may be considered as three prohibitions. Each of these has significant symbolic significance: multiplying for himself horses, women, and precious metals.

The lust for power: The prohibition regarding horses. Moses' first proscription on royal behavior prohibited the king from multiplying horses for himself. Horses were first domesticated in the Eurasian steppes and introduced to the Near East in the third millennium BCE. Unlike cattle and donkeys, which were widely used in the ancient Near East for agricultural purposes or to transport goods, horses were used primarily for pulling chariots.[21] Fleets of chariots gave a great military advantage over foot soldiers when battles were conducted in relatively flat terrain (Deut 20:1; Josh 17:16–18; Judg 1:19). Hittite and Ugaritic sources indicate that horses were used for military purposes north of Israel.[22] However, with a single exception, in the Pentateuch horses are mentioned only in connection with the Egyptians (Gen 47:17; Exod 9:3; 14:9, 23; 15:19; Deut 11:4; 17:16). Anticipating the temptation that surfaced later, not only for kings but also for the people, to look to horses and chariots as guarantors of security (Ps 20:7; Isa 30:16), Moses declared, "When you go out to battle against your enemies, and see horses and chariots and people more numerous than you, do not be afraid of them; for YHWH your God, who brought you up from the land of Egypt, is with you" (Deut 20:1).[23]

To the basic prohibition on the multiplication of horses, Moses added that the king must never send the people to Egypt to procure horses from there (v. 16b). Although the Egyptians were renowned for their use of horses and chariots in their military forces, they were generally im-

---

21. For illustrations, see *The Illustrated Bible Dictionary*, 1:260–61. For a brief discussion of the domestication and use of horses in the ancient Near East, see Firmage, "Zoology (Animal Profiles)," 1136–37. On chariots and chariotry, see Littauer and Crouwel, "Chariots," 888–92.

22. In a thirteenth century BCE text, the Ugaritic legend of Kirta, King Pabil seeks to persuade Kirtu to withdraw his siege of Pabil's city by offering him silver and gold, slaves, horses, and chariots (*Ugaritic Narrative Poetry*, 17).

23. For a dramatic fulfillment of this promise, see Judg 4:1–16.

porters rather than exporter of horses. Egypt is probably mentioned here as a potential source of horses because of Israel's memory of their involvement at the time of the Exodus, or because Moses realistically anticipated that Egypt would continue to be a force in Palestinian affairs in the future. This anticipation was fulfilled both in the days of the united monarchy (1 Kgs 11:40; 14:25), and on into the end of the eighth[24] and seventh centuries (2 Kgs 23:28–30).

But why did Moses warn against sending the people back to Egypt to get horses? The prohibition seems to be based on the fear that the king, as leader of the people, would reverse the exodus and lead them back into bondage, thereby undoing the great salvific acts that YHWH had accomplished on their behalf through Moses.[25] Whatever the reason, Moses strengthened his statement by appealing to an earlier utterance by YHWH that the Israelites were never to return to Egypt.[26]

The lust for status: The prohibition regarding women. The second command prohibited the king from multiplying women in his court (Deut 17:17). The word נָשִׁים, usually translated "wives," is better rendered more generically as "women," the reference being to the harem of a typical oriental king. Although the Old Testament provides numerous examples of men having more than one wife at a time,[27] this statement represents the closest the Old Testament comes to prohibiting more than one wife—though in this instance the focus is on the king.

In the ancient Near East, kings would amass large harems for several reasons. First, and most obviously, a harem provided the king with unlimited opportunity to satisfy his sexual cravings with the most beautiful women in the kingdom. Second, since marriages were often arranged

24. In Isaiah's pronouncement of woe on Israel, he associated going down to Egypt for help with reliance on horses, chariots, and horsemen (Isa 31:1).

25. This could account for later prophetic references to kings and kings as symbols of slavery. See especially Samuel's speech in 1 Sam 8:10–18 in response to the elders demand for a king.

26. The Scriptures record no such divine utterance before this. Perhaps the present statement, usually translated as a command, should also be interpreted as a promise: "For YHWH has said, 'You will never return that way again'" (so also Tigay, *Deuteronomy*, 167). If it is interpreted as a warning, the present statement declares that Israel may not on their own choose to go back to Egypt, for this would in effect annul their status as a people redeemed from slavery and in covenant relationship with YHWH.

27. Examples include Abraham (Gen 16; 25:1–2), Jacob (Gen 29:15–30), Esau (Gen 26:34; 36:2), Elkanah (1 Sam 1:2), David (1 Sam 18:17–30; 25:38–43; 2 Sam 3:2–5), and Solomon (1 Kgs 11:3).

to strengthen alliances with other states,[28] the institution of the harem enabled a king to be allied simultaneously with many outside rulers (see e.g., 1 Kgs 11:1). Third, just as the male members of a royal court served as "decoration" to reflect the glory and majesty of a king,[29] so the larger the harem and the more beautiful its members, the more impressed foreign visitors would be when they visited the king. In short, one of the functions of the harem was to enhance the status of the king among his international peers.

Remarkably Deut 17:17 says nothing about any of these considerations. Instead the motivation for the prohibition is simply though somewhat ambiguously stated, "So his heart may not be turned away." Since the prohibition does not explicitly prohibit marriage to foreign wives, who could lead the king into idolatry (cf. 7:3–4), the concern should probably not be restricted to the overt practice of idolatry. As in 6:5, the word לֵב, commonly rendered "heart," could also refer to the mind as the seat of thought and intellect. Like wine and strong drink, the lust for pleasure and status could lead to intoxication that would turn the king's heart away from God and his mind away from the rational exercise of his office (Prov 31:3–9). In light of what follows and in the context of the overall thrust of Deuteronomy, Moses' concern here may be defection from the Torah that he has been promulgating generally, which would of course also involve the Great Commandment to love YHWH their God exclusively.

The lust for wealth: The prohibition regarding silver and gold. Moses' third prohibition pertained to the king's excessive accumulation of silver and gold. Although Moses mentioned only these two metals, "silver and gold" probably stands for wealth and opulence in general. Moses did not speak about what might motivate a king to accumulate wealth, nor did he specify the actions a king might take to do so. However, in the broader context of ancient Near Eastern monarchies and in the light of the concern for the Israelite king not to consider himself superior to his countrymen (v. 20), he probably had in mind primarily the accumulation of private wealth by imposing heavy taxes on the citizenry.

28. See 1 Kgs 9:15–16 (Solomon and Pharaoh's daughter) and 16:31 (Ahab's marriage to Jezebel, a princess of Tyre, though she appears to have been his primary wife).

29. Daniel 1:3–4 focuses on the qualifications of candidates for the court of Nebuchadnezzar: youths without defect, handsome, intelligent in every branch of learning, discreet, wise, and knowledgable in the protocol of the court.

These three restrictions on common royal behavior address the three temptations that many have recognized as common to people in positions of leadership: an increasingly insatiable lust for power, a lust for status, and a lust for wealth.[30] It should be noted that Moses does not hereby prohibit the purchase of horses, or marriage, or the accumulation of some silver and gold within the country. What was banned was the king's accumulation of all of these by exploiting his leadership position for personal gain. Moses highlighted this concern through his threefold repetition of the prepositional expression לוֹ, "for himself." Persons are placed in positions of leadership for the sake of those they are called to lead, not for their own sakes.

The Demand: Submission (vv. 18–20)

The revolutionary nature of Moses' monarchic ideals becomes even more striking in the last verses of this paragraph. He expressed his ideals with three commands, all relating to the Torah: the king shall copy the Torah, the king shall have the Torah with him, and the king shall read the Torah. Given the way הַתּוֹרָה הַזֹּאת, "this Torah," and related expressions are used in the book,[31] it seems best to understand "this Torah" minimally as Moses' second address (5:1b—26:19 and 28:1–68), and maximally as the entire collection of Moses' speeches preserved in Deuteronomy and delivered as a series of farewell addresses to his people (1:6—4:40; 4:1b—

---

30. The titles of the following publications illustrate present-day infatuation with these tendencies: Stewart, *Money, Power and Sex*; Hartsock, *Money, Sex and Power: Toward a Feminist Historical Materialism*; Turner, *Sex, Money and Power: An Essay on Christian Ethics*; Foster, *The Challenge of the Disciplined Life: Christian Reflections on Money, Sex & Power*; Jackley, *Below the Beltway: Money, Sex, Power, and Other Fundamentals of Democracy in the Nation's Capital*; Sanders, *Power, Money & Sex: How Success Almost Ruined My Life*; Rosenfeld, *The Club Rules: Power, Money, Sex, and Fear: How It Works in Hollywood*; Rubin, *Power, Money, Fame, Sex: A User's Guide*.

31. The expression הַתּוֹרָה הַזֹּאת, "this Torah," occurs in 1:5; 4:8; 17:18–19; 27:3; 27:8; 27:26; 28:58; 28:61; 29:28[Eng 29]; 31:9; 31:11–12; 31:24; 32:46; סֵפֶר הַתּוֹרָה הַזֶּה, "this written document of the Torah," in 29:20[Eng 21]; 30:10; and 31:26; סֵפֶר הַזֶּה, "this written document," in 28:58; 29:19[Eng 20], 26[Eng 27].

26:19 and 28:1–68; 29:1—30:20), as well as the nation's "national anthem" (32:1–43)[32] and Moses' final benediction of the tribes (33:2–29).[33]

Moses began his positive instructions regarding the future king's conduct by referring to the time when he would sit on his throne over his kingdom (v. 18a), that is, in the course of his governing as king.[34] However, the timing of the first of these instructions should probably be distinguished from the second and third. The king would in all likelihood have made only one personal copy of the Torah, and he would have done so as soon as he assumed the kingship, perhaps even as part of his accession ritual. However, the command to have it with him bears a durative sense, and the final charge explicitly calls upon him to read it all the days of his life. These charges underlie YHWH's later injunction to Joshua to meditate on the Torah day and night (Josh 1:8) and the psalmist's congratulation of the person who does so (Ps 1:2).

The command to copy the Torah. Moses declared that the first duty of a king who accedes to the throne of Israel would be to produce a copy of the Torah that he (Moses) is currently promulgating for himself. This command is remarkable on five counts. First, it suggests that Moses recognized the canonical status of his teaching from the outset, necessitating its immediate transcription to writing and assuming its normativeness in perpetuity (cf. Deut 31:9).

Second, the first charge perceives the king not as one who writes the laws, but as one who receives them from a higher authority and is subject to them. Though Israel will have a human king, they will remain a theocracy, in which YHWH, the divine King, would rule everyone and reserve the authority to make laws. The addition of the prepositional expression לֹו, "for himself," presents an intentional contrast to the preceding words. Whereas Moses had earlier explicitly forbidden the king from amassing horses, women, and wealth "for himself," that is, for personal advantage,

32. This poem is generally referred to as the "Song of Moses." However, based on the description of the circumstances of the song in 31:19–22, it seems preferable to refer to this as the "Song of YHWH," inasmuch as he apparently dictated the words to Moses. In any case the narrative framework of the song suggests that it was to be memorized and sung in perpetuity, thereby serving as the national anthem.

33. For further discussion of these issues, see my essay, "Recovering the Voice of Moses," in Block, *The Gospel according to Moses,* chapter 1.

34. Though this could also be understood more narrowly as the time of his accession, that is, "when he takes his seat on the throne." Thus Mayes, *Deuteronomy,* 273; Tigay, *Deuteronomy,* 168.

now Moses declared emphatically that there is something the king must do "for himself," namely, write his own copy of the Torah.

Third, the charge assumes royal literacy from the outset of the monarchy. Many scholars continue to be skeptical about this level of literacy in ancient Israel. However, the invention of the twenty-two letter alphabet in the first half of the second millennium BCE certainly made the ability to read and write more accessible to much greater numbers of people than did Egyptian hieroglyphs and Akkadian cuneiform.[35] Furthermore there is no objective reason to doubt that compositions as extensive and complex as the individual speeches of Moses preserved in Deuteronomy could have been produced in the second half of the second millennium BCE.[36]

Fourth, the charge identifies the document to be copied as מִשְׁנֵה הַתּוֹרָה הַזֹּאת, "a copy of this Torah" (17:18). The translators of the Septuagint sent the history of interpretation of Deuteronomy in a wrong direction in the third century BCE when they rendered the phrase with τὸ δευτερονόμιον τοῦτο, "this second law." This unfortunate rendering is immortalized in the title of the book not only in the Greek version but in all English translations as well, obscuring not only the real meaning of phrase in this context but also the book's own title, אֵלֶּה הַדְּבָרִים, "These are the Words." The title "Deuteronomy" also clouds the fact that the overriding tone of the book is homiletical, expository, and rhetorical, rather than legal.

Fifth, Moses instructed the king to copy the Torah on a סֵפֶר[37] in the presence of the Levitical priests. Here Moses provides the first hint of the priests' role as custodians of the Torah that he was proclaiming and would shortly transcribe. Having committed his address to writing, Moses would

35. So also Sawyer, *Sacred Languages and Sacred Texts*, 49–51.

36. See the helpful study by Millard, "Books in the Late Bronze Age in the Levant," 171–81.

37. Although the word סֵפֶר is generally translated as "book," this rendering is misleading. Books with individual sheets of parchment or papyrus written on both sides so they could be read sequentially and bound together on one edge pages, were not produced until the Roman period (Lemaire, "Writing and Writing Materials," 1004). While סֵפֶר may refer to any written document, in this instance one should think of a specially tanned leather scroll of sheep or goat skin, which is known to have been used as writing material in Egypt from the early third millennium BCE (ibid., 1003). See also Millard, *Reading and Writing in the Time of Jesus*, 25–26; and Haran, "Book-Scrolls in Israel in Pre-Exilic Times," 166–67.

hand it over to the priests who carried the ark of the covenant and to the elders of Israel, charging them to read it before the people every seven years at the Festival of Booths (31:9–13). Responsibility for guarding the Torah fell to the priests by virtue of their role as custodians of YHWH's covenant.[38] At the accession of every king the priests were to retrieve the document, hand it to the king, and watch him as he copied it.

According to Philo, the demand for the king to copy the Torah was motivated by a concern for memorability—in the act of writing, the words of the text are impressed upon the mind more indelibly than if the text is only read.[39] However, this was much more than a mnemonic procedure; it was a sacral act in several respects. (1) It involved copying a sacred document that claims to have been uttered orally by Moses at the command of YHWH.[40] (2) It involved copying a document that was stored next to the most sacred object in Israel's possession—the ark of the covenant. (3) It involved copying a document in a sacred setting, presumably at the central sanctuary in the presence of the Levitical priests, who served both as custodians of the document and as witnesses and guarantors on YHWH's behalf. In the latter role they would ensure that the king would copy the entire document, without addition or omission,[41] and that he would be true to the Torah that he was copying. Copying the Torah is perceived here as a covenantal act, whereby the king bound himself to all its promises and demands. He thereby also declared nonverbally both his spiritual subordination to the priests and his subordination to the Torah as a symbol of the covenant that bound YHWH and Israel.

The command to wear the Torah. The second directive for the king with respect to the Torah consists of only two small words, וְהָיְתָה עִמּוֹ ("and it shall be with him"), but its significance is profound. In the ancient world of suzerain-vassal relationships, the vassal would receive a written copy of the covenant, which he then deposited in the temple of his chief

38. Deuteronomy 31:24–26 indicates that the song YHWH dictated to Moses was added to the Torah and the entire composition was then placed beside the ark of the covenant, symbolic of its immediate status as canonical and authoritative text.

39. Philo, *De Specialibus Legibus* 4.160; also cited by Tigay, *Deuteronomy*, 168.

40. The narrator and Moses both declared that he spoke to the people according to all that YHWH had commanded him (Deut 1:5; 4:5, 14; 6:1; 26:13–14).

41. The production of duplicate written copies of significant documents was widespread in ancient Mesopotamia. On completing the task, scribes would conventionally add a colophon declaring their fidelity to the original that commonly read, "according to its original, written, checked, and copied" (Leichty, "The Colophon," 150).

deity, who provided oversight of the document.[42] At stated intervals the document would be retrieved and read aloud before the subordinate at covenant renewal ceremonies.[43] However, the king of Israel was not to treat the Torah, which represented Moses' authoritative interpretation of YHWH's covenant with Israel, as a museum piece or an object to be retrieved only periodically and have read before him. Although it must never be treated as a good luck charm or an amulet,[44] the copy of the Torah was to accompany him wherever he went, as a constant written reminder of his personal vassal status and as a guide for his conduct.[45]

The command to read the Torah. The last charge to the king is the most complex, taking up the rest of verse 19 and all of verse 20. Moses began with a simple directive, "He shall read it all the days of his life," but this is followed by a series of four purpose clauses, which highlight the significance of this extraordinary royal duty. Whereas the first three identify specific responses that are dependent on the reading, the last announces the long-range reward for the king and his successors. Even so, all four statements echo earlier injunctions to the people.

First, faithful reading of the Torah is the key to a proper disposition toward YHWH, the divine Suzerain—fear, demonstrated in scrupulous obedience.[46] Second, faithful reading of the Torah is the key to a proper

42. See for example, the Hittite treaty between Suppiluliuma I of Hatti and Shattiwaza of Mittanni, which makes the following provision: "A duplicate of this tablet is deposited before the Sun-goddess of Arinna, since the Sun-goddess of Arinna governs kingship and queenship" (Beckman, *Hittite Diplomatic Texts*, 42 [6A§13]).

43. See for example, the Hittite treaty between Muwattalli of Hatti and Alaksandu of Wilusa: "This tablet which I have made for you, Alaksandu, shall be read out before you three times yearly, and you, Alaksandu shall know it. These words are by no means reciprocal. They issue from Hatti. Now you, Alaksandu must not do evil against My Majesty. Hatti must not prepare [evil] against you. I, Labarna, Great King, Beloved of the Storm-god of Lightning, have now summoned [the Thousand Gods] in this [matter] and have invoked them as witnesses. They shall listen" (ibid., 86 [13§16]). Moses later ordered that the Torah he proclaimed and transcribed be read before all the people every seven years at the Festival of Booths (31:9).

44. See Jeremiah's invective against his own people for treating the Torah this way (Jer 8:8).

45. This apparent linkage of the Torah with amulets is picked up in Proverbs and applied to parental commands and instructions (Prov 1:8–9; 3:3; 3:21–22; 6:20–21).

46. Like YHWH's own command in 4:10, the statement assumes that the fear of YHWH is not natural, and that it must be learned. From Moses' earlier statements it is clear that this fear is learned (A) by observing YHWH's victories over the enemies (2:25), (B) by hearing the voice of YHWH from the midst of the fire (4:10), (C) by observing the punishment imposed on those who violate the covenant (17:13; 19:20; 21:21). For the

disposition toward fellow members of the covenant community—humility toward one's own countrymen.[47] The Israelite king may have been chosen by YHWH and installed by the people as king over them,[48] but he must resist all temptation to consider himself in any way their superior. Third, faithful reading of the Torah is the key to staying on course in one's devotion to YHWH. Not turning "to the right or the left" is equivalent to walking in all the ways of YHWH.[49] Fourth, faithful reading of the Torah is the key to a secure future, described in terms of lengthened days over his kingdom in the midst of Israel for himself and his sons.[50]

By incorporating echoes of earlier texts that applied to the people of Israel, Moses reinforced the revolutionary nature of his paradigm for Israelite kingship. (1) Whereas the kings of other nations often gained power by sheer force and at the expense of their rivals and their subjects, the kingship was to be established in response to a democratic impulse and the favorable response of YHWH. (2) Whereas foreigners, illegiti-

---

first time Moses mentions hearing the Torah as the means by which the fear of YHWH would be instilled in the hearts of his people. When they heard the Torah that Moses has promulgated they would not fear the human whose voice they have heard and whose hands have penned the words, but the One in whose name and by whose authority he acted. Moses hereby cautioned his hearers not to become addicted to visual theophanies and extraordinary manifestations of divine power as the basis for a proper disposition toward YHWH. Rather, in the written record of Moses' interpretation of YHWH's past revelation, they would have constant reminders of the God who has fulfilled his promises to the ancestors by delivering his people from bondage, calling them to covenant relationship with himself, revealing to them his will, and delivering the land of the Canaanites into their hands (cf. 6:20–25).

47. In the idiom "that his heart may not be lifted up" echoes 8:13–14, where Moses had linked his warning to the people not to let their hearts be lifted up with an appeal not to forget YHWH. As in the earlier context, here the warning follows a triple reference to the multiplication of possessions.

48. The preposition עַל, "over [me/you]," is used four times in verses 14–15, three of which are found in Moses' speech.

49. See Deut 8:6; 10:12; 11:22; 19:9; 26:17; 28:9; 30:16; 32:4. The words "that he may not turn aside from the commandment to the right or to the left" (17:20) echo 5:31–32, where Moses had charged his people to observe the will of YHWH by acting in accord with that will, not turning aside to the right or to the left.

50. As noted earlier, the last clause is the only one of the four that promises a reward. But once again this clause echoes earlier statements, which appear in two versions. In some contexts, Moses spoke of the Israelites themselves lengthening their days on the land. The concept of lengthening days on the land occurs in 4:26, 40; 5:33; 11:9; 22:7; 30:18; 32:47. In others, Moses spoke of the days themselves lengthening. Variations of "your days may be prolonged" occur in 5:16; 6:2; 25:15.

mate usurpers from the outside or imperial overlords, often governed other states, the Israelites were to be governed by one of their own under the imperial reign of YHWH. (3) Whereas the kings of other nations regularly used their positions to satisfy their own lust for power, status, and wealth, the Israelite kings were forbidden from using their office to amass power and wealth for themselves. (4) Whereas other kings were perceived primarily as administrators of justice, a function they fulfilled by demanding absolute loyalty, the role of Israelite kings was to embody the divinely revealed standard of covenantal justice. (5) Whereas other kings codified laws to protect their own interests and to regulate the conduct of their subjects, rather than themselves,[51] YHWH himself codified the Israelite laws. He then had his spokesman, Moses, who had no vested interest in the kingship, interpret them, and then imposed them upon the king himself.[52] Written copies of treaties for vassal kings are well known, and numerous ancient law codes governing the conduct of the people have been discovered in the soil of the Near East. However, for Israel's king the response of the people is of secondary importance, if not irrelevant. He had no authority to teach or interpret the Torah, let alone amend it; he may only demonstrate its intent by modeling it.[53] (6) Whereas the kings of other ancient Near Eastern nations were elevated above their country-

---

51. This is obvious from the prologue to the Law Code of Hammurabi (Roth, *Law Collections from Mesopotamia and Asia Minor,* 76–81). This is not to say that other nations did not have codified ideals for their kings. Although the document known as *Advice to a Prince* found in the library of Ashurbanipal derives from an omen text, it reflects a Mesopotamian effort to remind kings of their responsibility to seek the welfare of their subjects. For the text, see Lambert, *Babylonian Wisdom Literature,* 113–15.

A similar awareness is reflected in the second millennium BCE Ugaritic *Kirta* epic in which King Kirta is said to be suffering because he has not pursued the widow's case nor taken up the claim of the wretched. For the text, see Parker, *Ugaritic Narrative Poetry,* 41. See also Job 29:7–17 and Prov 31:1–9, both of which present non-Israelite rulers as responsible for the well-being of their subjects. But none of these comes close to Deut 17:19–20 either in genre or in their intention to rein in the king's power.

52. Extra-biblical analogues to Moses' prescription for the king are difficult to find. According to an ancient Mesopotamian text, apparently at his enthronement, Enmeduranki, the antedeluvian king of Sippar in Babylonia, received "the tablet of the gods, the bag with the mystery of heaven and earth." This seems to have been some sort of pouch attached to god or king's chest (Widengren, *The Ascension of the Apostle and the Heavenly Book,* 11–12). For the text, see Craig, *Assyrian and Babylonian Religious Texts,* 1:64.

53. Knoppers, "Deuteronomy and the Deuteronomistic History," 402–4.

men with epithets like "son of God"[54] and "image of Baal/Shamash,"[55] in Deuteronomy the former title is reserved for the nation of Israel (14:1; 32:6, 18; cf. 1:31), and the latter is absent all together. The only epithet the king of Israel may claim is "brother" of his people.

The role of the king as model citizen of Israel and vassal of YHWH is highlighted not only by the echoes of earlier statements applied to Israel in this pericope, but also by the way in which exposure to the word of God is presented as a prerequisite to life and well-being. Although no single text contains all the elements, the complete chain of events follows this order:

Reading ⇨ Hearing ⇨ Learning ⇨ Fearing ⇨ Obeying ⇨ Living.

Fear is explicitly linked to obedience in several passages, as seen in this table:

Table 7: The Links between Exposure to the Word of God and Well-Being

Reference	Reading	Hearing	Learning	Fearing	Obeying	Living/ Well-being
4:10		✓	✓	✓		
5:23–29		✓		✓	✓	✓
6:1–3			✓	✓	✓	✓
17:13		✓		✓	✓	
17:19–20	✓	(✓)	✓	✓	✓	✓
19:20		✓		✓	✓	
31:11–13	✓	✓	✓	✓	✓	

Of all these texts, Deut 17:19–20 provides the most complete list, lacking only an explicit reference to hearing. However, since reading

54. In later texts, however, Davidic kings were referred to as "sons of God" (2 Sam 7:14; Ps 2:6; 22:10; 28:6; 89:27–28). For a summary discussion of the "divine sonship" of kings in ancient Mesopotamia, Syria, and Egypt, see Fossum, "Son of God," 788–89.

55. Esarhaddon was characterized in this way by his exorcist, Adad-Šumu-uṣur: "The father of the king, my lord, was the very image of Bel, and the king, my lord, is likewise the image of Bel" (Parpola, *Letters from Assyria and Babylonian Scholars*, 181).

involved "crying out" and the king is to "read" the Torah to himself, it could be argued that hearing is present implicitly. In drawing the link between reading and prolonged tenure on the throne (the equivalent to the people's long life in the land), Moses hereby presents the king as an exemplary Israelite and the embodiment of covenant fidelity. His countrymen should recognize that if they imitate him their own well-being in the land will be secured. At the same time, the consequences of not fearing and obeying YHWH are clearly spelled out in the covenant curses, specifically 28:58: "If you are not careful to do all the words of this Torah that are written in this book, out of fear for this glorious and awesome name, YHWH your God," then YHWH would impose all kinds of horrendous consequences upon Israel.

Concluding Reflections

Although we have spent most of our time trying to establish the BCE meaning of Deuteronomy 17:14–20, its significance extends far beyond the original cultural context to the life and administration of the church today. Specifically, this text offers the contemporary church some important guidelines for developing a theology of ministry—guidelines that run against the grain of the definitions of leadership offered at the beginning of this article.

First, the paradigm presented here suggests that the forms of leadership in the church need not necessarily follow a prescribed order. YHWH here accedes to the people's desire to have a king, which would inevitably challenge traditional tribal structures. Kingship was not hereby prescribed; it was *permitted*.

Second, those who lead the people of God must be chosen by God. The way in which the king would be called remained open. Presumably, since it was the people who initiated the request for a king, the identity of the person called will be revealed to the people (perhaps even before it was known by the person himself). In Israel's own history this election ultimately led to David, "whom YHWH had in mind from the beginning" (1 Sam 13:14). Just as the early church was led by persons recognized to have been called by God,[56] so churches today must be led by persons whom all recognize are called by God.

---

56. In Rom 1:1 Paul referred to himself as "a servant of Christ Jesus, called to be an apostle, set apart for the gospel of God."

Third, leaders are installed in office to serve the well-being of those they lead and are not to exploit their positions for personal advantage or selfish gain. The lust for power (horses), the lust for status and self-gratification (women), and the lust for wealth (silver and gold), remain paramount temptations in every age. In the Bible responsible headship is never about power or privilege; it is always about securing the well-being of those under one's charge.

Fourth, functionally and for the sake of the ministry, leaders may be perceived as *primi inter pares/frates*, "the first among peers/brothers," but they must acknowledge their subordination to God. The king envisioned by Moses was to write a copy of the Torah *for himself* in the presence of the priests, who, as representatives of God, would hold him accountable for his personal conduct. Significantly not a word is said about administrative gifts or persuasive talent. [57]

Fifth, while a few leaders in Israel's history modeled the ideals of the Torah presented here (Joshua, Josh 1:8–9 [though not a king]; Hezekiah, 2 Kgs 18:3–7; and Josiah, 2 Kgs 22:18–19), ultimately the role would be fulfilled perfectly only by Jesus the Messiah, the son of David, who came, not to bring an end to the Torah, but to fulfill it (Matt 5:17). He serves as the perfect embodiment of the ideals of covenant relationship as represented in the Torah.

Sixth, before leaders can presume the right to teach the people the Torah or to create visions of growth and destiny for them, they must embody personally the ideals of covenant relationship to which the people have bound themselves. This may call for a modification of Maxwell's favorite leadership proverb: "He who thinks he leads, but has no followers, is only taking a walk." Leaders in the church had better be taking a walk—walking according to what they read in the Torah *for themselves* so they may learn to fear YHWH and obey his will. Then their tenure will receive the blessing of God and they will model for people the direct link between knowing the Torah and fearing and obeying YHWH (cf. 31:9–13). Paul had obviously grasped the significance of Moses' words

---

57. This understanding of leadership contrasts sharply with that of Carnes Lord of the Naval War Academy, who asserts (in *The Modern Prince: What Leaders Need to Know Now*) that leadership presupposes some element of "such traditionally manly qualities as competitiveness, aggression, or, for that matter, the ability to command . . . Leadership that is not prepared to disadvantage anyone is hardly leadership at all." As cited by George Will in an editorial column, "Ending the 'Feminization' of Politics," A7.

when he counseled Timothy on how to approach his own ministry. He may have had this very text in mind when he wrote: "Until I come, devote yourself to the public reading of Scripture, to exhortation, to teaching. Do not neglect the gift you have, which was given you by prophecy when the council of elders laid their hands on you. Practice these things, devote yourself to them, so that all may see your progress. Keep a close watch on yourself and on the teaching. Persist in this, for by so doing you will save both yourself and your hearers" (1 Tim 4:13–16).

Long before church leaders perform the tasks involved in their role they must accept their primary responsibility, namely, standing before God and his people as models of godliness, fidelity, and virtue, leading with their own lives before they lead with their ideas and gifts. May the Lord inspire and equip a new generation of church leaders in our day to lead according to the paradigm Moses established in Deut 17:14–20 and in so doing to shepherd the flock "according to God" (1 Pet 5:2).

7

The Privilege of Calling
The Mosaic Paradigm for Missions (Deut 26:16–19)[1]

Introduction

FOR ALMOST TWO DECADES George W. Peters, one of the great missiological statesmen of the previous century, held high the torch of missions not only on the campus of Dallas Seminary but also around the world.[2] In his teaching he emphasized the contrasts between the missiological strategies in the Old and New Testaments. Although one may recognize a universal agenda in both Testaments, the differences in the strategies may be summed up in the phrases, "centripetal universality" and "centrifugal universality" (See fig. 7 below).

Peters wrote, "Centrifugal universality is in effect when a messenger of the gospel crosses frontiers and carries the good news to the people of no faith. Centripetal universality, often mistaken for particularism, operates like a magnetic force, drawing distant peoples to a central place, people, or person. The latter is the methodology of the Old Testament, with Israel and the temple as the center designed to draw people to themselves and to YHWH."[3]

---

1. This essay was previously published in *Bibliotheca Sacra* 162 (2005) 387–405.
2. George W. Peters was the uncle of the author's wife.
3. Peters, *Biblical Theology of Missions*, 52.

Figure 7: Centripetal and Centrifugal Paradigms for Missions

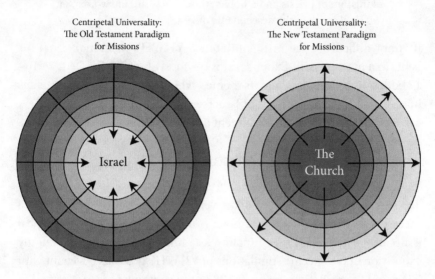

Centripetal Universality:
The Old Testament Paradigm
for Missions

Centripetal Universality:
The New Testament Paradigm
for Missions

Israel

The
Church

The centripetal feature of God's missiological strategy in the Old Testament is seen in YHWH's rescuing Israel from slavery and drawing Israel into a covenant relationship with himself as a glorious trophy of grace so that the world might know that he alone is God and that he alone can meet their deepest needs if they, like Caleb, or Rahab, or Ruth, cast themselves on Him.

Although Deut 26:16–19 is not cited by Peters in his book on missions, this remarkable passage can help in developing a theology of missions that is truly biblical. This short paragraph is not an isolated text. On the contrary, it is intimately linked both to Moses' preceding exposition of the law revealed at Sinai and to what follows, that is, the covenant blessings and curses dealt with in chapter 28. Deuteronomy 26:16–19 functions as a critical hinge in the overall flow of this second address. But this text is also linked to Exod 19:3–6. It seems that as Moses made this profound statement in Deuteronomy, words he heard from YHWH himself forty years earlier at the top of Mount Sinai were ringing in his ears:

> This is what you shall say to the family of Jacob and declare to the descendants of Israel: "You yourselves have seen what I did to the Egyptians, and how I bore you on eagles' wings and brought you to myself. Now therefore, if you will indeed obey my voice and

keep my covenant, you shall be my treasured possession (סְגֻלָּה) among all peoples, for all the earth is mine; and you shall be to me a kingdom of priests and a holy nation." These are the words that you shall speak to the descendants of Israel.

It is not difficult to see in this utterance YHWH's missionary goal for Israel in a nutshell. This Exodus text is obviously linked with Deut 26:16–19 both by its vocabulary and its themes, which presented to the Israelites in barest outline (A) the basis of Israel's calling, (B) the essence of Israel's calling, (C) the keys to the fulfillment of Israel's calling.

The Literary Context, Structure, and Style of Deuteronomy 26:16–19

The significance of these four short verses is quite out of proportion to their length. They provide a summary of several of the key theological issues of the book, and they function as a hinge between Moses' lengthy exposition of the specific stipulations of YHWH's gracious covenant with Israel and the recitation in chapter 28 of the consequences for the nation depending on their response. Verse 16 functions as a colophon bringing to a conclusion what is generally referred to as the "Deuteronomic Law Code," and verses 17–19 serve as a reminder of the primary goals of the covenant that YHWH established with his people.

The style and vocabulary of verse 16 are typically deuteronomic. In verses 1–15 Moses had looked forward to the time when Israel would be well established in the land. But with the opening phrase, הַיּוֹם הַזֶּה, "this day," he brought the attention of his hearers back to the present moment of decision on the plains of Moab. Like the other sixty-one occurrences of הַיּוֹם, "today," in the Old Testament,[4] in Deuteronomy this expression highlights the "emphatic contemporaneity" of the entire book.[5] In this instance Moses reminded those gathered before him that in his address they were actually hearing the revelatory voice of YHWH their God.[6] Still there is something fresh in this statement. Whereas everywhere else in

---

4. The expression הַיּוֹם הַזֶּה occurs in Deut 2:22, 25, 30; 3:14; 4:20, 38; 5:24; 6:24; 8:18; 10:8, 15; 11:4; 26:16; 27:9; 29:3, 27; 32:48; 34:6. For a listing of the remainder, see Millar, "Living at the Place of Decision," 43 n. 61.

5. Thus von Rad, *The Problem of the Hexateuch*, 26.

6. Cf. Millar, "Living at the Place of Decision," 42–44.

the book Moses presented his words as his own commands, here he spoke exceptionally of YHWH commanding the people directly.[7]

The reference to these "decrees and laws" (חֻקִּים וּמִשְׁפָּטִים) links this verse with several earlier texts where הַחֻקִּים and הַמִּשְׁפָּטִים have been combined. Specifically this pair of substantives, combined with the verbs שָׁמַר, "to keep," and עָשָׂה, "to do, practice," links this statement stylistically and thematically with 12:1. These two verses serve as bookends to Moses' exposition on the specific ordinances that YHWH had revealed at Sinai and that he now seeks to apply to life in the Promised Land. And the word pair חֻקִּים וּמִשְׁפָּטִים, "decrees and laws," which occurs nine times in Moses' second pastoral address (chapters 5–26),[8] also serve as a shorthand expression for the entire revelation received at Horeb. Of course, this does not mean that chapters 12–26 are merely a recitation of the Sinai revelation or even a restatement of the laws promulgated there. Like chapters 5–11, the genre of 12–26 is best represented by the term תּוֹרָה, "instruction,"[9] and the "decrees and laws," refer specifically to the laws that underlie this second address. Through this address Moses seeks to impress upon the people their relevance for life in the land beyond the Jordan.

If Deut 26:16 displays strong lexical and thematic links with the paraenetic first part of the second address (chapters 5–11), these connections are even more pronounced in verses 17–19: (A) "to walk in his ways" (26:17; cf. 8:6; 10:12; 11:22; also 28:9; 30:16); (B) the threefold designation of the covenant stipulations, "his decrees, his commands, and his laws" (26:17; cf. 5:31; 6:1; 7:11; 8:11; 11:1; also 30:16); (C) "listen to [obey] his voice" (26:17; cf. 9:23; also 28:1; 30:2, 8, 20); (D) to be his "treasured people" (26:18; cf. 7:6; also 14:2); (E) "a holy people belonging to YHWH your God" (26:19; cf. 7:6; also 14:2, 21; 28:9). Besides looking back these verses also look forward, particularly to 28:1, וְהָיָה אִם־שָׁמוֹעַ תִּשְׁמַע בְּקוֹל יְהוָה אֱלֹהֶיךָ לִשְׁמֹר לַעֲשׂוֹת אֶת־כָּל־מִצְוֺתָיו אֲשֶׁר אָנֹכִי מְצַוְּךָ הַיּוֹם וּנְתָנְךָ יְהוָה אֱלֹהֶיךָ עֶלְיוֹן עַל כָּל־גּוֹיֵי הָאָרֶץ, "And if you *faithfully listen to the voice of YHWH your God, keeping all his commands* that I command you *today by doing*

7. The participial construction, "YHWH your God is commanding you," with God as the subject only here. Elsewhere Moses is always the subject of "[am] commanding you."

8. 5:1, 31; 6:1, 20; 7:11; 11:32; 12:1; 26:16–17.

9. This designation for this address has been encountered earlier in 17:18–19, and will be used repeatedly in the following chapters: 27:3, 8, 23, 26; 28:58, 61; 29:20 [Eng 21], 28 [Eng 29]; 30:10; 31:9, 11–12.

[them], then YHWH your God will set you high above all the nations of the earth."[10] [italics repeated expressions]

The Basis of Israel's Calling

According to the Exod 19:4–6 Israel's missionary calling was based on YHWH's previous gracious actions on her behalf. YHWH reminded Moses of three divine actions for which the Israelites should be eternally grateful: (A) he rescued them from the Egyptians; (B) he took care of the Israelites throughout their history, but especially during the last weeks and months; (C) he brought Israel to Himself. This reminder contains an extremely important principle of missions. Those who are called to missionary service are the products of God's gracious saving and covenantal action. The last expression is especially important for our understanding of Israel's place in God's scheme of things. God did not call Israel basically to a code of conduct, but to a relationship with himself. Moses developed this note emphatically in Deut 26:16–19.

In Deut 26:17–19 Moses alluded to the ceremony by which YHWH and the present generation of Israelites had confirmed their covenant relationship. These verses catch the reader by surprise, in both their syntax and their content.[11] In keeping with the general tone of the entire second address, Moses' intent here was to emphasize that Israel's obedience to YHWH was not to be driven merely by the sense of duty on the part of a vassal toward the suzerain, but by keen awareness of the special nature of their relationship. In so doing he alluded to a formal juridical procedure—that he had apparently supervised in the context of delivering this address—by which YHWH and the generation of Israelites that stood before him had formalized their covenant relationship.

The previous chapters leave few clues as to when this might have occurred. A logical place would have been between 11:32 and 12:1, that is, between Moses' extended appeal for loyalty and adherence to the Great Command (exclusive love for YHWH) in chapters 5–11 and his exposition of the specific covenant stipulations. In 11:26–32 Moses explicitly set before the people "today" the options of blessing or curse, depend-

10. Chapter 28 may originally have been linked directly to chapter 26, with chapter 27 having been inserted between chapters 26 and 28 in the final editing of the book.

11. In characterizing the style of these verses as "ponderous and overloaded," Dale Patrick (*Old Testament Law*, 238) fails to recognize their rhetorical and homiletical function.

ing on their response to YHWH's claim to exclusive allegiance, demonstrated by their obedience to his will.[12] We may recognize an approximate analogue in Exod 19–24. In this complex narrative YHWH's formal announcement of the covenant and general declaration of its demands and privileges (19:4–6) is separated from the specific revelation of his will in the Decalogue (Exod 20:3-17) and the Book of the Covenant (Exod 21–23) by Moses' mediation of the offer of covenant to the people and the people's formal declaration of acceptance: "All that YHWH has spoken we will do," which Moses then relayed back to God (19:8). However, the dialogical and reciprocal ceremony implied in Deut 26:17–19 also recalls the covenant blood ritual at Sinai. Whereas in the present instance the two parties to the covenant had apparently declared their commitments to each other verbally, according to Exod 24:5–8 these had been declared by the nonverbal gesture of sprinkling the blood of the sacrificial animals first on the altar (representing YHWH), and then on all the people.

Deuteronomy 26:17–19 divides into two parts, which are unequal in size but otherwise display a remarkable parallelism. The corresponding features are highlighted in the following synopsis of a fairly literal translation:

17	Today you have had YHWH declare to be your God,	18	Today YHWH has had you declare to be his as a treasured people—just as he promised you,
	and to walk in his ways, and to keep his decrees, laws, and commands, and to listen to his voice.	19	and to keep all his commands, and to set you high above all the nations that he has made—for praise, and renown and honor—and to be a holy people belonging to YHWH your God—just as he promised.[13]

While the parallelism is clear, it is not quite so clear who says what or how it was said. Obviously YHWH did not declare that he would "walk in his ways," etc.—these expressions always apply to Israel. And obviously Israel does not set herself high above the nations, etc. As the presiding of-

12. This paragraph is framed by "I am setting before you today." "This day," occurs in 26:17 and 18.

13. The syntactical parallelism does not match the rhetorical parallelism. For detailed discussion of the complex grammatical issues involved, see Guest, "Deuteronomy 26:16–19 as the Central Focus," 72–129.

ficer in the covenant ratification rituals, Moses summarizes the privileges each party accepts and the obligations to which they commit themselves, but he does so through indirect speech, and in so doing creates some syntactical ambiguities. The issues can be clarified by recasting the content of the declarations into direct speech, in which case what the parties to the covenant actually said would have sounded something like this:

Moses' Voice:	Today, you have had YHWH declare:
God's Voice:	*"I will be your God,*
	And you shall walk in my ways,
	And you shall keep my ordinances, and my
	commands, and my laws,
	And you shall listen to my voice."
Moses' Voice:	Today, YHWH has had you declare:
The People's Voice:	*"We will be Your treasured people—*
	just as You promised us—
	And we will keep all Your commands;
	And You shall set us high above all the nations
	You have made for praise, fame, and honor;
	And we will be a holy people belonging to YHWH our
	God—just as You promised."[14]

Each speech consists of two parts: the status within the relationship that the respective speakers accept for themselves (*italics*), and the obligations to which they recognize the other to have committed themselves (**bold**). The former are expressed fundamentally with infinitives involving the verb הָיָה, "to be." Accordingly YHWH accepts the status of Israel's God, in fulfillment of the oft-repeated promise embodied in the covenant formula,[15] and Israel accepts the status of YHWH's treasured people and a holy people belonging to YHWH.[16] Here Moses observes expressly that this is in fulfillment of his earlier promises. Additionally, the Israelites

14. Cf. ibid., 117–26.

15. The basic form of the formula is "I will be your God and you shall be my people" (אֶהְיֶה לָכֶם לֵאלֹהִים וְאַתֶּם תִּהְיוּ־לִי לְעָם). See Jer 7:23; cf. the reverse order in Jer 11:4; 30:22; Ezek 36:28; also Exod 6:7. On the formula, see Sohn, "I Will Be Your God and You Will Be My People," 364; Hugenberger, *Marriage as a Covenant*; Rendtorff, *The Covenant Formula*; Kalluveettil, *Declaration and Covenant*; Baltzer, *The Covenant Formulary*.

16. The infinitive form, לִהְיוֹת, "to be," with reference to both Yahweh and the Israelites' speech highlights the status that is being accepted.

commit themselves to keeping all YHWH's commands, in fulfillment of YHWH's charge in verse 17b. The obligations to which each party recognizes the other to have committed himself are expressed with active verbs. YHWH calls on Israel to walk in his ways, to keep all his commands, and to listen to his voice, and Israel recognizes YHWH's commitment to set them high above all the nations he has made, for praise, fame, and honor.

The opening declaration of each part is particularly striking because they represent the only occurrences in the entire Old Testament of the hiphil form of אָמַר, "to say, declare," which raises special problems for interpretation.[17] Based on the normal significance of the hiphil stem one should expect a causative sense in each case: "You have caused YHWH to say this day," and "YHWH has caused you to say this day."[18]

Although these statements are remarkably parallel, the following verses demonstrate that the parties involved in these declarations (YHWH and Israel) are far from equals. In any case, it would be quite out of place for a human vassal to force the divine Suzerain into saying anything.[19] It is preferable, therefore, to assume a softer sense, something like "You have had or let YHWH say" (or even "You have accepted or acknowledged YHWH's declaration") "that he will be your God," and "YHWH has had or let you say," that is, "YHWH has accepted or acknowledged your declaration that you will be his treasured people."[20] Even though the term בְּרִית, "covenant," is missing from this paragraph, it is evident from the declarations that follow that these verses involve the formalization of a covenant relationship. Accordingly, the hiphil of אָמַר is best interpreted in a quasi-juridical sense; each party hears the other party declare its commitment to the stipulations of the agreement.

17. Most English translations misconstrue the significance of these statements not only by rendering this unique construction blandly as "declared," but also by attributing the respective statements to the wrong person.

18. Thus Nelson, *Deuteronomy*, 304.

19. Thus Lohfink, *Great Themes from the Old Testament*, 26. For Lohfink's full discussion of the issues involved, see "Dt 26,17–19 und die 'Bundesformel,'" 229–35. Tigay rightfully observes (*Deuteronomy*, 393 n. 47), "It would not make sense to say that Israel caused *God* to say that Israel will accept him as their God and walk in his ways and obey him (v. 17), or that God induced Israel to say that it would be his treasured people and that he will elevate it above the nations (v. 19)."

20. Cf. NRSV and NJB, "You have obtained YHWH's agreement/this declaration from YHWH." For discussion of the present form, see Vriezen, "Das hiphil von אָמַר in Deut 26,17.18," 207–10.

The mutuality of these declarations is remarkable, though not without precedent either in the making of ancient Near Eastern treaties or in the establishment of personal covenantal relationships. This phenomenon is illustrated most dramatically by the treaty between Rameses II of Egypt and the Hittite king Hattusili III in the thirteenth century BCE. The treaty has been preserved in both Egyptian and Hittite versions.[21] The former, which represents a translation into Egyptian of the Akkadian original, was carved in Egypt on the walls of the Temple of Amon in Karnak and the Ramesseum, while the latter has been preserved on three fragmentary cuneiform tablets discovered at Boğasköy. The procedure underlying these texts appears to have transpired as follows: (1) Diplomats representing both states settled on the terms of the agreement. (2) Representatives of each side produced a version styled as the words of the respective monarchs. (3) These versions were inscribed in cuneiform in the Akkadian language (the language of international diplomacy) on tablets of precious metal (silver in this case). (4) These tablets were exchanged and taken home. (5) The texts were translated into the native language, providing the Egyptians and Hittites respectively with constant reminders of the obligations to which the other parties had bound themselves. This explains why the version produced by the Hittite chancellery has been preserved in Egypt and vice versa.[22] Deuteronomy 26:16–19 seems to presuppose an oral version of this procedure in which Israel heard YHWH declare his commitment to them (probably through the mediation of Moses), and YHWH heard the people declare their commitment to Him.

Such declarations represented the means by which relations that did not exist naturally were created.[23] Thus when Israel heard YHWH declare orally his commitment to be their God, and when YHWH heard Israel declare orally that they would be his treasured people, the present generation standing before Moses was (re)constituted the privileged people of YHWH (עַם יהוה). Whatever the historical and chronological relationship between chapter 27 and the chapters between which it is sandwiched, in

21. These are conveniently juxtaposed in *ANET*, 199–203.

22. The procedure is helpfully summarized by Beckman, *Hittite Diplomatic Texts*, 91.

23. According to Falk (*Hebrew Law in Biblical Times*, 136), such utterances represented "a constitutive declaration," by which a relationship could be created. With reference to Deut 26:17–18, he adds, "The ceremony of covenanting between God and Israel . . . included perhaps a mutual statement of the stipulations implied in the covenant. This, again, is reminiscent of marriage" (ibid.).

27:9 Moses and the Levitical priests formally declared the significance of this event: "Silence! Hear, O Israel. This day you have been constituted the people of YHWH your God." This special covenant relationship provides the foundation for Israel's call to reach the nations with the gospel of God's grace.[24]

The Nature/Essence of Israel's Calling

Having observed *how* the present generation had confirmed their acceptance of the covenant relationship that God had promised Abraham and ratified with their parents at Sinai, we may now ask *why* this relationship has been created. To *what* has YHWH called Israel? The answer can be highlighted by plotting the privileges and obligations that Israel and YHWH heard each other affirm, as in the following synopsis:

Verse 17, What Israel heard YHWH declare
Privilege: I promise to be your God.
Obligation: You are to walk in my ways.
Obligation: You are to keep all my commands.
Obligation: You are to listen to my voice.

Verse 18, What YHWH heard Israel declare
Privilege: We accept our status as Your treasured people.
Obligation: We will keep all Your commands.
Obligation: We accept our status above all the nations.
Obligation: We accept out status as a holy people of YHWH.

What Israel has heard YHWH declare in verse 17 is much simpler stylistically (four simple infinitive construct phrases) and with respect to substance (a declaration of YHWH's commitment to be Israel's God followed by a triad of demands for obedience) than what YHWH heard Israel declare in verses 18–19. These three verses highlight four privileges for Israel, all of which relate to their missiological calling.

24. Contra Peters (*Biblical Theology of Missions,* 52), who asserts that "there is no real gospel message—good news—for the Gentiles before the cross and the resurrection of Christ."

1. Israel Has Been Called to Be the People of YHWH

This privilege is declared from two sides. On the one hand, the Israelites have heard YHWH declare his commitment to be their God (v. 17). Moses already expressed Israel's special relationship with YHWH more than 300 times in Deuteronomy with the expression, "YHWH your/our God" (including three times IN verses 16–19). In addition YHWH had introduced himself as the God of Israel in the preamble to the Decalogue (5:6). Remarkably the infinitive clause לִהְיוֹת לְךָ לֵאלֹהִים, "to be your God" (26:17), represents the first explicit reference to the covenant formula in the book. The bilateral nature of YHWH's covenant relationship with Israel is presented more fully in 29:11–12 [Eng 12–13]. There the goal of the covenant (בְּרִית) and the oath (אָלָה) that YHWH made with his people is stated as follows: "that he may establish you today as his people, and that he may be your God, as he promised you, and as he swore to your fathers, to Abraham, to Isaac, and to Jacob." The promise to the ancestors to which Moses referred is recorded in Gen 17:7: "I will establish my covenant between Me and you and your descendants after you throughout their generations for an everlasting covenant, to be God to you and to your descendants after you." The present generation of Israelites heard YHWH declare his fulfillment of the ancient promise.

As the creator of all, YHWH is indeed the master of all (אָדוֹן); but by virtue of his saving and covenantal acts, he made Israel his people in a particular sense. According to one form of YHWH's self-introduction formula, the goal of the exodus was to establish Israel as YHWH's own people (italics added below):

"I am YHWH who sanctifies you, who brought you out from the land of Egypt *to be your God.* I am YHWH." (Lev 22:33)

"But for their sake I will remember my covenant with their ancestors whom I brought out from the land of Egypt in the sight of the nations *that I might be their God.* I am YHWH." (Lev 26:45)

"I am YHWH your God who brought you out from the land of Egypt *to be your God;* I am YHWH your God." (Num 15:41)

In the divinely inspired "National Anthem of Israel" (chapter 32), YHWH claims Israel as his portion (חֵלֶק), his people (עַם), and his allotted possession (חֶבֶל נַחֲלָה). The reference to "His people" indicates that this relationship is also described from the other side as well. Not only had Israel heard YHWH commit himself to be Israel's God, but he had heard the Israelites commit themselves to being "His people" (26:18), that is, "a people belonging to YHWH" (v. 19). Although the expression "people of YHWH" (עַם יהוה) is not found in Deuteronomy,[25] variations of the present construction "a people belonging to YHWH" (עַם לַיהוה) occur repeatedly (7:6; 14:2, 21; 27:9).

Whatever else it means to be "a people belonging to YHWH," this should not be interpreted as a casual relationship. On the contrary, this is an intimate covenantal association, analogous to that which exists between a husband and wife or a father and son (cf. 14:1).[26] Although the relationship between YHWH and Israel in Deuteronomy is often understood primarily as a covenant relationship between a divine Suzerain and his human vassals, the *Sitz im Leben* of the "covenant formula,"[27] to which the present declarations allude, may actually derive from the context of family law. It has long been recognized that the formula, "I will be your God and you shall be my people,"[28] bears a striking resemblance to both the ancient Hebrew marriage formula, "I will be your husband, and you shall be my wife,"[29] and the adoption formula, "I will be your father, and

25. The expression עַם יְהוָה, "the people of YHWH," occurs only nine times in the Old Testament. In the Song of Deborah and Barak (Judg 5:11, 13) the expression bears a pronounced military sense. In 2 Sam 1:12; Ezek 36:20; and Zeph 2:10, "the people of YHWH" are seen in relation to foreign nations. Second Sam 6:21 and 2 Kgs 9:6 refer to kings appointed over "the people of YHWH." The phrase appears three more times (Num 11:29, 17:6 [Eng 16:41], and 1 Sam 2:24). Judges 20:2 and 2 Sam 14:13 speak of Israel as עַם הָאֱלֹהִים, "the people of God." Numbers 21:29 and Jer 48:46 refer to Moabites as עַם־כְּמוֹשׁ, "the people of Chemosh."

26. Lohfink (*Great Themes*, 117–33) argues that in these contexts עַם יהוה should be translated as "family of YHWH," rather than "people of YHWH."

27. In 26:17 YHWH declared that he would be Israel's God. On the formula, see Rendtorff, *The Covenant Formula*; Smend, *Die Bundesformel*.

28. The basic wording of the formula is "I will be your God and you shall be my people" (Jer 7:23). The clauses appear in reverse order in Jer 11:4; 30:22; and Ezek 36:28. In Exod 6:7 the marital connection is even more pronounced: "I will take you to be my people and I will be your God." On the use of לָקַח + לְ as an expression for marriage, see Sohn, "'I Will Be Your God and You Will Be My People,'" 364–68; Sohn, *The Divine Election of Israel*, 11–16. Third-person variations of the formula ("I will be their God, and they shall be my people") are even more common than second-person forms (Jer 31:33; Ezek 37:27; in reverse order, Jer 24:7; 32:38; Ezek 11:20; 37:23; Zech 8:8).

29. The formula is represented most clearly in the Elephantine papyri. See Cowley, *Aramaic Papyri of the Fifth Century B.C.*, #2 and #4. Cf. Porten, *Archives from Elephantine*, 206. Hosea 2:4 [Eng 2] suggests that the opposite action, namely, the breakup of a mar-

you shall be my son."[30] These forms of the formula may seem to represent only the statements made by the husband in the marriage ceremony or by the father in the adoption ceremony.[31] But such contracts were mutual. Presumably the marriage ceremony would involve the husband saying, "I will be your husband, and you shall be my wife," to which the wife would respond orally, "I will be your wife, and you shall be my husband." Similarly in an adoption ceremony, the father would declare, "I will be your father, and you shall be my son," to which the son would respond, "I will be your son, and you shall be my father" (cf. Ps 89:26–27). Support for the latter interpretation may be found in Deut 14:1–2, where the words "You are sons belonging to YHWH your God" are followed with the words "You are a [holy] people belonging to YHWH your God."[32]

2. Israel Has Been Called to Be YHWH's "Special Treasure"

While Israel welcomed YHWH's affirmation of himself as their God, YHWH no doubt also delighted in hearing the Israelites declare their acceptance of their position in the relationship with לִהְיוֹת לוֹ לְעַם סְגֻלָּה, "to be his treasured people" (26:18). This is the third and climactic occurrence of the expression עַם סְגֻלָּה in the book (cf. 7:6; 14:1). The word סְגֻלָּה is rare, occurring only eight times in the Old Testament. In six of these passages it is used in the present metaphorical sense (Exod 19:5; Deut 7:6; 14:2; Mal 3:17; Ps 135:4). But its concrete usage in the other two provides the key to its metaphorical significance. In 1 Chr 29:3 and Eccl 2:8 the word is used of valued possessions, especially the treasure of kings.[33]

---

riage, was formalized with the opposite formula: "She is not my wife, and I am not her husband." For discussion of this text and these issues, see Freedman, "Israel's Response in Hosea 2:17b," 199–204.

30. Cf. 2 Sam 7:14 (= 1 Chr 17:13); 1 Chr 22:10; Ps 2:7.

31. See the helpful evidence gathered by Sohn, "'I Will Be Your God and You Will Be My People,'" 355–72; Sohn, *Divine Election of Israel*, 62–73.

32. Note the parallelism of the Hebrew construction in 14:1–2:

בָּנִים אַתֶּם לַיהוָה אֱלֹהֵיכֶם	You are sons belonging to YHWH your God;
עַם קָדוֹשׁ אַתָּה לַיהוָה אֱלֹהֶיךָ	You are a [holy] people belonging to YHWH your God.

33. This interpretation is confirmed by the usage of its Akkadian cognate, *sikiltum*, in extrabiblical inscriptions. A second-millennium seal impression from Alalakh reads, "the servant of Adad, the beloved (*na-ra-am*) of Adad, the *sikiltum* of Adad." Collon, *The Seal Impressions from Tell Atchana/Alalakh*, 12–13. Note also the personal name,

According to Deut 14:1, Israel was granted this status through divine election. Of all the peoples in the world Israel was chosen by YHWH for this privileged status. Israel's declared acceptance of this status as YHWH's treasure alludes to Exod 19:5, where this metaphor first occurs: "You shall be my treasured possession (סְגֻלָּה) among all peoples, for all the earth is Mine." Just as the crown jewels in London reflect the glory of the monarchs of England, so Israel was specially chosen to reflect the glory of God among the nations.

3. Israel Has Been Called to Be a Light of God's Grace to the Nations

Isaiah used the words "light to the nations" to describe the mission of the Servant of YHWH (Isa 42:1; 49:6). The metaphor is missing in Deuteronomy, but the concept is certainly present in 26:19, which represents one of the most remarkable statements in all of Deuteronomy. Despite Israel's insignificant size (7:6–7) and her moral discredits (cf. 9:1–24), YHWH assigned her a status superior "to all the nations that he has made." In previous references in Deuteronomy to Israel's relationship to the nations (גּוֹיִם), the word referred to the groups that occupied the land of Canaan, over whom the Israelites would demonstrate superiority by defeating them and occupying their land.[34] With the statement of purpose, "to set you high above the nations," Moses casts his gaze far beyond Canaan to the world as a whole—all the nations that YHWH had made.

Sikilti–Adad, "Treasured one of Adad." For further discussion, see Greenberg, "Hebrew *segullā*: Akkadian *sikiltu*," 172–74; Weinfeld, *Deuteronomy and the Deuteronomic School*, 226 n.2. For additional attestation, see Brinkman et al., "*sikiltu*," 244–45. Juxtaposing "servant," "beloved," and *sikiltum* to describe the vassal relationship of the king to his god is especially telling.

A similar usage is attested also in a thirteenth-century BCE letter from the Hittite emperor to Ammurapi, the last king of Ugarit, in which the former reminds the latter that he is his servant and his *sglt*. Dietrich et al., eds., *Cuneiform Alphabetic Texts from Ugarit*, 179 (*KTU* 2.39:7, 12 = *PRU* V.18:38:7, 12). The rendering of the Hebrew term as "peculiar" in the Authorized Version is not to be understood as "odd or weird," but in the sense of the underlying Latin, *peculium*, that is "personal/private property." The Septuagint translates the word, λαὸν περιούσιον, "a people of his special possession." Similarly Titus 2:14, Eph 1:14, and 1 Pet 2:9 read περιούσιον, "possession, property."

34. Deut 4:38; 7:1, 17, 22; 9:1; etc.

This interpretation is confirmed by the echo of this verse heard in 28:1.[35] There Moses stated that if Israel would scrupulously listen to the voice of YHWH their God and obey all his commands, then YHWH would set them "high above all the nations of the earth." "All the nations of the earth" in 28:1 is equivalent to the nations "that he has made," in 26:19. The "Song of YHWH" (Deut 32) seems to provide further commentary on this verse: "When the Most High [עֶלְיוֹן][36] gave to the nations their grant, when he divided humankind, he fixed the borders of the peoples according to the number of the sons of God. But YHWH's allotment is his people, Jacob his allotted grant" (32:8–9). Whereas other nations are governed through mediatorial agents,[37] YHWH has claimed Israel as his special grant to be administered directly.

Deuteronomy 26:19 does not specify how Israel's superiority over the nations would be expressed. However, in 15:6 Moses had provided hints of what this might mean. There YHWH's full blessing of Israel was described in terms of economic hegemony ("You will lend to many nations, but you will not borrow") and political superiority ("You will rule over many nations, but they will not rule over you"). This sense is reinforced in 28:2–14, where Moses described in detail the blessings that would accrue to Israel if they were faithful to YHWH. Moses referred to the other nations explicitly only three times,[38] but the dimensions of hegemony include economic (vv. 2–6, 8, 11–12), military (v. 7), and psychological (v. 10) superiority. In short, Israel will be the head over all and the tail to no one (v. 13).[39]

---

35. Verse 28:1 bears an even closer resemblance to Exod 19:6 than to 26:17, as the following translations of the texts demonstrate:

Exod 19:6 "If you will conscientiously listen to my voice . . .";
Deut 28:1 "If you will conscientiously listen to the voice of YHWH your God . . ."

36. The divine appellation עֶלְיוֹן, "Most High," provides a direct homonymous link with 26:19 and 28:1, both of which employ the term עֶלְיוֹן, though in an adverbial sense, namely, "high."

37. The translation "sons of God," rather than "sons of Israel," follows the reading in 4QDeut[j] (בני אלים) and the Septuagint (ἀγγέλων θεοῦ).

38. They are called "many nations" (28:12), "the peoples of the earth" (v. 10), and "your enemies" (v. 7).

39. The roots of the international concern of the present statement may also be found in Exod 19:5–6, where YHWH not only claimed that the entire world is his own but also declared Israel's exalted status among all the peoples as his treasured people.

Although 26:19 does not describe how Israel will be elevated above the nations, the verse summarizes the effects: לִתְהִלָּה וּלְשֵׁם וּלְתִפְאָרֶת, "for praise and fame and honor." The word תְּהִלָּה, "praise," occurs elsewhere in the book only in 10:21, where Moses had said YHWH is Israel's praise, because of all that he had done for them. In that context Israel's experience of divine favor brought praise to Him. The word שֵׁם is literally "name," but as in several other instances outside Deuteronomy (Gen 6:4; 11:4; Zeph 3:20; Job 30:8), here it denotes "renown or reputation." The third expression, תִּפְאָרֶת, refers to "glory, fame, splendor."[40]

However, scholars and translations disagree on how "praise, fame, and honor" are to be understood in this context. The New International Version rendering suggests that the honor us Israel's.[41] To be set high above the nations for praise, fame, and honor describes a fate for Israel that is the opposite of that envisioned in 9:14, where YHWH threatened to destroy Israel and blot out their name from under heaven. This understanding seems to find support in Zeph 3:19–20, where echoes of the present text can be heard:

"See, at that time I will deal with all your oppressors.
And I will save the lame and gather the outcast,
and I will change their shame into praise (לִתְהִלָּה)
and fame (לְשֵׁם) in all the earth.
At that time I will bring you home,
at the time I will gather you together;
for I will make you a name (לְשֵׁם) and praise (לִתְהִלָּה)
among all the peoples of the earth,
when I restore your fortunes before your eyes," says YHWH.

However, this interpretation of Deut 26:19 is not as certain as it seems. Some translations preserve the ambiguity of the original with readings like, "for him to set you high above all nations that he has made, in praise and in fame and in honor" (NRSV; cf. NASB, NJB). This allows for the praise and fame and honor to be ascribed to either Israel or YHWH. Within the context of the book and in view of later echoes of this text it seems preferable to ascribe the glory to God. The New English Bible and

40. In Exod 28:2, 40, the word is paired with כָּבוֹד, "glory," to describe the magnificence of Aaron's priestly vestments.

41. The NLT is even more explicit, "Then you will receive praise, honor, and renown." So also Tigay, *Deuteronomy*, 246; McConville, *Deuteronomy*, 383.

the Revised English Bible rightly read, "to bring him praise and fame and glory."

First, Israel's standing among the nations was never to be a source of national pride.[42] Moses repeatedly diffused any temptation to arrogance because of numerical (7:7) or moral superiority (9:4–24), or personal achievement (8:17–18).

Second, as already noted, in the only other occurrence of תְּהִלָּה in the book (10:21), Israel was to recognize YHWH as her praise, because of all that he had done for her. This interpretation is reinforced by Moses' later comments in 28:9–10: "YHWH will establish you as a holy people (עַם קָדוֹשׁ) for Himself, as he has sworn to you, if you keep the commands of YHWH your God and walk in his ways. And all the peoples of the earth shall see that you are called by the name of YHWH, and they shall fear you."

Third, Jer 13:11 and 33:9 echo the present text, describing how Israel's fortunes brought praise to YHWH among the nations. Both verses include the same Hebrew words for name, praise, and glory.

Just as in a later time the temple would be designed and designated in Isa 60:7 as "My glorious house" (בֵּית תִּפְאַרְתִּי, literally, "the house of my honor"),[43] so YHWH's intention for Israel was that her well-being would reflect the glory and grace of the God whose name they bore, and the nations would fear them because of that name. According to Deut 28:1–14, because of YHWH's blessing, Israel will be acknowledged worldwide as the most privileged nation on earth. But this would have nothing to do with any innate glory; it will be the consequence of divine favor alone.[44]

4. Israel Has Been Called to Be a Holy People

As a fourth privilege YHWH heard them accept their status as a holy people belonging to YHWH. On three previous occasions Moses referred to Israel as a holy people belonging to YHWH their God. In both 7:6 and 14:2 her status as an עַם קָדוֹשׁ ("holy people") was associated with YHWH's election of her to be his treasured possession (סְגֻלָּה). And in

42. Wright, *Deuteronomy*, 272–73; *HALOT*, 1773.

43. In 1 Chr 22:5 David commented that "the house that is to be built for YHWH must be exceedingly magnificent for fame (שֵׁם) and glory (תִּפְאָרֶת) throughout all lands."

44. Israel was recognized by the peoples to be the most privileged because they had a God who was near and responded to their cries to him and revealed his will to them (Deut 4:6–8).

14:21 the prohibition of consuming the meat of any animal that had died a natural death is based on her status as a holy people. Sojourners and foreigners may eat it, but Israel may not.

The present text does not explain what it means to be a holy people. However, as in verse 18 the added clause כַּאֲשֶׁר דִּבֶּר, "as he has promised,"[45] recalls Exod 19:5–6, where YHWH promised Israel that if they will keep his covenant and listen to his voice, they would be YHWH's special treasure among all the peoples, his kingdom of priests, and his "holy nation."

This statement of Israel's holy status has great significance for understanding Israel's missionary role. God did not separate Israel from the nations so that he might merely lavish his attention on her as if she were a pet kitten or a china dish on a shelf. Just as the Levitical priests were set apart to serve as YHWH's agents of grace between him and Israel, so Israel collectively was to serve as a link between God and the world. The need for mediation was created by the estrangement of the world from its Creator. As YHWH's priests, Israel was to declare the light of his revelation to the nations and to intercede on their behalf before Him.

The Burden of Israel's Calling

Whereas God's call of Israel to salvation was absolutely unconditional, the nation's effectiveness in fulfilling her call to mission was conditional, as seen in Exod 19:5–6: "*If* you will indeed obey my voice and keep my covenant . . ." The success of Israel's mission as a light to the nations depended on her listening to YHWH's voice and keeping his covenant. Deuteronomy repeatedly stresses the importance of fidelity to the covenant.

With his emphasis on "doing" (Deut 26:16), Moses declared that God's will was not revealed to Israel simply to be stored in a museum or even to be displayed publicly as a source of pride. Nor did he intend merely to give them a resource for analysis or philosophical reflection. The purpose of the law was to serve as a guide for conduct. This is seen in the words "you shall keep and do them with all your heart and your entire being." The verbs "keep" and "do" function as a hendiadys, meaning "diligently apply," which is then reinforced by an appeal to unqualified and total compliance with the will of God, the divine Suzerain.[46] Israel's obli-

---

45. For discussion of the significance of this expression, see Milgrom, "Profane Slaughter," 1–17, esp. 10.

46. The phrase "with all your heart and all your being" is typically deuteronomic, being applied elsewhere to unreserved love (אָהֵב) for the divine Suzerain (6:5; 30:6),

gations are summarized in verse 17 in three typically deuteronomic claus-es: the Israelites must "walk in his ways,"[47] keep all YHWH's commands,[48] and listen to his voice.[49] To "keep all his commands" (v. 18) summarizes the three obligations YHWH laid on them in verse 17.

Conclusion

With Moses' final declaration of Israel's holiness, he concluded his ex-position on the stipulations of the covenant (Deut 12:1—26:19). All that remained for him in this address was to present the consequences for Israel of her response to the challenge and privilege of this special cov-enant relationship with YHWH (28:1–69). The manner in which Moses concluded this section has profound implications not only for a biblical theology of the law but also for a biblical understanding of Israel's role in the divine program of revelation and redemption.

It is tempting to view God's election of Israel and his revelation of his will to this people either as ends in themselves or merely to represent the means whereby Israel's security and her possession of the land would be guaranteed. A superficial reading of the accounts of the Sinai revela-tion (Exod 19–Num 9) might support this interpretation. Apart from the Egyptians, from whose clutches YHWH delivered the Israelites, and the Canaanites, whose land YHWH was about to deliver into the Israelites' hands, references to the world outside of Israel are rare. Twice YHWH had declared that he had separated Israel from the peoples (Lev 20:24, 26). On several occasions the nations were mentioned as witnesses to what YHWH was doing with Israel (Exod 34:10; Lev 26:45; Num 14:15). In Num 24:8 Balaam foresaw Israel's victory over the nations. However,

---

unreserved rendering of vassal service (עָבַד, 10:12; 11:13; 13:4 [Eng 3]), unreserved obe-dience (שָׁמַע) to the voice of YHWH (30:2), unreserved turning (שׁוּב) to YHWH (v. 10), and unreserved searching (בָּקַשׁ) for him (4:29).

47. The expression appears elsewhere in 8:6; 19:9; 28:9; 30:16 (cf. "to walk in *all* his ways," in 5:30; 10:12; 11:22).

48. As in 6:5, the three words for commands (חֻקָּיו, "His decrees"; מִצְוֹתָיו, "His com-mands"; מִשְׁפָּטָיו, "His laws") express totality, in this case all the stipulations of the cove-nant. The use of the verb שָׁמַר, "to keep," provides another link with Exod 19:5–6, suggest-ing that "to keep his decrees, commands, and laws," should be interpreted as equivalent to שָׁמַר אֶת־בְּרִיתִי, "to keep my covenant," in the earlier context.

49. The phrase "to listen to his voice" ties this verse even more tightly to Exod 19:5–6, where the call to keep YHWH's covenant is preceded by the charge to listen to his voice diligently.

the tables would be reversed in the covenant curses, in which YHWH warned Israel that if they would persist in infidelity they would be scattered and would perish among the nations (Lev 26:33, 38).

Israel's missionary function does not receive much space in the record of the Sinai revelation, but this does not mean it is lacking. On the contrary, YHWH had set the context and parameters for his covenant at the very beginning when he promised Israel that if they would keep his covenant and listen to his voice they would be his treasured possession, his kingdom of priests, and his holy nation (Exod 19:5–6). With the addition of "for all the earth is mine" (v. 5), YHWH's implicit universal concern is rendered explicit. And only from this perspective can Israel's law be understood. God gave the law to his people *in order* to declare to the world what his glory and grace could accomplish in the lives of the destitute and enslaved (cf. 4:8).

In general, the treatment of the nations in Deuteronomy follows the pattern set by the Sinai revelation. References to Egypt and the Canaanite nations are frequent, but Israel's relationship to other nations or the world at large receives scant attention. YHWH is said to have created the nations (26:19) and assigned to them their respective territories (32:8; cf. 2:1–25). Elsewhere they are presented as witnesses to YHWH's actions on behalf of or against Israel (2:25; 4:6–8; 28:10, 37; 29:24) or as those who would tempt the Israelites to emulate them (4:19; 13:8[Eng 7]; 17:14; 32:21). In a single poetic text Moses predicted that the tribe of Joseph would be victorious over the nations (33:17). Like the curses in Leviticus, Deuteronomy frequently refers to the nations as agents of divine judgment against Israel, and/or the place to which YHWH would drive them in his fury (4:27; 28:33, 36, 49–50, 64–65; 30:1, 3).

Deuteronomy presents the nations as the context from which YHWH chose Israel, and before whom he established them as his treasured and holy people (7:6–7; 10:15; 14:2), with the goal of setting them above all the nations. To achieve this goal YHWH would grant to Israel extraordinary prosperity and economic and political hegemony over the nations (7:14; 15:6; 28:12). However, as God himself had expressed so forcefully in Exod 19:5, this status and role would be contingent on their fidelity to Him, demonstrated in obedience to the covenant stipulations (28:1).

According to Moses' second address, four critical factors were to be involved in Israel's life and service as the people of YHWH. First, they were the products of YHWH's gracious and unmerited saving actions. By obeying him they showed their gratitude for deliverance and their loyalty to their Deliverer. Second, Israel's occupation of Canaan was contingent on their fidelity to Him. Apart from faith and obedience they would have no title to the land, as the covenant sanctions in chapter 28 demonstrated. Third, through their obedience to the will of YHWH, as revealed in his laws, the Israelites were to declare to the world not only how righteous are his statutes (4:6–8), but also how righteous and gracious is their God. Finally, through their obedience to YHWH's will they were to demonstrate the glorious privilege that attends their status as his special treasure and his holy people (cf. 4:5–8).

If these facts are not recognized, then the law is distorted, either in antinomianism or in legalism. The Israelites would be the means of God's blessing the whole world only if they would walk in his ways and listen to his voice. When YHWH called Abraham to covenant relationship with Himself, and when he confirmed this covenant with Israel at Sinai, and again on the plains of Moab, he had the nations in view.

In Deuteronomy the pattern for missions is fundamentally centripetal. While the world watched, YHWH delivered Israel from her Egyptian bondage, entered into a covenant relationship with her, put Canaan into her hands, and blessed her. As his covenant partner, his special treasure, and his holy people, Israel became an example of the power of divine grace and glory to the praise and renown and honor of YHWH. What YHWH had done for Israel he sought to do for all, but like Caleb, and Rahab, and Ruth, they must come to Israel. Nowhere does the Pentateuch include a missionary mandate anything like the Great Commission in Matt 28:18–20 that commanded Israel to go to the nations and proclaim YHWH to them. It should have happened more naturally. The prevailing formula was simple:[50] demonstrate gratitude for divine grace through loyal living and experience YHWH's blessings, thereby attracting the attention of the nations, who would give praise and glory to YHWH, and join Israel in their covenant relationship with Him.

In the face of Israel's failure and the resulting exile, the missionary strategy in the New Testament changed. However, to conclude that a centrifugal approach displaces the centripetal strategy is too simplistic. Peter wrote in 1 Pet 2:9–12 that the missionary role of New Testament believers was similar to that of Israel. There is no hint here that the believ-

---

50. Jonah's mission to Nineveh demonstrates that the centrifugal paradigm is not excluded in the Old Testament.

ers who were scattered among the Gentiles had traveled to Gentile lands in a conscious missionary effort. Rather, like ancient Israel among the nations, these Christians were residing in pagan communities. By their having experienced God's grace and by their godly conduct they were to proclaim the excellencies of God who had called them out of darkness into his marvelous light. Jesus' words in Matt 5:13–16 about his followers being salt and light also suggest that believers are to engage in the centripetal aspects of missionary witness.

However, at the end of the Gospel of Matthew Jesus himself shifted the strategy from "Come see what God has done for his people" to "Go tell the world what God has done for his people" (28:18–20)—from a centripetal focus to a centrifugal one. The community of believers then expanded far beyond ethnic and territorial Israel,[51] and specific individuals such as Paul were called to carry the gospel of divine grace to the Gentiles. The Scriptures close with a glorious vision of people from every tribe and nation redeemed and gathered around the Lamb to worship him (Rev 5:9; 7:4). Ironically this represents the supreme example of centripetal strategy. May believers be faithful in proclaiming his grace wherever they are, and may many heed his call to go to the ends of the earth, so that everyone may know that YHWH, incarnate in Jesus Christ, is God and Lord of all—to the praise of his glory.

---

51. The pattern is illustrated dramatically in the book of Acts with the successive outpourings of the Holy Spirit on Jews in Jerusalem (Acts 2), Samaritans (Acts 8), Gentile God-fearers in the land (Acts 10), and the Ephesians as representatives of Gentiles on foreign soil (Acts 19).

8

The Power of Song
Reflections on Ancient Israel's National Anthem (Deuteronomy 32)

Introduction

WHAT IS MORE MOVING than the spirited singing of a national anthem? By all accounts, national anthems are a recent phenomenon.[1] "Het Wilhelmus," the Dutch national anthem, written between 1568 and 1572 during the Dutch revolt against Phillip II of Spain, is apparently the oldest, though the Japanese claim that the lyrics to their Kimigayo were written in the ninth century.[2] While national anthems vary considerably, they tend to be dominated by the eighteenth- to nineteenth-century martial style of Europe, when nationalism was on the rise. National anthems are almost always laudatory, presenting a positive picture of a nation, often by praising those who have shaped its political history or by celebrating the natural beauty of its countryside. Some national an-

---

1. For a collection of national anthems, see Bristow, ed., *National Anthems of the World*.

2. The exact date is unknown. Although it was not set to music until 1880, the poem derives from the Heian period (794–1185 CE).

thems were commissioned by governments,[3] and some were written by unknowns,[4] but only a few were composed by renowned musicians.[5]

It may surprise some to learn that the history of national anthems is actually 2,500 years older than we had previously thought, for in Deut 32 we find the national anthem of ancient Israel. Identified in virtually all translations as "The Song of Moses,"[6] readers of the New Testament book of Revelation will naturally think of this text when they read of heavenly worshipers singing "the song of Moses the servant of God, and the song of the Lamb" (τὴν ᾠδὴν Μωϋσέως τοῦ δούλου τοῦ θεοῦ καὶ τὴν ᾠδὴν τοῦ ἀρνίου) in Rev 15:3. However, this label is not entirely satisfactory on several grounds. First, "the song of Moses" in Rev 15:3 may just as well refer to Exod 15, which explicitly celebrates YHWH's deliverance of the Israelites from their tyrannical Egyptian overlords, an event that is paradigmatic of the salvation provided by the Lamb. In any case Rev 15:3–4 represents a collage of Old Testament motifs and texts, with only faint allusions either to Exod 15 or to Deut 32.[7] Second, within the context of Deut 31–32 it is misleading to label this song as "the Song of *Moses*," because he was neither its composer nor its subject; Moses was merely a conduit for its communication. The narrative introduction to the song in Deut 31:14–22 suggests the lyrics were dictated by YHWH to Moses and Joshua in the tent of meeting, and that Moses then recited (דִּבֶּר) them all to the people (31:30; cf. 32:44–47). In the immediate context the speaker represented by the first person in the exordium (vv. 1–4) would have been

3. *O Canada* was commissioned by Théodore Robitaille, Lieutenant Governor of Quebec, for the 1880 Saint-Jean-Baptiste Day celebration. While the lyrics were composed in French by judge and poet Sir Adolphe-Basile Routhier, they were set to music by Calixa Lavallée. The English version, originally written by Robert Stanley Weir in 1908, is not a literal translation of the French. While the French lyrics remain unchanged, the English version has been revised several times; the present form dates to 1980.

4. E.g., France's *La Marseillaise*, by Claude Joseph Rouget de Lisle; the United States of America's *The Star-Spangled Banner*, based on "The Anacreontic Song," by John Stafford Smith.

5. Having been composed by Franz Joseph Haydn, Germany's *Das Lied der Deutschen*, is a notable exception. Some credit Austria's *Land der Berge, Land am Strome* to Wolfgang Amadeus Mozart, but this is doubtful.

6. NIV, TNIV, ESV, NLT, HCSB, NRSV (notes to Coogan, *The New Oxford Annotated Bible*, 300); NJPSV (notes to Berlin and Brettler, *The Jewish Study Bible*, 440).

7. Though some argue Rev 15:3–4 is influenced more by Deut 32 than Exod 15. See Ford, *Revelation*, 257. For fuller discussion of the Old Testament background to Rev 15:3–4, see Beale, *The Book of Revelation*, 792–800.

Moses, but then in original assembly he would have been the speaker of the entire Song. However, the Song is not presented as the composition of Moses, but as the speech of YHWH, and crafted in such a way that it speaks for the voices of generations of Israelites into the distant future. The words of the opening stanza represent anyone who sings this Song in the present or in time to come. However, thereafter the singer disappears and the first person is reserved for YHWH Himself. Accordingly, if we insist on labeling the Song by its composer or its subject, rather than by its genre, we should call it "The Song of YHWH."[8]

The Genre of Deuteronomy 32

The genre of Deut 32 is widely discussed in the scholarly literature.[9] Based on the opening call for witnesses and the argumentation of the Song, especially its presentation of the evidence against Israel, and several legal details within the text,[10] many have interpreted it as a רִיב, a prophetic lawsuit.[11] The opening call to the heavens and the earth resembles a similar call in Isa 1:2, and links this text thematically to earlier appeals in Deuteronomy to the heavens and the earth to function as witnesses (4:26;

8. In Jewish tradition it is called *Shirat Haʾazinu*, "The Song of 'Give Ear,'" after the opening word, הַאֲזִינוּ.

9. See especially, Sanders, *The Provenance of Deuteronomy 32*, and most recently, Lee, "The Narrative Function of the Song of Moses in the Contents of Deuteronomy and Genesis–Kings"; Weitzman, *Song and Story in Biblical Narrative*; Britt, "Deuteronomy 31–32 as a Textual Memorial," 358–74; Leuchter, "Why is the Song of Moses in the Book of Deuteronomy?" 295–317; Watts, *Psalm and Story*, 63–81; Giles and Doan, *Twice Used Songs*.

10. E.g., YHWH's reference to raising his hand as a gesture associated with an oath in verse 40.

11. This interpretation was first developed in detail by Huffmon, "The Covenant Lawsuit in the Prophets," 285; Wright, "The Lawsuit of God," 26–67. Variations of this interpretation are common. See Thompson, *Deuteronomy*, 297; Luyten, "Primeval and Eschatological Overtones in the Song of Moses (Dt 32, 1–43)," 341–47; Miller, *Deuteronomy*, 226; Wright, *Deuteronomy*, 298. For a recent defense of this view see Wiebe, "The Form, Setting and Meaning of the Song of Moses," 119–63. Wiebe links the Song to an annual covenant renewal ceremony and dates it to the time of Samuel. He identifies the following components of the legal process: Introduction (vv. 1–6); the prosecutor's speech (vv. 7–14); the indictment of Israel (vv. 15–18); the sentence (vv. 19–26); a complaint and dirge (vv. 27–33); deliberation by the judge (v. 34); the final decision concerning Israel, her pardon, and the transfer of the punishment on the nations (vv. 35–42); a concluding hymn (v. 43).

30:19; 31:28). As in the lawsuits of later prophets, this song includes an indictment (vv. 15–18) followed by the sentence (vv. 19–25).

However, this interpretation overlooks both the expansions that have nothing to do with lawsuits (vv. 2, 30–43), and elements that are more closely associated with wisdom literature than with legal proceedings.[12] Peter Craigie suggested it was written for recitation at covenant renewal ceremonies, as a means of reminding the Israelites of the terms and implications of the covenant.[13] Others have proposed variations of this liturgical interpretation. Dennis Olson understands Deut 32 as a catechetical song;[14] Matthew Thiessen refers to it as a "hymn or liturgy";[15] and Mark Allen calls it a "hymn of witness."[16] Moving in a less obviously liturgical direction, Richard Nelson interprets the Song as "theodicy that explains national catastrophe" and "gives confidence and builds trust in YHWH."[17] In the most recent full-length study of the Song, Andrew Lee argues that "the Song functions as a prophetic criticism of Israel to focus its audience on the central command of the Torah, the moral issue of 'remembering YHWH,' and sheds light on Israel's vocation as witness to the nations, resulting in a theology of history for all nations."[18] In so doing, "the Song expresses the heart of Deuteronomy. It does it by fusing its thematic affinities and differences to bear on the Deuteronomic demand for covenantal loyalty and worship, and showing how these ideas of loyalty and worship must translate into a quality of character in Israel that befits the people of YHWH."[19]

12. According to Solomon A. Nigosian, this text had a unique form involving a "covenantal lawsuit inverted to forge a salvation oracle and the whole presented in a didactic mode." See "The Song of Moses (DT 32)," 8. Among others who recognize its didactic features, perhaps influenced by wisdom, see Boston, "The Wisdom Influence upon the Song of Moses," 198–202; Sanders, *Provenance of Deuteronomy 32*, 91–93; Labuschagne, "The Song of Moses," 93. Watts (*Psalm and Story*, 76) characterizes it as "unique invention" with a significant didactic function.

13. Craigie, *The Book of Deuteronomy*, 373.

14. Olson, *Deuteronomy and the Death of Moses*, 139.

15. Thiessen, "The Form and Function of the Song of Moses (Deuteronomy 32:1–43)," 402.

16. Allen, "Deuteronomic Re-presentation in a Word of Exhortation," 25.

17. Nelson, *Deuteronomy*, 369.

18. Lee, "The Narrative Function of the Song of Moses," 6–7.

19. Ibid., 230.

In summary, while legal features are actually quite muted, the Song exhibits a strong liturgical stamp, and bears a stronger resemblance to several psalms in the Psalter than to prophetic lawsuits.[20] Whatever technical term we wish to ascribe to the poem, its didactic function is clear. In addition to proclaiming the greatness of YHWH, the Song provides a constant reminder to Israelites of their origins and ascendancy—rooted in YHWH's grace—and their demise—rooted in their perfidious response to grace—demonstrating YHWH's justice in punishing them, and pointing to the resolution of the broken relationship through YHWH's future acts of grace.[21]

Ultimately the best clues to the genre of Deut 32 are found within the Song itself and in the surrounding narrative.[22] As noted earlier, YHWH commanded Moses to teach the Song to the Israelites from beginning to end, not only that they might take it with them across the Jordan into the Promised Land, but that it might be passed on to their descendants and never be forgotten from the lips of future generations (31:19–21; cf. 32:44–47). Both Torah and Song were taught and transcribed by Moses. However, whereas the Torah was deposited beside the Ark and placed in the custody of Levitical priests and elders, who were to read it to the people [minimally] every seven years (31:9–13) at the Festival of Booths (Sukkoth), this Song was placed on the lips of all the people to go with them wherever they went and to be transmitted by the people to succeeding generations. This suggests that the narrator perceived the Song

20. The features that have been associated with the רִיב genre also appear in the psalms: the opening appeal for attention (Pss 49:2 [Eng 1]; 78:1); the summary of Israel's history, including YHWH's grace to which Israel responded with rebellion (Pss 78; 105; 106; 135; cf. also the prayer of the Levites in Neh 8); and the concluding exhortation to praise (v. 43; cf. Pss 105:45; 106:47–48).

21. Similarly Boston, "The Song of Moses," 191, 149–52, 187–91.

22. The historical value of the surrounding narrative is completely ignored or discounted by most critical scholars. Leuchter ("Why is the Song of Moses in the Book of Deuteronomy? 314) admits a Mosaic connection when he characterizes the Song as "an old poem penned by Mushite priests who had known only David to be a monarchic supporter [of the law code]." He suggests that the Song was "a northern staple," recited and performed among Levites in the former northern kingdom of Israel. He adds, "To these Levites, The Song would have been *their* text, emerging from *their* liturgy and representing *their* culture." In so doing he seems to assume that the order of functionaries identified as Levitical priests in Deuteronomy originated with Moses, the Levite *par excellence*. For a welcome alternative, see Lee, "Narrative Function of the Song of Moses," who recognizes its significance within the surrounding narrative framework (31:1–30; 32:44–47), the book of Deuteronomy as a whole, and within the narrative plot of Genesis–Kings.

as a sort of national anthem for the people of YHWH. By declaring its function as a "witness" (31:19; עֵד), in perpetuity testifying (31:21; עָנָה) against them and in YHWH's defense, the Song assumes a quasi-legal, even constitutional status. In this respect it exhibits a *gravitas* that is absent from contemporary national anthems, whose primary function is to inspire pride in one's country. Instead of painting a utopian and idealistic picture of the nation of Israel, it portrays them realistically as ungrateful beneficiaries of divine grace and rebellious against their national deity, and warns them of the dangers of abandoning YHWH in favor of other gods whenever it is heard or sung. Indeed the only notes of praise in the Song are addressed to YHWH, who, despite His people's persistent perfidy, in the end remains true to His immutable covenant promises and takes His people back to Himself. At the same time, like the rainbow in Gen 9:12–17, it would provide the Israelites with a constant sign of YHWH's commitment to them as a nation. These were the messages that Moses had personally communicated in word and deed throughout the past forty years, and these were the messages he had been delivering in the addresses preserved in the book. Therefore, it should not surprise modern readers that although the Song casts the message in a different form, it is the same message his people had heard eloquently proclaimed as Torah from the very beginning of the book. This anthemic function also explains why the Song avoids explicit references to historical events.[23] If it was to be relevant for every future generation, it could not be identified with any specific context. On the contrary, as a profoundly theological explanation of Israel's past and the nature of her relationship with YHWH in principle, its relevance in perpetuity was guaranteed. The vagueness of the text with respect to historical events is best understood in the light of the context within which it is embedded. This is not a response to Israel's rebellion and YHWH's judgment, but like the covenant blessings and curses at the end of Moses' second address (chap. 28), an advance warning of the consequences of infidelity to Him.

The Nature and Style of Deuteronomy 32

Deuteronomy 32 provides a perfect model on which to base exploring the nature of Hebrew poetry.[24] Curiously, the Old Testament never formally

---

23. On attempts to date the Song based on historical allusions, see Lee, "The Narrative Function of the Song of Moses," 12–15.

24. Craigie (*Deuteronomy*, 375) observes that this Song is more polished in its poetic parallelism and the length of its lines than other early songs.

distinguishes between poetry and prose. Biblical Hebrew has words for "chronicle" (דִּבְרֵי הַיָּמִים), "writing" (כְּתָב), "document" (סֵפֶר), "genealogy" (תּוֹלְדֹת), "proverb" (מָשָׁל), "song" (שִׁיר), "psalm" (מִזְמוֹר), "lament" (קִינָה), "songs of praise" (תְּהִלָּת/תְּהִלִּים), but it has no words for "prose" or "poetry." Some have argued that there is no poetry in the Bible—only a "continuum" from loosely parallelistic structures in what we think of as *prose* texts to a more "heightened rhetoric" of parallelistic devices misleadingly labeled as verse, and that the distinction is a Hellenistic imposition upon a Semitic construct.[25] However, it is not that simple. As is the case when we move from Exod 14 to 15 and Judg 4 to 5, when we move from Deut 31 to 32 we encounter a dramatic new literary environment. Although examples of the features cited below may also be found in prose texts, in texts commonly perceived as poetic we find a heightened use of (1) assonantal plays on sound;[26] (2) meter and rhythm,[27] though the stress is on literary symmetry, the harmony of ideas and concepts, rather than sounds, and biblical poets were extremely creative and effective in their freedom to break rhythmic forms;[28] (3) grammatical and syntactical modifications;[29]

25. Kugel, *The Idea of Biblical Poetry*, 85; Kugel, "Poetry," 806.

26.

32:6	הֲלוֹא־הוּא אָבִיךָ קָּנֶךָ	Is not he your father, who <u>created you</u>,
	הוּא עָשְׂךָ וַיְכֹנְנֶךָ	He who made you and <u>established you</u>?
32:8–9	בְּהַנְחֵל עֶלְיוֹן גּוֹיִם	When Elyon assigned the nation<u>s</u> as a grant,
	בְּהַפְרִידוֹ בְּנֵי אָדָם	when he divided humankind,
	יַצֵּב גְּבֻלֹת עַמִּים	He fixed the borders of the peoples
	לְמִסְפַּר בְּנֵי אֵלִים׃	according to the number of the sons of <u>God</u>.
	כִּי חֵלֶק יְהֹוָה עַמּוֹ	See, YHWH's portion is <u>His</u> people,
	יַעֲקֹב חֶבֶל נַחֲלָתוֹ	Jacob is <u>His</u> allotted heritage.
32:14	חֶמְאַת בָּקָר וַחֲלֵב צֹאן	Curds from the herd, and <u>milk</u> from the flock,
	עִם־חֵלֶב כָּרִים וְאֵילִים בְּנֵי־בָשָׁן	with <u>fat</u> of lambs and ram<u>s</u>,
	וְעַתּוּדִים עִם־חֵלֶב כִּלְיוֹת חִטָּה	bulls of Bashan and goat<u>s</u>,
	וְדַם־עֵנָב תִּשְׁתֶּה־חָמֶר	with the very <u>finest</u> of the wheat—
		and the blood of the grapes—
		you drank foaming wine.

27. On Deut 32 see especially Fokkelman, *Major Poems of the Hebrew Bible*, 144–49. For studies of the issue of parallelism more broadly, see Stuart, *Studies in Early Hebrew Meter*; Geller, *Parallelism in Early Biblical Poetry*.

28. Alter (*The Art of Biblical Poetry*, 9) abandons the term "meter" with reference to Hebrew poetry.

29. Diminished use of the article (only 3x in the Song, all in the opening verses: הַשָּׁמַיִם, "the heavens" [v. 1]; הָאָרֶץ, "the earth" [v. 1]; הַצּוּר, "the Rock" [v. 4]); the sign of

(4) disproportionate frequency of *hapax legomena*[30] and other rare words,[31] and other forms of free and loose expressions;[32] (5) figurative language;[33] (6) semantic and other forms of parallelism, based on stan-

---

the definite direct object, אֵת (absent in the Song); the relative particle אֲשֶׁר, "who, which" (it occurs only in v. 38a, though implicit [asyndetic] relative clauses are common: vv. 6c, 17 [4x], 18 [2x], 20e, 27d, 28a, 35b, 37c); *waw* consecutive (+ imperfect of past events occurs 10x, but it also uses the simple imperfect for past events). Despite these tendencies, Nicholas Lunn has demonstrated that the basic rules of grammar in prose also apply to poetry (*Word-Order Variation in Biblical Hebrew Poetry*).

30. See שְׂעִירִם, "rain" (v. 2); פְּתַלְתֹּל, "twisted" (v. 5); יְלֵל, "howling"; בּוֹנֵן, "to care for" (v. 10); כָּשָׂה, "to become obstinate" (v. 15); שָׂעַר, "to be aghast, appalled" (v. 17); שׁיה, "to forget" (v. 18, though תֶּשִׁי may be a corruption of נשה [*HALOT*, 1477]); אֵמֻן, "faithfulness" (v. 20); מְזֶה, "to be weakened"; מְרִירִי, "poisonous" (v. 24); הִפְאָה (from אפה), "to cut off" (v. 26); כָּמַס, "to store up" (v. 34); שִׁלֵּם, "to pay back" (v. 35); נָסִיךְ, "libation"; סִתְרָה, "protection" (v. 38).

31. See עָרַף, "to drip" (v. 2; cf. 33:28); the feminine plural יְמוֹת, "days," instead of יָמִים (v. 7); גּוֹזָל, "young eagle" (v. 11; in Gen 15:9 it refers to a turtle dove); חֵמֶר, "fermenting wine" (v. 14; cf. Ps 75:9); יְשֻׁרוּן, "Jeshurun," YHWH's name of honor for Israel (v. 15; cf. 33:5, 26; Isa 44:2); בָּעַט, "to kick" (v. 15; cf. 1 Sam 2:29; Jer 2:17); עָבָה, "to become fat" (v. 15; cf. 1 Chr 10:10); שֵׁדִים, "demons" (v. 17; cf. Ps 106:37); לָחַם, "to eat" (v. 24; denominative verb from לֶחֶם, "bread"; cf. Ps 141:4; Prov 4:17; 9:5; 23:1, 6); קֶטֶב, "pestilence" (v. 24; cf. Isa 28:2; Hos 13:14; Ps 91:6); זָחַל, "to crawl" (v. 24; cf. Mic 7:17); נכר, in the sense of "to misjudge" (v. 27; 1 Sam 23:7; Jer 19:4); פְּלִילִים, "concede" (v. 31; this interpretation is doubtful; cf. Exod 21:22; Job 31:11); מְרֹרֹת, "bitter grapes" (v. 32; used of bitter herbs in Exod 12:8; Num 9:11); עֲתִדֹת, "destiny" (v. 35; cf. Job 15:24; Isa 10:3 with different senses); אָזַל, "to disappear" (v. 36; cf. 1 Sam 9:7; Job 14:11; Prov 20:14); עָצוּר, "ruler" (v. 36; apparently a *qatul* noun form; Tigay, *Deuteronomy*, 312; cf. 1 Kgs 14:10; 21:21; 2 Kgs 9:8; 14:26); עָזוּב, "helper" (v. 36; see previous comment; these two expressions always appear together); פַּרְעֹת, "head hair" (v. 42; cf. Num 6:5; Ezek 44:20). To these rare words we should also add the archaic third masculine singular suffix נֵהוּ (v. 10), and the plural suffix מוֹ– (עָלֵימוֹ, "on them" [v. 23]; צָרֵימוֹ, "their enemies" [v. 27]; אֱלֹהֵימוֹ, "their gods" [v. 37]; זִבְחֵימוֹ, "their sacrifices" [v. 38]); as well as the form חָסָיוּ, "they sought refuge" with the preserved final *yod* (v. 37) and the rare *taw* feminine ending of אָזְלַת, instead of אזלה (v. 36). Elsewhere the Song tends to use the more common forms for these morphemes.

32. The use of negative particles is especially striking. Not only do לֹא, "no," and אֵין, "There is not," appear with remarkable frequency (לֹא: vv. 5b, 6b, 6c, 17a, 17b, 17d, 21a, 21c, 27b, 31a, 34a; אֵין: vv. 4c, 12b, 28b, 39c, 39f), but they are also combined with nouns and adjectives to create a series of unusual phrases in nominative expressions: אֵין עָוֶל, literally, "There is no perversity" used attributively, "without perversity" (v. 4c); לֹא בָנָיו, "not-his-sons" (v. 5a); וְלֹא חָכָם, "and there is no wisdom," used attributively, "without wisdom" (v. 6b); לֹא אֱלֹהַּ, "non-god" (v. 17a); לֹא־אֵל, "non-god" (v. 21a); לֹא־עָם, "non-people" (v. 21c). To these expressions we should add the particle אֶפֶס, "nonexistent" (v. 36d), and the odd construction involving the participle אֹבֵד, from אָבַד, "to perish," in v. 28a: כִּי־גוֹי אֹבַד עֵצוֹת הֵמָּה, which means something like, "They are a nation devoid of sense."

33. Similes occur in v. 2, where the life-giving words of this Song are compared to rain/dew, using four different expressions (רְבִיבִים, שְׂעִירִים, טַל, מָטָר), in v. 10d, where Israel is compared to "the apple" of YHWH's eye (אִישׁוֹן עֵינוֹ), and 11a, where YHWH is com-

dardized word-pairs for concretizing and focusing purposes,[34] so that in the oral reading the hearer appreciates the balance in sense, assonance, and rhythm; and (7) impressionistic portraiture. Whereas prose conveys its theological message more or less through chronological description, Hebrew poetry may allude to it, but rarely includes enough detail to reconstruct what happened. If prose creates an image of the represented scene in the mind of the hearer, like romantic landscape painting, then poetry seeks to create a mood and disposition toward the event, like impressionistic art.

Because of the frequency of verbs for speech within the song, Deut 32 exhibits a profoundly dialogical tone and style.[35] Some of these verbs mark the beginning of extended speeches that have been embedded in the Song (v. 20 [introducing vv. 20b–25]; 37 [introducing vv. 37b–42]). However, some apparently embedded speeches are not signaled by an introductory verb: the proclamation of the singer (v. 4); the recollections of the father (vv. 8–14); an embedded speech by YHWH (vv. 39–42). Furthermore, within some of the embedded speeches we find an additional level of embedding in fragments of speeches. This is true of YHWH's utterances. Some of these embedded speeches are signaled with the verb אָמַר (YHWH's speech, vv. 26, 40–42; the adversaries' speech, v. 27), some are unmarked. Verse 30 exhibits the quality of a gnomic utterance, apparently declared by an unnamed interlocutor; he speaks of YHWH, Israel and the enemies as an outsider. The first person plural of verse 31 suggests this is an embedded utterance of an Israelite. The result

---

pared to an eagle lovingly guarding its nest. Metaphors dominate the Song's portrayal of YHWH: he is הַצּוּר, "the Rock" (vv. 4a, 15d, 18a, 30c, 31a) creator (קָנָה, v. 6c), the Lord of the manor distributing land among his subjects (vv. 8–9), Israel's mother (v. 18b–c). But in his expressions of fury YHWH is also portrayed as the divinity who shoots his arrows at the objects of his wrath (v. 23), and who dispatches his agents Famine (רָעָב), Plague (רֶשֶׁף), Pestilence (קֶטֶב), wild beasts (בְּהֵמוֹת), and the sword (חֶרֶב) to do his deadly work (vv. 24–25). Indeed the poet paints a picture of YHWH with a storehouse filled with vengeance waiting to be released on Israel's enemies (34–35).

34. See the discussion by Alter, *Art of Biblical Poetry*, 3–26.

35. Words for speech, either in verb or noun forms, occur fourteen times. The verb אָמַר, "to say," occurs six times (vv. 7d, 20a, 26a, 27c, 37a, 40b); the noun אֹמֶר, "word, speech" (vv. 1b); אִמְרָה, "word, speech" (v. 2d); also דִּבֶּר, "to speak" (v. 1a); קָרָא, "proclaim" (v. 3); הַב, "ascribe" by speech (v. 3b); שָׁאַל, "ask" (v. 7c); הִגִּיד, "declare" (v. 7c); רָנַן, hiphil, "rejoice" (v. 43).

is an extremely complex Song, involving three levels of direct discourse, which may be represented as follows:[36]

Figure 8: The Levels of Discourse in the Song of YHWH

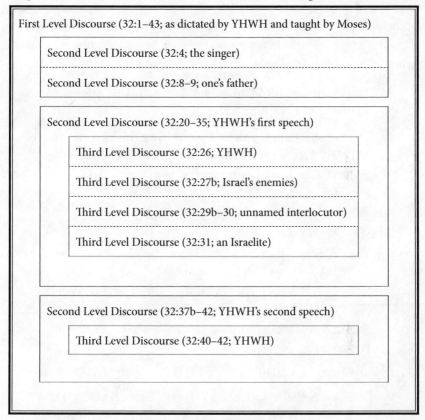

First Level Discourse (32:1–43; as dictated by YHWH and taught by Moses)

Second Level Discourse (32:4; the singer)

Second Level Discourse (32:8–9; one's father)

Second Level Discourse (32:20–35; YHWH's first speech)

Third Level Discourse (32:26; YHWH)

Third Level Discourse (32:27b; Israel's enemies)

Third Level Discourse (32:29b–30; unnamed interlocutor)

Third Level Discourse (32:31; an Israelite)

Second Level Discourse (32:37b–42; YHWH's second speech)

Third Level Discourse (32:40–42; YHWH)

In the immediate context the speaker represented by the first person in the exordium (vv. 1–4) would have been Moses, but then in original assembly Moses would have been the speaker of the entire Song. But if this Song was composed, not as the speech of Moses, but of YHWH, to speak for the voices of generations of Israel in the distant future, then the opening stanza represents anyone who sings this Song at any time. Hereafter the singer disappears and the first person is reserved only for YHWH Himself.

36. Cf. the discussion by Fokkelman, *Major Poems*, 58–62. Lee ("Narrative Function of the Song of Moses," 55) recognizes only two speakers, Moses and YHWH.

The demarcations of the respective speeches and speeches within speeches are not the only signals of structure. The boundaries between strophes are often signaled grammatically. Important clues are provided by the focus particle, כִּי, which occurs no fewer than a dozen times,[37] the marking of initial lines in a parallel pair by departing from the canonical verb-subject-object/modifier order, and the explicit identification of new subjects. These features may appear alone or in combination. On these grounds we may divide the Song into sections and stanzas as follows:[38]

A. The Exordium: A Call to Acknowledge the Perfections of YHWH (vv. 1–4)

B. The Recollection: A Call to Acknowledge the Imperfections of YHWH's People (vv. 5–18)
   Stanza I: The Thesis Statement (vv. 5–6)
   Stanza II: A Call to Remember YHWH's Grace (vv. 7–14)
   Stanza III: Trampling Underfoot the Grace of YHWH (vv. 15–18)

C. The Confession: A Call to Recognize the Justice of YHWH (vv. 19–35)
   Stanza I: YHWH's Justice in Dealing with His Own People (vv. 19–25)
   Stanza II: YHWH's Justice in Dealing with Israel's Enemies (vv. 26–35)

D. The Gospel: A Call to Treasure YHWH's Compassion (vv. 36–42)

E. The Coda: A Call to Celebrate YHWH's Deliverance (v. 43)

37. In view of the exhaustive work on this particle by Follingstad (*Deictic Viewpoint in Biblical Hebrew Text*), the prevailing interpretation of כִּי as a fundamentally causal conjunction should now be abandoned. The only instance in this chapter where a causal interpretation of the particle might be warranted is found in verse 20, but even here this is doubtful. A temporal sense is plausible in verse 36c.

38. For alternative presentations of the structure of the Song, see Lee, "Narrative Function of the Song of Moses," 55–56; Skehan, "The Structure of the Song of Moses in Deuteronomy (Deut 32:1–43)," 153–63; Wright, "Lawsuit," 33; Labuschagne, "The Song of Moses in Deuteronomy 32"; Christensen, *Deuteronomy 21:10—34:12*, 787.

The Function and Use of Deuteronomy 32

But how was this song to be used in ancient Israel? If it was intended as Israel's anthem, as I have proposed, then it would probably have been recited or sung at corporate worship events. This conclusion is reinforced by its pervasively liturgical flavor. Scholars have identified a series of liturgical features within the song: (1) the designation of this text as a שִׁירָה, "song, poem," rather than a רִיב, "legal case"; (2) the frequent alternation of persons moving back and forth among first and second and third persons; (3) the alternation of speakers, some identified explicitly,[39] some implicitly;[40] (4) the series of commands (vv. 3, 7, 39, 43) and interrogatives (vv. 6, 30, 34, 37–38);[41] and (5) the concluding call to praise (v. 43). In addition to these internal features, we should note the narrative context in which the revelation of this song is given. The narrator has juxtaposed instructions for its recitation with the report of Moses' committing his preceding addresses to writing, his placement of this Torah beside the ark, and his charge to the Levitical priests to read the Torah every seven years in a cultic setting (Sukkoth, Festival of Booths; 31:9–13). If the valedictory pastoral addresses of Moses in Deuteronomy have incorporated many elements of ancient Near Eastern covenant forms, this Song has embedded and adapted the features of a covenant רִיב to create a powerful corporate hymn of praise.

If the Song was composed in a liturgical context for liturgical purposes, when was it composed and for which liturgical context was it intended? Concentrating on evidences of influence of this Song on later biblical writings, especially Isa 40–66, Jeremiah, and Ezekiel,[42] some have argued that the Song's provenance should be sought in late prophetic circles.[43] However, the influence of the Song on earlier texts, including

39. The singer (vv. 1, 3); the addressee's father (v. 7); YHWH (vv. 20, 26, 37, 40); Israel's enemies (v. 27).

40. An Israelite observer (v. 30), the singer (v. 31).

41. For full discussion of the liturgical interpretation see Thiessen, "The Form and Function of the Song of Moses," 407–24. For a reconstruction of how the liturgy might have been performed see pp. 416–18. Thiessen's liturgical interpretation is cited with approval by Leuchter, "Why Is the Song of Moses in the Book of Deuteronomy?" 314.

42. For an examination of the influence of the Song on the portrayal of the nations in Ezekiel see Gosse, "Deutéronome 32,1–43 et les redaction des livre d'Ezéchiel et d'Isaïe," 110–17.

43. Mayes, *Deuteronomy*, 381. For further discussion, see Bergey, "The Song of Moses

Isa 1–39, which derives from the eight century BCE, is becoming increasingly apparent, suggesting we should seek an earlier date.[44] Based on what are interpreted to be historical allusions, the Song's conceptual framework, and its archaic and late lexical and syntactical features,[45] many have defended an earlier date for the Song.[46] Unfortunately, like many psalms, whose contexts are notoriously difficult to date, this Song provides few, if any, concrete hints of a specific historical circumstance that might have precipitated it.[47] As for the linguistic and syntactical evidence, the rich combination of archaic and late features may be accounted for in any one of three ways: (1) The archaic features point to an early date (fourteenth to tenth century BCE), with the late features reflecting inevitable updating of the text as the Song was sung and performed over the centuries. (2) The late features point to a late date (eighth century BCE and following), the archaic features being the result of deliberate archaizing to give the Song an authentically Mosaic flavor.[48] (3) The combination of early and late features points to a transitional period (tenth to eighth centuries BCE), when older forms had not yet given way completely to younger forms.[49] I accept the first position.

(Deuteronomy 32.1–43) and Isaianic Prophecies," 34–36; also Nigosian, "The Song of Moses (DT 32)," 5–7.

44. See especially Bergey's essay noted above. For a full study of the issue, see Sanders, *The Provenance of Deuteronomy 32*. According to Sanders, "There is every appearance that many scholars preponderantly elaborated the relationship with specific prophets because of their prejudices concerning the date of the song. Some of them had a blind spot for the correspondences with prophecy from different periods" (ibid., 64).

45. The distribution and proportions of these are helpfully catalogued and discussed by Nigosian, "Linguistic Patterns of Deuteronomy 32," 206–24. Full bibliography of previous studies is provided.

46. Many have dated the Song to the eleventh or tenth centuries BCE. The time of Samuel: Eissfeldt, *Das Lied Moses Deuteronomium 32 1–43 und das Lehrgedicht Asaphs Psalm 78 samt einer Analyse der Umgebung des Mose–Liedes*; more recently, Wiebe, "The Form, Setting and Meaning of the Song of Moses," 119–63. For a date in the time of the Judges, see Cassuto, "The Prophet Hosea and the Books of the Pentateuch," 99; Cassuto, "The Song of Moses (Deuteronomy Chapter xxxii 1–43)," 41–46. For full discussion of the history of scholarship on Deut 32, see Sanders, *Deuteronomy 32*, 1–98; for a summary, see Lee, "Narrative Function of the Song of Moses," 12–32.

47. So also Fokkelman, *Major Poems*, 142–43.

48. Mayes, *Deuteronomy*, 381.

49. This is the view adopted by Nigosian, "Linguistic Patterns," 209–24. He does not even consider the first option.

How the Song might have been used liturgically in early Israelite worship we may only speculate. Although echoes of the Song are often heard in later texts, they offer few clues concerning its usage in Israel's ritual. Josephus offers interesting insight into early Jewish tradition concerning the song: "He [Moses] recited to them a poem in hexameter verse, which he has moreover bequeathed in a book preserved in the temple, containing a prediction of future events, in accordance with which all has come and is coming to pass, the seer having in no whit strayed from the truth. All these books he consigned to the priests, together with the ark, in which he had deposited the Ten Words (δέκα λόγους) written on two tablets, and the tabernacle" (*Ant.* 4.303).

According to Rabbinic tradition, Levites would read portions of the song in the temple on the Sabbath over a six-week cycle, while worshipers presented their Additional Offerings (מוסף), and when they came to the end, they would repeat the cycle.[50] Since a separate scroll apparently containing only Deut 32 has surfaced in Qumran (4QDeut^q),[51] it seems this text was used separately either as part of a liturgy or for instructional purposes. However, the Song may contain its own clues concerning its liturgical use. The expressed and implied shifts in speaker may suggest an antiphonal and multi-character liturgy, something like the following:[52]

Table 8: The Liturgical Structure of the Song of YHWH

Verses	Content	Speaker
1–3	Introduction	Leader of the Service
4	Creedal Affirmation	Congregation
Pause		
5–6	Summary Declaration of the Indictment	Leader of the Service
7	Call to Remember YHWH's Grace	Leader of the Service
8–14f	Recitation of YHWH's Grace	Men
14g–18	Declaration of the Indictment of the People	Leader of the Service

50. For references, see Tigay, *Deuteronomy*, 546 n. 35.

51. See Skehan, "A Fragment of the 'Song of Moses' (Deut 32) from Qumran," 12–15.

52. This is an adaptation of Thiessen's reconstruction. See "The Form and Function of the Song of Moses," 407–24.

Verses	Content	Speaker
Pause		
19–20a	Declaration of YHWH's Sentence	Leader of the Service
20b–27c	Recitation of YHWH's Judgment Speech	Priest or Cultic Prophet
27d–e	Declaration by the Nations	Appointed Man in the Assembly
28–29	Description of the Nations	Priest or Cultic Prophet
30	Question Asked of the Nations	Leader of the Service
31	Declaration of the Israelites	Congregation
32–35	Recitation of YHWH's Description of Israel's Enemies	Priest or Cultic Prophet
Pause		
36–37a	Declaration of YHWH's Commitment to His People	Priest or Cultic Prophet
37b–38	Recitation of Israel's Challenge to the Nations	Congregation
39–42	Recitation of YHWH's Judgment Speech against the Nations	Priest or Cultic Prophet
43	Concluding Summons to Praise	Congregation

Although this reconstruction of the Song's liturgical use is admittedly speculative, we should consider its power to shape lives apart from the liturgy at the sanctuary. As the anthem of the people committed to memory, its influence was not limited to liturgical contexts. On the lips of all the people it should have been recited and heard in the far corners of the land—wherever Israelites lived. YHWH outlined the need for the Song in the narrative preamble (31:14–22), and Moses affirmed YHWH's analysis of the situation (31:29). According to verse 21, the sorry state of the people's hearts created the need for it. YHWH knew what kind of people the Israelites were. Looking back, the past forty years had provided plenty of time and opportunity to demonstrate how fickle they were. Only recently, at Baal Peor, this new generation had rebelled with shameful apostasy (Num 25). But looking forward, both the narrative (vv. 1–22) and the Song anticipate a chain of reactions that the death of Moses (31:16a) would trigger.[53]

53. The imminent death of Moses hangs over the entire book of Deuteronomy, which Moses himself anticipated from the beginning (3:23–29; 31:2). Indeed, as soon as he

First, the people will become apostate and abandon YHWH (31:16b). YHWH is keenly aware of the Israelites' fickleness; the moment Moses' restraining influence would be removed they would adopt the pagan religious practices and beliefs of the surrounding nations. The pain in YHWH's heart is evident in His description of their apostasy: they would play the harlot after the gods of the land;[54] they would abandon Him; and they would break His covenant. How quickly Israel would forget the grace of the One who had redeemed them, called them to himself to be His people, His holy nation, His kingdom of priests, His royal treasure (Exod 19:1–5), and for forty years had cared for them in the desert! At the proverbial drop of a hat they would abandon him for the gods of the nations.

Second, YHWH will respond with fury, abandoning His people and hiding His face from them (31:17–18). They will accuse him of infidelity, but as the covenant blessings and curses had predicted (Deut 28), this would be His response. YHWH is not obligated to favor those who persist in behaving like Canaanites. Consequently, no matter how hard they searched for him or how loudly they cried, he would not respond.

Third, troubles and disasters will overcome them (31:17b). The expression "many evils and troubles" (רָעוֹת רַבּוֹת וְצָרוֹת) is shorthand for all the curses built into the covenant (Lev 26; Deut 28).[55]

Fourth, the people will respond with false charges and blame (31:17c). Their words will be correct: "Have not all these things happened to us because our God has abandoned us?" But their tone is wrong and the accusation erroneous. Instead of acknowledging their own responsibility, they will pass blame on God. But YHWH emphasizes again in verse 18 that it was their action that ignited His fury: they have violated the first and great command by turning to other gods.

If this is the problem, then what is the solution? A song! Not a prophet like Moses, or a priest like Aaron, or a patriarch like Abraham, or a king like David. The replacement for Moses to keep the people spiritually on course is a *song*. Herein we learn the prophetic purpose of Israel's national anthem: to keep alive the memory of YHWH's grace, especially

has taught the people the Song, YHWH will call him up Mount Nebo to die (32:48–52; 34:1–12). See further Olson, *Deuteronomy and the Death of Moses*.

54. Judges 2:10–23 suggests this happened one generation after the death of Joshua.

55. The threat and experience of divine abandonment, and the consequent disasters are common motifs in ancient literature. See Block, *The Gods of the Nations*, 113–47; Block, "Divine Abandonment," 15–42.

when they prosper and delight in the fulfillment of His promises (vv. 1–14), and to warn them of the consequences of abandoning him for other gods (vv. 18–25). However, as Moses had done in Deut 4:25–31 and chapters 29–30, the Song also concludes with a magnificent proclamation of the steadfast commitment of YHWH, who cannot let the judgment be the last word (vv. 26–42). In the midst of prosperity the Song sends a caution—Remember YHWH!—and in the midst of judgment it offers hope—Remember YHWH! Herein lies the Song's rhetorical power.

Moses, the servant of YHWH, had been able to lead the people spiritually because he was a physical presence before a coherent though mobile community camped around the tabernacle of YHWH. Joshua, his replacement, could continue playing this inspirational role, for his charge was to lead the entire nation in battle against the Canaanites. However, once the land had been taken and the tribes scattered to their territorial allotments, no human leader could be before all the people all the time, preventing them all from doing what was right in their own eyes. Apparently the system of Levitical cities was designed that the influence of the central sanctuary could extend to the whole population, but even godly Levites could not accompany all the people all the time as they went back and forth from their fields or engaged in everyday commerce. In our day we would have solved the problem by placing a copy of the Scriptures in the hands of the people. But this was not an option, for several reasons. First, assuming the credibility of the note in 31:9–13, even if Moses had transcribed all his addresses in this book, at this time there would have been only one copy of each address, and it would have been stored in the sanctuary in the custody of the Levitical priests. Furthermore, while we do not know when the book of Deuteronomy (or the Pentateuch, for that matter) was cast in its present form,[56] the Scriptures available to the nation would have been fragmentary, a collection of scrolls containing texts that were eventually incorporated in the Pentateuch.[57] Second, although the book of Deuteronomy assumes the Levitical priests were literate, and eventually the king would be as well (17:14–20), most Israelites would not have known what to do with a written Scripture. However, in a preliterate society a text like Deut 32 could easily have been memorized by all the

56. For discussion of possibilities, see chapter 1.

57. These might have included written records of patriarchal stories, the revelation at Sinai (Exod 24:1–7), Israel's battles (Exod 17:14), and a diary of their forty-year trek from Egypt to the plains of Moab (Num 33:1–49).

people, and having been committed to memory, its lyrics summarizing the gospel the Israelites had experienced would ring in the people's minds wherever they went. The purpose of this anthem was obviously not to celebrate the beauty of the homeland or to instill national pride in the people—the view of Israel is actually quite negative. Its function was to raise the people's aspirations by fixing their eyes on YHWH and instilling in them gratitude for His undeserved favors.

Conclusion

The narrator of Deuteronomy reports that Moses was able to teach the anthem preserved in Deut 32 to the people (Deut 31:30; 32:44–47), which suggests that as the Israelites crossed the Jordan under Joshua's leadership this Song should have been ringing in their ears. However, the historian of Judg 2:8–15 shows how quickly the Song was forgotten and how quickly YHWH's words in Deut 31:16–18 were fulfilled:

> Joshua son of Nun, the servant of the LORD, died at the age of one hundred ten years. So they buried him within the bounds of his inheritance in Timnath-heres, in the hill country of Ephraim, north of Mount Gaash. Moreover, that whole generation was gathered to their ancestors, and another generation grew up after them, who did not know the LORD or the work that he had done for Israel. Then the Israelites did what was evil in the sight of the LORD and worshiped the Baals; and they abandoned the LORD, the God of their ancestors, who had brought them out of the land of Egypt; they followed other gods, from among the gods of the peoples who were all around them, and bowed down to them; and they provoked the LORD to anger. They abandoned the LORD, and worshiped Baal and the Astartes. So the anger of the LORD was kindled against Israel, and he gave them over to plunderers who plundered them, and he sold them into the power of their enemies all around, so that they could no longer withstand their enemies. Whenever they marched out, the hand of the LORD was against them to bring misfortune, as the LORD had warned them and sworn to them; and they were in great distress. (NRSV)

If the Torah was largely neglected throughout Israel's history,[58] the same must have been true of this song. But it was not forgotten by ev-

58. When the Torah scroll was discovered in the temple in the late seventh century BCE, it was passed through several hands (Hilkiah the priest, Shaphan the scribe, Josiah the king), before Huldah the prophet was finally able to instruct Josiah and his court on the full significance of the document (2 Kgs 22:1–20).

eryone. While a full study of the influence of this song is beyond the scope of this inquiry, scholars are recognizing increasingly the influence of the song on later prophecy,[59] but its influence is also apparent in wisdom writings,[60] and even in the New Testament.[61] Sadly, modern readers are scarcely aware of this treasure in the Old Testament. Rediscovery of Israel's national anthem could go a long way toward recovering the gospel in the Old Testament and in recovering Jesus' and the apostles' sense of the unity of biblical revelation.

Israel's National Anthem: The Song of YHWH

A. The Exordium: A Call to Acknowledge the Perfections of YHWH (vv. 1–4)

[1] Give ear, O heavens, and I will speak,
and let the earth hear the words of my mouth.
[2] May my teaching drop as the rain,
my speech distill as the dew,
like gentle rain upon the tender grass,
and like showers upon the herb.
[3] See, I will proclaim the name of YHWH;
Ascribe greatness to our God!
[4] "The Rock, His work is perfect;
See, all His ways are justice.
A God of faithfulness and without iniquity,
Righteous and upright is He."

59. E.g., Bergey, "The Song of Moses (Deuteronomy 32.1–43) and Isaianic Prophecies," 34–36; Keiser, "The Song of Moses as a Basis for Isaiah's Prophecy," 486–500; Gosse, "Deutéronome 32,1–43 et les redaction des livre d'Ezéchiel et d'Isaïe," 110–17; Gile, "Ezekiel 16 and the Song of Moses," 87–108.

60. Cassuto, "The Prophet Hosea and the Books of the Pentateuch," 79–100; Holladay, "Jeremiah and Moses: Further Observations," 18–21; Boston, "Wisdom Influence," 198–202, concludes there is "a definite relationship between this song and the wisdom traditions." However, his hypothesis that wisdom influenced the Song seems to have the direction of influence wrong, especially if Deut 32 is to be dated early, as most scholars do.

61. According to Aland et al., eds., *Novum Testamentum Graece et Latine*, 778, allusions to and quotations from Deut 32 occur in Matt 4:8, 10; 10:37; 12:39; 17:17; 25:31; Luke 13:34; 14:26; 19:42; 21:22; John 5:21; Acts 2:40; 6:6; 7:35, 38, 45, 53; 15:3; 17:26; 20:32; Rom 9:14; 10:19; 12:19; 15:10; 1 Cor 10:20, 22; 2 Cor 6:14; 2 Thess 2:13; Eph 1:6; Phil 2:15; Heb 1:6; 2:5; 10:30; 1 John 1:9; Jude 10:30; 14; Rev 1:18; 6:10; 9:20; 10:5; 12:12; 15:3, 4; 16:5; 19:2. See further Bell, "Deuteronomy 32 and the Origin of the Jealousy Motif in Romans 9–11," 200–85.

B. *The Recollection: A Call to Acknowledge the Imperfections of YHWH's People (vv. 5–18)*

STANZA I: THESIS STATEMENT

> ⁵ They have dealt corruptly with Him;
> they are no longer His children because they are blemished;
> they are a crooked and twisted generation.
> ⁶ Is this how you respond to YHWH,
> you foolish and senseless people?
> Is not he your father, who created you,
> He who made you and established you?

STANZA II: A CALL TO REMEMBER YHWH'S GRACE

> ⁷ Remember the days of old;
> consider the years of many generations;
> Ask your father, and he will declare to you,
> your elders, and they will tell you.
> ⁸ When Elyon assigned the nations as a grant,
> when he divided humankind,
> He fixed the borders of the peoples
> according to the number of the sons of God.
> ⁹ See, YHWH's portion is His people,
> Jacob is His allotted heritage.
> ¹⁰ Hound him in a desert land,
> and in the howling waste of the wilderness;
> He encircled him, he cared for him,
> He kept him as the pupil of His eye.
> ¹¹ Like an eagle that stirs up its nest,
> that flutters over its young,
> spreading out its wings, catching them,
> bearing them on its pinions,
> ¹² YHWH alone guided him,
> no foreign god was with him.
> ¹³ He made him ride on the high places of the land,
> and he ate the produce of the field,
> and he suckled him with honey out of the rock,
> and oil out of the flinty rock.
> ¹⁴ Curds from the herd,
> and milk from the flock,
> with fat of lambs and rams,
> bulls of Bashan and goats,
> with the very finest of the wheat,
> and the blood of the grapes—you drank foaming wine

STANZA III: TRAMPLING UNDERFOOT THE GRACE OF YHWH

> [15] But Jeshurun grew fat, and kicked;
> you grew fat, grew stout, and grew sleek;
> then he forsook God who made him
> and scoffed at the Rock of his salvation.
> [16] They inflamed his passion with strange gods;
> with abominations they provoked him to anger.
> [17] They sacrificed to demons that were no gods,
> to gods they had never known,
> to new gods that had come recently,
> whom your fathers had never dreaded.
> [18] Of the Rock that bore you, you were unmindful,
> and you forgot the God who gave you birth.

C. The Confession: A Call to Recognize the Justice of YHWH

STANZA I: YHWH's JUSTICE IN DEALING WITH HIS OWN PEOPLE

> [19] YHWH saw it and spurned them,
> because of the provocation of His sons and His daughters.
> [20] And he said,
> I will hide my face from them;
> I will see what their end will be,
> See, they are a perverse generation,
> children in whom is no faithfulness.
> [21] They have inflamed my passion with what is no god;
> they have provoked Me to anger with their idols.
> So I will inflame their passion with those who are no people;
> I will provoke them to anger with a foolish nation.
> [22] See, a fire is kindled in my nose,
> and it burns to the depths of Sheol,
> it devours the earth and its increase,
> and sets on fire the foundations of the mountains.
> [23] And I will heap upon them disasters;
> My arrows I will spend on them;
> [24] They shall be wasted with hunger,
> and devoured by plague and poisonous pestilence;
> I will send the teeth of beasts against them,
> with the venom of things that crawl in the dust.
> [25] Outdoors the sword shall bereave,
> and indoors terror,
> for young man and woman alike,
> the nursing child with the man of gray hairs.

Stanza II: YHWH's Justice in dealing with Israel's Enemies

26 I would have said,
I will cut them to pieces;
I will wipe them from human memory,
27 had I not feared provocation by the enemy,
lest their adversaries should misunderstand,
lest they should say,
Our hand is triumphant,
it was not YHWH who did all this.
28 See, they are a nation void of counsel,
and in them there is no understanding.
29 If they were wise, they would understand this;
they would discern their latter end!
30 How could one have chased a thousand,
and two have put ten thousand to flight,
unless their Rock had sold them,
and YHWH had given them up?
31 See, their rock is not like our Rock;
our adversaries are by themselves.
32 See, their vine comes from the vine of Sodom
and from the terraces of Gomorrah;
their grapes are grapes of poison;
their clusters are deadly;
33 their wine is the poison of serpents
and the cruel venom of vipers.
34 Is not this laid up in store with Me,
sealed up in my treasuries?
35 Vengeance is mine, and recompense,
for the time when their foot shall slip;
See, the day of their calamity is at hand,
and their doom comes swiftly.

D. The Gospel: A Call to Treasure YHWH's Compassion

36 See, YHWH will champion the cause of His people
and have compassion on His servants,
when he sees that their power is gone
and there is none remaining, neither ruler nor helper.
37 Then he will say,
Where are their gods,
the rock in which they took refuge,
38 who ate the fat of their sacrifices
and drank the wine of their drink offering?

Let them rise up and help you;
let them be your protection!
[39] Pay attention, now.
See, I, even I, am He,
and there is no god beside Me;
I kill and I make alive;
I wound and I heal;
and there is none that can deliver out of my hand.
[40] See, I lift up my hand to heaven
and I say,
As I live forever!
[41] if I sharpen my flashing sword
and my hand takes hold on judgment,
I will take vengeance on my adversaries
and will repay those who hate Me.
[42] I will make my arrows drunk with blood,
and my sword shall devour flesh—
with the blood of the slain and the captives,
from the long-haired heads of the enemy.

E. The Coda: A Call to Celebrate YHWH's Deliverance [62]

[43] Rejoice, O heavens with Him,
and bow down to Him, all sons of God.
Rejoice, O nations, with His people.
And let all the angels of God strengthen themselves.
See, the blood of His sons he will avenge;
and avenge and take vengeance on His enemies.
He will pay back those who hate Him,
and atone for the land of his people.

---

62. Following LXX. See Excursus B below for a brief introduction to the text-critical issues involved. The versions are not agreed on the ending of the song. MT has a 4-cola stanza; 4QDeut[q] and Targum Neofiti 6-cola; LXX 8-cola. Scholarly consensus tends to favor the 6-cola reading. See Nelson, *Deuteronomy*, 379–80; van der Kooij, "The Ending of the Song of Moses: On the Pre-Masoretic Version of Deut 32:43," 93–100; McCarthy, *BHQ*, 152*–54*. Rofé ("The End of the Song of Moses [Deuteronomy 32:43]," 164) prefers a 4-cola reading, but different from MT:

Rejoice heavenly beings with Him
And let the divine ones exult,
for he will avenge the blood of His servants
And he will cleanse the land of His people.

Excursus B:
Text-Critical Issues
in Deuteronomy 32:43

F ROM A TEXT CRITICAL point of view, Deuteronomy 32:43 is argu-
ably the most difficult verse in the chapter, if not in the book. NIV
and most English translations follow MT in presenting a short four-line
ending to the Song. The lines themselves seem complete and the strophe
makes sense as it stands. However, even a cursory glance raises questions
as to whether or not the verse is either complete or original. The middle
two lines exhibit the kind of parallelism we have come to expect in the
Song, but the first and last lines lack corresponding cola. The situation
would have been ameliorated if lines 1 and 4 displayed some correspon-
dence, in which case the cola could have formed an *abba* pattern. But this
is not the case.

Suspicions regarding MT are reinforced by the evidence of the versions and the texts from Qumran. The evidence of MT, LXX, and Qumran
may be juxtaposed as follows:

Table 9: Text-Critical Evidence (Deuteronomy 32:43)

MT	4QDeut[q]	MS Underlying LXX[63]
	הַרְנִינוּ הַשָּׁמַיִם עִמּוֹ	הַרְנִינוּ הַשָּׁמַיִם עִמּוֹ
	וְהִשְׁתַּחֲווּ לוֹ כָּל אֱלֹהִים	וְהִשְׁתַּחֲווּ לוֹ כָּל בְּנֵי אֱלֹהִים
הַרְנִינוּ גוֹיִם עַמּוֹ		הַרְנִינוּ גוֹיִם אֶת עַמּוֹ
		וְיַחֲזְקוּ לוֹ כָּל מַלְאֲכֵי אֱלֹהִים
כִּי דַם־עֲבָדָיו יִקּוֹם	כִּי דַם־בָּנָיו יִקּוֹם	כִּי דַם־בָּנָיו יִקּוֹם
וְנָקָם יָשִׁיב לְצָרָיו	וְנָקָם יָשִׁיב לְצָרָיו	וְנָקָם וַיָּשִׁיב נָקָם לְצָרָיו
	וְלִמְשַׂנְאָיו יְשַׁלֵּם	וְלִמְשַׂנְאָיו יְשַׁלֵּם
וְכִפֶּר אַדְמָתוֹ עַמּוֹ	וַיְכַפֵּר אַדְמַת עַמּוֹ	וְכִפֶּר יְהוָה אַדְמַת עַמּוֹ

	Rejoice, O heavens with Him	Rejoice, O heavens with Him
	and bow down to him all gods.	and bow down to Him, all sons of God.
Rejoice, O nations, with his people.		Rejoice, O nations, with his people.
		And let all the angels of God strengthen themselves.
See, the blood of his servants he will avenge;	See, the blood of his sons he will avenge;	See, the blood of his sons he will avenge;
and take vengeance on his enemies.	and take vengeance on his enemies.	and avenge and take vengeance on his enemies.
	He will pay back those who hate Him;	He will pay back those who hate Him,
He will atone for his land and people.	and atone for the land of his people.	and atone for the land of his people.

To this list of versions we might add Targum Neofiti, which reads as follows:

63. LXX reads: εὐφράνθητε οὐρανοί ἅμα αὐτῷ καὶ
προσκυνησάτωσαν αὐτῷ πάντες υἱοὶ θεοῦ
εὐφράνθητε ἔθνη μετὰ τοῦ λαοῦ αὐτοῦ
καὶ ἐνισχυσάτωσαν αὐτῷ πάντες ἄγγελοι θεοῦ
ὅτι τὸ αἷμα τῶν υἱῶν αὐτοῦ ἐκδικᾶται
καὶ ἐκδικήσει καὶ ἀνταποδώσει δίκην τοῖς ἐχθροῖς
καὶ τοῖς μισοῦσιν ἀνταποδώσει
καὶ ἐκκαθαριεῖ κύριος τὴν γῆν τοῦ λαοῦ αὐτοῦ.

Acclaim before him, O you nations;
Praise him, O you his people, the house of Israel.
For he avenges the humiliations and the blood of his servants the just,
and he shall take revenge on (their) enemies.
For the sins of the people the land shall be smitten,
But in his good mercies he will make atonement for the land and for his people.

While a full discussion of the text critical issues involved in the coda is beyond the scope of this paper, we note that scholars have varied greatly in their assessment of this evidence. Some argue for retaining MT;[64] some for a reading as short as MT, but differing significantly;[65] others for a reading the length of Qumran (six-cola), but with some modifications.[66]

Although few support the eight-cola reading of a Hebrew *Vorlage* underlying LXX,[67] this reading should not be discounted too readily.[68] First, the conservative translation theory underlying LXX Pentateuch renders unlikely the suggestion that the translator created line 4 to balance line 3 or line 7 to balance line 8, or that these represent a conflated reading intent on preserving alternative textual traditions.[69]

Second, admittedly according to accepted rules of textual criticism, shorter readings tend to be preferred, while longer readings are viewed as secondary expansions for the sake of clarity. However, in this case, not only does LXX provide the more difficult reading, but it is also easier to account for the four- and six-cola readings as corruptions of an original eight-cola reading than vice versa. Given the similar openings to the coda

64. Fokkelman, *Major Poems of the Hebrew Bible*, 130-32

65. Rofé ("The End of the Song of Moses [Deuteronomy 32:43]," 164) and Phillip Marshall ("Deut 32:43 and Textual Criticism," end the Song as follows:

Rofé	Marshall
Rejoice heavenly beings with him	Ring out for joy, O heavens, with him
And let the divine ones exult,	And bow down to him, all gods.
for he will avenge the blood of him servants	For he will exact vengeance on the blood of his sons,
And he will cleanse the land of him people.	And he will make expiation for the land of his people.

66. Nelson, *Deuteronomy*, 379–80; van der Kooij, "The Ending of the Song of Moses," 93–100; McCarthy, *BHQ*, 152*–54*.

67. See Albright, "New Light on Early Recensions of the Hebrew Bible," 27–33. English translations reflect these differences in scholarly opinion. NAS and NIV follow MT; NRS, ESV and NLT follow the six–cola reading.

68. So also Jason S. DeRouchie, in personal communication, which triggered some of the observations that follow.

69. Cf. Tov, *Textual Criticism of the Hebrew Bible*, 241.

in MT and 4QDeut[q] it is easy to imagine that a scribe's eye skipped from הַרְנִינוּ in line 1 of the *Vorlage* to LXX to line 3 (homoeoarkton, "similar beginning"), resulting in the omission of the first two lines of the original coda. As for line 4 of LXX, with its reference to heavenly beings, this line may have been dropped by a Jewish scribe responsible for MT for theological reasons, perhaps in association with the change of בְּנֵי אֱלֹהִים, "sons of God," to בְּנֵי יִשְׂרָאֵל, "sons of Israel," in verse 8. It is difficult to explain why line 7 of LXX would have been dropped by MT. Perhaps the scribe wished to keep an even number of lines or to preserve a total of 140 cola for the Song (70 lines, corresponding to the seventy sons of Israel who went down into Egypt) (Deut 10:22).[70]

Third, this interpretation is reinforced by the clear echo of the Hebrew underlying line 2 of LXX we hear in Psalm 97:7, הִשְׁתַּחֲווּ־לוֹ כָּל־אֱלֹהִים, "Bow down to him all gods," which in turn is cited in Hebrews 1:6, Καὶ προσκυνησάτωσαν αὐτῷ πάντες ἄγγελοι θεοῦ, "And bow to him all angels of God."[71] Fourth, to demonstrate the inclusion of the Gentiles in the eschatological people of God in Romans 15:10, Paul quotes the third line of Deuteronomy 32:43 LXX verbatim as Scripture: Εὐφράνθητε, ἔθνη, μετὰ τοῦ λαοῦ αὐτοῦ, "Rejoice, O Gentiles with his people."[72] Significantly Paul prefaces this citation with καὶ πάλιν λέγει, "And again it says," the assumed subject being ἡ γραφή, "the Scriptures."[73] Apparently he deemed the LXX version of Deuteronomy 32:43 to be authoritative Scripture.

70. Thus van der Kooij, "The Ending," 100; McCarthy, *BHQ*, 153*–54*.

71. Psalm 96:6 LXX reads, προσκυνήσατε αὐτῷ πάντες οἱ ἄγγελοι αὐτοῦ, "Bow down to him all his angels"; cf. Deut 32:43b, καὶ προσκυνησάτωσαν αὐτῷ πάντες υἱοὶ θεοῦ.

72. It is possible that the immediate inspiration for this quotation came from Ode 2:43, the second of fourteen odes collected and place immediately after the Psalms in LXX[A]. On these odes, see Bell, *Provoked to Jealousy*, 229–30. For a discussion of Romans 15:10, see ibid., 259–62. According to Wevers, *Notes on the Greek Text of Deuteronomy*, 534, LXX translates line 1 of MT incorrectly: "The Hi verb is addressed to the nations גוים/ἔθνη, but the Hebrew verb has עמו, "his people" as a verbal modifier, thus "make his people ring out (for joy)." LXX plays on עמו in a double entendre, as עם, "with," and עם, "people," so μετὰ τοῦ λαοῦ αὐτοῦ.

73. Cf. Rom 4:3; 9:17; 10:11; 11:2. Similarly Bell, *Provoked to Jealousy*, 259.

Bibliography

Ackerman, Susan. "The Personal is Political: Covenantal and Affectionate Love (*āhēb, āhăbâ*) in the Hebrew Bible." *Vetus Testamentum* 52 (2002) 437–58.

Aland, K. et al. *Novum Testamentum Graece et Latine.* 26th ed. Stuttgart: Deutsche Bibelgesellschaft, 1986.

Albertz, Rainer. *A History of Israelite Religion in the Old Testament Period.* Translated by J. Bowden. 2 vols. OTL. Louisville: Westminster John Knox, 1994.

Albright, W. F. "Discussion." In *City Invincible: A Symposium on Urbanization and Cultural Development in the Ancient Near East,* edited by C. H. Kraeling and R. M. Adams, 94–123. Chicago: University of Chicago Press, 1960.

———. *From Stone Age to Christianity: Monotheism and the Historical Process.* 2nd ed. Garden City, NY: Doubleday, 1957.

———. *YHWH and the Gods of Canaan: A Historical Analysis of Two Contrasting Faiths.* Garden City, NY: Doubleday, 1968.

Allen, David M. "Deuteronomic Re-presentation in a Word of Exhortation: An Assessment of the Paraenetic Function of Deuteronomy in the letter to the Hebrews." PhD diss., University of Edinburgh, 2007.

Allen, Leslie C. *Psalms 101–150.* Word Biblical Commentary 21. Waco, TX: Word, 1983.

Alt, Albrecht. "The Origins of Israelite Law." In *Essays in Old Testament History and Religion,* translated by R. A. Wilson, 101–71. Garden City, NY: Doubleday, 1967.

Alter, Robert. *The Art of Biblical Poetry.* New York: Basic, 1987.

Amir, Y. "The Decalogue according to Philo." In *The Ten Commandments in History and Tradition,* edited by Ben-Zion Segal, 121–60. Jerusalem: Magnes, 1990.

Andersen, Francis I. *The Hebrew Verbless Clause in the Pentateuch.* Journal of Biblical Literature Monograph Series 14. Nashville: Abingdon, 1970.

Arnold, Bill T. "Deuteronomy as the *Ipsissima Vox* of Moses." *Journal of Theological Interpretation* 4 (2010) 53–74.

Austin, J. L. *How to Do Things with Words.* 2nd ed. Edited by J. O. Urmson and M. Sbisà. Cambridge: Harvard University Press, 1975.

Averbeck, Richard E. "זבח." In *New International Dictionary of Old Testament Theology & Exegesis.* Edited by Willem VanGemeren, 1:1066–73. Grand Rapids: Zondervan, 1997.

———. "מִנְחָה." In *New International Dictionary of Old Testament Theology & Exegesis.* Edited by Willem VanGemeren, 2:978–90. Grand Rapids: Zondervan, 1997.

———. "עֹלָה." In *New International Dictionary of Old Testament Theology & Exegesis.* Edited by Willem VanGemeren, 3:407–15. Grand Rapids: Zondervan, 1997.

———. "שֶׁלֶם." In *New International Dictionary of Old Testament Theology & Exegesis.* Edited by Willem VanGemeren, 4:135–43. Grand Rapids: Zondervan, 1997.

Avigad, N. "Jerahmeel and Baruch." *Biblical Archaeologist* 42 (1979) 114–18.

Baillet, M. *Les "Petites Grottes" de Qumrân. Exploration de la falaise. Les grottes 2Q, 3Q, 5Q, 6Q, 7Q à 10Q.* Discoveries in the Judaean Desert 3. Oxford: Clarendon, 1962.

Baltzer, Klaus. *The Covenant Formulary: In Old Testament, Jewish, and Early Christian Writings.* Philadelphia: Fortress, 1971.

Baly, D. "The Geography of Monotheism." In *Translating and Understanding the Old Testament: Essays in Honor of Herbert Gordon May,* edited by H. T. Frank and W. L. Reed, 253–78. Nashville: Abingdon, 1970.

Barr, James. *The Concept of Biblical Theology: An Old Testament Perspective.* Minneapolis: Fortress, 1999.

Bass, B. M., editor. *Stogdill's Handbook of Leadership.* Rev. ed. New York: Free, 1981.

Beale, G. K. *The Book of Revelation.* New International Greek Testament Commentary. Grand Rapids: Eerdmans, 1999.

Beckman, Gary. *Hittite Diplomatic Texts.* Edited by Harry A. Hoffner Jr. 2nd ed. Writings from the Ancient World 7. Atlanta: Scholars, 1999.

Bell, Richard H. "Deuteronomy 32 and the Origin of the Jealousy Motif in Romans 9–11." In *Provoked to Jealousy: The Origin and Purpose of the Jealousy Motif in Romans 9–11,* 200–85. Wissenschaftliche Untersuchungen zum Neuen Testament 2/63. Tübingen: Mohr (Siebeck), 1994.

Bennis, Warren G. "About the Teal Trust." No pages. Online: http://www.teal.org.uk/about.htm.

———. "Leadership Theory and Administrative Behavior: The Problems of Authority." *Administrative Science Quarterly* 4 (1959) 259–301.

Benz, F. L. *Personal Names in the Phoenician and Punic Inscriptions.* Studia Pohl 8. Rome: Pontifical Biblical Institute, 1972.

Bergen, Robert D. "Preaching Old Testament Law." In *Reclaiming the Prophetic Mantle: Preaching the Old Testament Faithfully,* edited by G. L. Klein, 51–69. Nashville: Broadman, 1992.

Bergey, R. "The Song of Moses (Deuteronomy 32.1–43) and Isaianic Prophecies: A Case of Early Intertextuality?" *Journal for the Study of the Old Testament* 28 (2003) 33–54.

Berlin, A., and M. Z. Brettler. *The Jewish Study Bible.* Oxford: Oxford University Press, 2004.

Berry, R. J. *The Care of Creation: Focusing Concern and Action.* Downers Grove, IL: InterVarsity, 2000.

———, editor. *Environmental Stewardship: Critical Perspectives—Past and Present.* New York: Continuum, 2006.

Betz, O. "στίγμα." In *Theological Dictionary of the New Testament.* Edited by G. Kittel and G. Friedrich, and translated by G. W. Bromiley, 7:657–64. Grand Rapids: Eerdmans, 1971.

Blenkinsopp, J. *The Pentateuch: An Introduction to the First Five Books of the Bible.* New York: Doubleday, 1992.

———. *Prophecy and Canon: A Contribution to the Study of Jewish Origins.* South Bend, IN: University of Notre Dame Press, 1977.

Block, Daniel I. *The Book of Ezekiel Chapters 1–24.* New International Commentary on the Old Testament. Grand Rapids: Eerdmans, 1997.

———. *The Book of Ezekiel Chapters 25–48.* New International Commentary on the Old Testament. Grand Rapids: Eerdmans, 1998.

———. *Deuteronomy.* New International Version Application Commentary. Grand Rapids: Zondervan, forthcoming.

———. "Divine Abandonment: Ezekiel's Adaptation of an Ancient Near Eastern Motif." In *Perspectives on Ezekiel: Theology and Anthropology*, edited by Margaret S. Odell and John T. Strong, 15–42. Society of Biblical Literature Symposium Series 9. Atlanta: Scholars, 2000.

———. *The Gods of the Nations: Studies in Ancient Near Eastern National Theology.* Rev. ed. Evangelical Theological Society Monographs. Grand Rapids: Baker, 2000.

———. *The Gospel according to Moses: Theological and Ethical Reflections on the Book of Deuteronomy.* Eugene, OR: Cascade, forthcoming (2012).

———. "Leadership, Leader, Old Testament." In *New Interpreter's Dictionary of the Bible.* Edited by K. D. Sakenfeld, 3:620–26. Nashville: Abingdon, 2008.

———. "Marriage and Family in Ancient Israel." In *Marriage and Family in the Biblical World,* edited by K. Campbell, 33–102. Downers Grove, IL: InterVarsity, 2003.

———. "My Servant David: Ancient Israel's Vision of the Messiah." In *Israel's Messiah in the Bible and the Dead Sea Scrolls,* edited by Richard. S. Hess and M. Daniel Carroll R., 17–56. Grand Rapids: Baker, 2003.

———. "Nations." In *New International Dictionary of Old Testament Theology & Exegesis.* Edited by Willem VanGemeren, 4:966–72. Grand Rapids: Zondervan, 1997.

———. "Sojourner; Alien; Stranger." In *International Standard Bible Encyclopedia.* Rev. ed. Edited by G. W. Bromiley, 4:561–64. Grand Rapids: Eerdmans, 1988.

———. "To Serve and to Keep: Toward a Biblical Understanding of Humanity's Responsibility in the Face of the Biodiversity Crisis." In *Keeping God's Earth: Creation Care and the Global Environment,* edited by Daniel I. Block and Noah J. Toly, 116–42. Downers Grove, IL: InterVarsity, 2010.

———. "Unspeakable Crimes: The Abuse of Women in the Book of Judges." *The Southern Baptist Theological Journal* 2 (1998) 46–55.

———. "Who do Commentators say 'the Lord' is? The Scandalous Rock of Romans 10:13." In *On the Writing of New Testament Commentaries. Festschrift for Grant R. Osborne on the Occasion of His 70th Birthday,* edited by Stanley E. Porter and Eckhard J. Schnabel. Leiden: Brill, forthcoming (2012).

Blum, E. *Studien zur Komposition des Pentateuch.* Beihefte zur Zeitschrift für die alttestamentliche Wissenschaft 189. Berlin: de Gruyter, 1990.

Bord, L. J., and D. Hamidović. "Écoute Israël (Deut. VI 4)." *Vetus Testamentum* 52 (2002) 13–29.

Borowski, O. *Every Living Thing: Daily Use of Animals in Ancient Israel.* Walnut Creek, CA: AltaMira, 1998.

Boston, James R. "The Song of Moses: Deuteronomy 32:1–43." PhD diss., Union Theological Seminary, 1966.

———. "The Wisdom Influence upon the Song of Moses." *Journal of Biblical Literature* 87 (1968) 198–202.

Botterweck, G. J., and H. Ringgren, editors. *Theological Dictionary of the Old Testament.* Translated by J. T. Willis, G. W. Bromiley, and D. E. Green. 15 vols. Grand Rapids: Eerdmans, 1974–.

Bouma-Prediger, S. *For the Beauty of the Earth: A Christian Vision for Creation Care.* Grand Rapids: Baker, 2001.

Braulik, Georg. "Commemoration of Passion and Feast of Joy." In *The Theology of Deuteronomy: Collected Essays of Georg Braulik, O.S.B.* Translated by U. Lindblad, 67–85. Bibal Collected Essays 2. N. Richmond Hills, TX: Bibal, 1994.

———. "Die Abfolge der Gesetze in Deuteronomium 12–26 und der Dekalog." In *Das Deuteronomium: Entstehung, Gestalt und Botschaft,* edited by N. Lohfink, 252–72. Bibliotheca ephemeridum theologicarum Lovaniensium 68. Leuven: Leuven University Press, 1985.

———. *Die deuteronomischen Gesetze und der Dekalog.* Stuttgarter Bibelstudien 145. Stuttgart: Katholisches Bibelwerk, 1991.

———. "Deuteronomium 4,13 und der Horebbund. " In *Für immer verbündet: Studien zur Bundestheologie der Bibel,* edited by Christoph Domen and Christian Frevel. Stuttgart: Katholisches Bibelwerk, 2007.

———. "Gesetz als Evangelium: Rechtfertigung und Begnadigung nach der deuteronomischen Tora." *Zeitschrift für Theologie und Kirche* 79 (1982) 127–60.

———. "The Joy of the Feast." In *The Theology of Deuteronomy: Collected Essays of Georg Braulik.* Translated by U. Lindblad, 27–65. Bibal Collected Essays 2. N. Richland Hills, TX: Bibal, 1994.

———. "Law as Gospel: Justification and Pardon according to the Deuteronomic Torah." *Interpretation* 38 (1984) 5–14.

———. "The Sequence of the Laws in Deuteronomy 12–26." In *A Song of Power and the Power of Song: Essays on the Book of Deuteronomy,* edited by D. L. Christensen, translated by L. M. Maloney, 313–35. Studies in Biblical Theology 3. Winona Lake, IN: Eisenbrauns, 1993.

———. "Wisdom, Divine Presence and Law: Reflections on the Kerygma of Deut 4:5–8." In *The Theology of Deuteronomy: Collected Essays of Georg Braulik, O.S.B.* Translated by U. Lindblad, 1–25. Bibal Collected Essays 2. N. Richmond Hills, TX: Bibal, 1994.

Braulik, G., and N. Lohfink. "Deuteronomium 1,5 באר את־התורה הזאת: 'er verlieh dieser Tora Rechstkraft.'" In *Textarbeit: Studien zu Texten und ihrer Rezeption aus dem Alten Testament und der Umwelt Israels:Festschrift für Peter Weimar zur Vollendung seines 60. Lebensjahres mit Beiträgen von Freunden, Schülern und Kollegen,* edited by K. Kiesow and T. Meurer, 35–51. Alter Orient und Altes Testament 294. Münster: Ugarit, 2003.

Breuer, Mordechai. "Dividing the Decalogue into Verses and Commands." In *The Ten Commandments in History and Tradition,* edited by Ben-Zion Segal and Gershon Levi, 291–330. Jerusalem: Magnes, 1990.

Brichto, H. C. *Toward a Grammar of Biblical Poetics.* Oxford: Oxford University Press, 1992.

Briggs, C. A. *A Critical and Exegetical Commentary on the Book of Psalms.* International Critical Commentary. Edinburgh: T. & T. Clark, 1907.

Briggs, Richard S. "Speech-Act Theory." In *Dictionary for Theological Interpretation of the Bible,* edited by K. J. Vanhoozer et al., 763–66. Grand Rapids: Baker, 2005.

———. *Words in Action: Speech Act Theory and Biblical Interpretation: Toward a Hermeneutic of Self-Involvement.* Edinburgh: T. & T. Clark, 2001.

Brinkman, John A. et al. "*sikiltu.*" *The Assyrian Dictionary of the Oriental Institute of the University of Chicago.* Vol. 15, 244–45. Chicago: University of Chicago Press, 1956.

Bristow, M. J., editor. *National Anthems of the World.* 11th ed. London: Weidenfeld & Nicholson, 2006.

Britt, Brian M. "Deuteronomy 31–32 as a Textual Memorial." *Biblical Interpretation* 8 (2000) 358–74.

———. *Rewriting Moses: The Narrative Eclipse of the Text.* Journal for the Study of the Old Testament Supplement Series 402. Gender, Culture, Theory 14. London: T. & T. Clark, 2005.

Bronner, L. *The Stories of Elijah and Elisha as Polemics against Baal Worship*. Leiden: Brill, 1968.

Brown, F., S. R. Driver, and C. A. Briggs. *A Hebrew and English Lexicon of the Old Testament*. Oxford: Clarendon, 1907.

Brown, W. P., editor. *The Ten Commandments: The Reciprocity of Faithfulness*. Louisville: Westminster John Knox, 2004.

Bulmer, R. "The Uncleanness of the Birds of Leviticus and Deuteronomy." *Man* 24 (1989) 304–21.

Burkitt, F. C. "The Hebrew Papyrus of the Ten Commandments." *Jewish Quarterly Review* 15 (1903) 392–408.

Calvin, John. *Commentaries on the Four Last Books of Moses*. Translated by Charles William Bingham. Grand Rapids: Eerdmans, 1950.

———. *Institutes of the Christian Religion*. Edited by J. T. McNeill. Library of Christian Classics. London: SCM, 1961.

———. *John Calvin's Sermons on the Ten Commandments*. Edited and translated by B. W. Farley. Grand Rapids: Baker, 1980.

Cassuto, Umberto. *A Commentary on the Book of Exodus*. Translated by I. Abrahams. Jerusalem: Magnes, 1967.

———. "The Prophet Hosea and the Books of the Pentateuch." In *Biblical and Oriental Studies*. Vol. 1, 79–100. Jerusalem: Magnes, 1973.

———. "The Song of Moses (Deuteronomy Chapter xxxii 1–43)." In *Biblical and Oriental Studies*. Vol. 1, 41–46 Jerusalem: Magnes, 1973.

Chan, Kim-Kwong. "You Shall Not Eat These Abominable Things: An Examination of Different Interpretations on Deuteronomy 14:3–20." *East Asia Journal of Theology* 3 (1985) 95–104.

Chaney, M. L. "'Coveting Your Neighbor's House' in Social Context." In *The Ten Commandments: The Reciprocity of Faithfulness*, edited by W. P. Brown, 302–18. Louisville: Westminster John Knox, 2004.

Chapman, David W. "Marriage and Family in Second Temple Judaism." In *Marriage and Family in the Biblical World*, edited by K. M. Campbell, 183–239. Downers Grove, IL: InterVarsity, 2003.

Childs, Brevard S. *The Book of Exodus: A Critical Theological Commentary*. Old Testament Library. Philadelphia: Westminster, 1974.

———. *Introduction to the Old Testament as Scripture*. Philadelphia: Fortress, 1985.

Christensen, Duane L. *Deuteronomy 21:10—34:12*. Word Biblical Commentary 6B. Nashville: Nelson, 2002.

Christensen, Duane L., and M. Narucki. "The Mosaic Authorship of the Pentateuch." *Journal of the Evangelical Theological Society* 32 (1989) 465–71.

Clarke, Ernest G. *Targum Pseudo-Jonathan: Deuteronomy*. Aramaic Bible 5B. Collegeville, MN: Liturgical, 1998.

Clines, David J. A. "The Ten Commandments, Reading from Left to Right." In *Interested Parties: The Ideology of Writers and Readers in the Hebrew Bible*, 25–48. Journal for the Study of the Old Testament Supplement Series 205. Sheffield: Sheffield Academic Press, 2009.

———. "The Ten Commandments, Reading from Left to Right." In *Words Remembered, Texts Renewed: Essays in Honour of John F. A. Sawyer*, edited by J. H. G. Davies and W. G. E. Watson, 96–112. Journal for the Study of the Old Testament Supplement Series 195. Sheffield: Sheffield Academic Press, 1995.

———, editor. *Dictionary of Classical Hebrew*. 7 vols. to date. Sheffield: Sheffield Academic Press, 1993–.

Coats, George W. *Moses: Heroic Man, Man of God.* Journal for the Study of the Old Testament Supplement Series 57. Sheffield: JSOT Press, 1988.

Cogan, M., and H. Tadmor. *II Kings: A New Translation with Introduction and Commentary.* Anchor Bible 11. Garden City, NY: Doubleday, 1988.

Collon, D. *The Seal Impressions from Tell Atchana/Alalakh.* Alter Orient und Altes Testament 27. Neukirchen-Vluyn: Neukirchener, 1975.

Coogan, M. D., editor. *The New Oxford Annotated Bible.* 3rd ed. Oxford: Oxford University Press, 2001.

Cowley, A. E., editor. *Aramaic Papyri of the Fifth Century B.C.* London: Clarendon, 1923.

Craig, J. A. *Assyrian and Babylonian Religious Texts.* Vol. 1. Leipzig: Hinrichs, 1895.

Craigie, Peter C. *The Book of Deuteronomy.* New International Commentary on the Old Testament. Grand Rapids: Eerdmans, 1976.

———. "The Comparison of Hebrew Poetry: Psalm 104 in the Light of Egyptian and Ugaritic Poetry." *Semitics* 4 (1974) 10–21.

Cribb, Bryan H. *Speaking on the Brink of Sheol: Form and Message of Old Testament Death Stories.* Piscataway, NJ: Gorgias, 2009.

Crüsemann, F. *Bewahrung der Freiheit: Das Thema des Dekalogs in sozialgeschichtlicher Perspektive.* Kaiser Traktate 78. München: Kaiser, 1983.

———. *The Torah: Theology and Social History of Old Testament Law.* Translated by A. W. Mahnke. Minneapolis: Fortress, 1996.

Curtis, Edward M. "Idol, Idolatry." In *Anchor Bible Dictionary*, edited by D. N. Freedman, 3:376–81. Garden City, NY: Doubleday, 1992.

Dahood, M. "Yahweh our God is the Unique." In *Ras Shamra Parallels*, edited by L. R. Fisher et al. Vol. 1. Analecta orientalia 49. Rome: Pontifical Biblical Institute, 1972.

Dandamaev, Muhammad A. *Slavery in Babylonia: From Nabopolassar to Alexander the Great (626–331 B.C.).* Edited by M. A. Powell and D. B. Weisberg, and translated by V. A. Powell. DeKalb, IL: Northern Illinois University Press, 1984.

Davidson, R. "Which Torah Laws Should Gentile Christians Obey? The Relationship between Leviticus 17–18 and Acts 15." Paper presented to the Evangelical Theological Society, San Diego, November 15, 2007.

Davies, Graham. "A Samaritan Inscription with an Expanded Text of the Shema." *Palestine Exploration Quarterly* 131 (1999) 3–19.

Day, J. "New Light on the Mythological Background of the Allusion to Resheph in Habakkuk III 5." *Vetus Testamentum* 29 (1979) 259–74.

De Wette, W. M. L. "Dissertatio critico-exegetica qua Deuteronomium a propribus pentateuchi libris diversum, alius cuiusdam recentioris auctoris opus esse monstratur." PhD diss., Jena University, 1805.

DeRouchie, Jason S. *A Call to Covenant Love: Text Grammar and Literary Structure in Deuteronomy 5–11.* Gorgias Dissertations 30. Piscataway, NJ: Gorgias, 2007.

Dick, M. B. "Worshiping Idols: What Isaiah Didn't Know." *Bible Review* 18.2 (2002) 30–37.

Dietrich, Manfried et al. *The Cuneiform Alphabetic Texts: From Ugarit, Ras Ibn Hani and Other Places (KTU).* Munster: Ugarit, 1995.

Dijkstra, Meindert. "Moses, the Man of God." In *The Interpretation of Exodus: Studies in Honour of Cornelis Houtman*, edited by Riemer Roukema, 17–36. Biblical Exegesis and Theology 44. Leuven: Peeters, 2006.

Donbaz, V. "An Old Assyrian Treaty from Kültepe." *Journal of Cuneiform Studies* 57 (2005) 63–68.

Donner, H., and W. Röllig. *Kanaanäische und aramäische Inschriften.* 2nd ed. 3 vols. Wiesbaden: Harrassowitz, 1966–69.

Douglas, J. D., editor. *The Illustrated Bible Dictionary.* 3 vols. Downers Grove, IL: InterVarsity, 1980.

Douglas, Mary. *Purity and Danger: An Analysis of the Concepts of Pollution and Taboo.* New York: Ark, 1984.

Driver, S. R. *A Critical and Exegetical Commentary on Deuteronomy.* International Critical Commentary. Edinburgh: T. & T. Clark, 1902.

Drucker, P. "Forward: Not Enough Generals Were Killed." In *The Leader of the Future,* edited by F. Hesselbein, M. Goldsmith, and R. Beckhard, vii. San Francisco: Jossey-Bass, 1996.

Duff, J. "Should the Ten Commandments Be Posted in the Public Realm? Why the Bible and the Constitution Say, 'No.'" In *The Ten Commandments: Reciprocity of Faithfulness,* edited by W. P. Brown, 159–70. Louisville: Westminster John Knox, 2004.

Dunn, James D. G. *Christology in the Making: An Inquiry into the Origins of the Doctrine of the Incarnation.* London: SCM, 1980.

Durham, John I. *Exodus.* Word Biblical Commentary 3. Waco, TX: Word, 1987.

Eissfeldt, O. *Das Lied Moses Deuteronomium 32 1–43 und das Lehrgedicht Asaphs Psalm 78 samt einer Analyse der Umgebung des Mose-Liedes.* Beihefte zur Zeitschrift für die alttestamentliche Wissenschaft 104/5. Berlin: Akademie, 1958.

Exum, J. Cheryl, and H. G. M. Williamson. *Reading from Right to Left: Essays in Honour of David J. A. Clines.* London: Sheffield Academic Press, 2003.

Falk, Ze'ev W. *Hebrew Law in Biblical Times.* 2nd ed. Provo, UT: Brigham Young University Press, 2001.

Finsterbusch, Karin. "Bezüge zwischen Aussagen von Dtn 6,4–9 und 6,10–25." *Zeitschrift für die alttestamentliche Wissenschaft* 114 (2002) 433–37.

Firmage, Edwin. "Zoology (Animal Profiles)." In *Anchor Bible Dictionary,* edited by D. N. Freedman, 6:1136–37. Garden City, NY: Doubleday, 1992.

Fishbane, M. *Biblical Interpretation in Ancient Israel.* Oxford: Clarendon, 1985.

Fleming, Daniel E. "The Etymological Origins of the Hebrew *nābî*': The One Who Invokes God." *Catholic Biblical Quarterly* 55 (1993) 217–24.

———. *The Installation of Baal's High Priestess at Emar.* Harvard Semitic Studies 42. Atlanta: Scholars, 1992.

Fokkelman, J. P. *Major Poems of the Hebrew Bible: At the Interface of Hermeneutics and Structural Analysis.* Vol. 1, *Ex. 15, Deut. 32, and Job 3.* Studia Semitica Neerlandica. Assen, the Netherlands: Van Gorcum, 1998.

Follingstad, C. M. *Deictic Viewpoint in Biblical Hebrew Text: A Syntagmatic and Paradigmatic Analysis of the Particle* כי. Dallas: SIL, 2001.

Ford, J. Massyngberde. *Revelation: A New Translation with Introduction and Commentary.* Anchor Bible 38. Garden City, NY: Doubleday, 1975.

Fossum, Jarl E. "Son of God." In *Dictionary of Deities and Demons in the Bible,* edited by K. van der Toorn, B. Becking, and P. W. van der Horst, 788–94. Rev. ed. Leiden: Brill, 1999.

Foster, B. R. "Animals in Mesopotamian Literature." In *A History of the Animal World in the Ancient Near East,* edited by B. J. Collins, 271–88. Handbuch der Orientalistik I/64. Leiden: Brill, 2002.

———. *Before the Muses: An Anthology of Akkadian Literature.* 2 vols. Bethesda, MD: CDL, 1993.

Foster, Paul. "Why did Matthew get the *Shema* wrong? A Study of Matthew 22:37." *Journal of Biblical Literature* 133 (2003) 309–33.

Foster, Richard J. *The Challenge of the Disciplined Life: Christian Reflections on Money, Sex & Power.* Rev. ed. San Francisco: Harper & Row, 1989.

Fox, Michael V. *Character and Ideology in the Book of Esther.* Columbia, SC: University of South Carolina Press, 1991.

Freedman, D. N. "Israel's Response in Hosea 2:17b: 'You are my Husband.'" *Journal of Biblical Literature* 99 (1980) 199–204.

———. *The Nine Commandments: Uncovering the Pattern of Crime and Punishment in the Hebrew Bible.* New York: Doubleday, 2000.

———. "Pentateuch." In *The Interpreter's Dictionary of the Bible*, edited by G. A. Buttrick, 3:711–27. Nashville: Abingdon, 1964.

Freedman, Mordechai A. "Israel's Response in Hosea 2:17b: 'You are My Husband.'" *Journal of Biblical Literature* 99 (1980) 199–204.

Fritz, Volkmar. "Temple Architecture: What Can Archaeology Tell Us about Solomon's Temple?" *Biblical Archaeology Review* 13.4 (1987) 38–49.

Fyall, R. S. *Now My Eyes See You: Images of Creation and Evil in the Book of Job.* New Studies in Biblical Theology 12. Downers Grove, IL: InterVarsity, 2002.

Geisler, Norman L., editor. *Inerrancy.* Grand Rapids: Zondervan, 1979.

Geller, Stephen. *Parallelism in Early Biblical Poetry.* Missoula, MT: Scholars, 1979.

Gerstenberger, E. "תעב *tʿb*, pi. to abhor." In *Theological Lexicon of the Old Testament*, edited by E. Jenni and C. Westermann, and translated by M. E. Biddle, 3:1428–31. Peabody, MA: Hendrickson, 1997.

———. *Wesen und Herkunft des "Apodiktischen Rechts."* Wissenschaftliche Monographien zum Alten und Neuen Testament 20. Neukirchen-Vluyn: Neukirchener, 1965.

Gibson, J. C. L. *Textbook of Syrian Semitic Inscriptions.* Vol. 2, *Aramaic Inscriptions.* Oxford: Clarendon, 1975.

Gile, J. "Ezekiel 16 and the Song of Moses: A Prophetic Transformation?" *Journal of Biblical Literature* 130 (2011) 87–108.

Giles, Terry, and William J. Doan. *Twice Used Songs: Performance Criticism of the Songs of Ancient Israel.* Peabody, MA: Hendrickson, 2009.

Goldingay, J. *Daniel.* Word Biblical Commentary 30. Dallas: Word, 1989.

Goody, J. *The Logic of Writing and the Organization of Society.* Cambridge: Cambridge University Press, 1986.

Gordon, Cyrus H. "His Name is 'One.'" *Journal of Near Eastern Studies* 29 (1970) 198–99.

Gosse, B. "Deutéronome 32,1–43 et les redaction des livre d'Ezéchiel et d'Isaïe." *Zeitschrift für die alttestamentliche Wissenschaft* 107 (1995) 110–17.

Gottlieb, R. S. *A Greener Faith: Religious Environmentalism and Our Planet's Future.* Oxford: Oxford University Press, 2006.

Gowan, Donald E. *Theology of the Prophetic Books: The Death and Resurrection of Israel.* Louisville: Westminster John Knox, 1998.

Grant, Jamie A. *The King as Exemplar: The Function of Deuteronomy's Kingship Law in the Shaping of the Book of Psalms.* Atlanta: Society of Biblical Literature, 2004.

Greenberg, Moshe. "Biblical Reality toward Power: Ideal and Reality in Law and Prophets." In *Religion and Law: Biblical-Judaic and Islamic Perspectives*, edited by E. B. Firmage et al., 101–12. Winona Lake, IN: Eisenbrauns, 1990.

———. "Decalogue (The Ten Commandments)." In *Encyclopaedia Judaica.* 2nd ed. Edited by Fred Skolnik, 5:520–25. Farmington Hills, MI: Gale, 2007.

———. "Hebrew *segulla*: Akkadian *sikiltu*." *Journal of the American Oriental Society* 71 (1951) 172–74.

————. "The Vision of Jerusalem in Ezekiel 8–11: A Holistic Interpretation." In *The Divine Helmsman: Studies on God's Control of Human Events*. Festschrift Lou H. Silverman, edited by J. L. Crenshaw and S. Sandmel, 143–64. New York: Ktav, 1980.

Grisanti, M. A. "שָׁקַץ." In *New International Dictionary of Old Testament Theology & Exegesis*, edited by Willem VanGemeren, 5:243–46. Grand Rapids: Zondervan, 1997.

Gröndahl, F. *Die Personnenamen der Texte aus Ugarit*. Studia Pohl 1. Rome: Pontifical Biblical Institute, 1967.

Grosheide, F. W. *Commentary on the First Epistle to the Corinthians*. New International Commentary on the New Testament. Grand Rapids: Eerdmans, 1953.

Grudem, Wayne. *Systematic Theology: An Introduction to Biblical Doctrine*. Grand Rapids: Zondervan, 1994.

Guest, Steven Ward. "Deuteronomy 26:16–19 as the Central Focus." PhD diss., Southern Baptist Theological Seminary, 2009.

Guinness, Os, and John Seel, editors. *No God but God: Breaking with the Idols of Our Age*. Chicago: Moody, 1992.

Gutbrod, W. "νόμος." In *Theological Dictionary of the New Testament*, edited by G. Kittel, and translated by G. W. Bromiley, 4:1022–91. Grand Rapids: Eerdmans, 1967.

Hafemann, Scott J. *Paul, Moses, and the History of Israel: The Letter / Spirit Contrast and the Argument from Scripture in 2 Corinthians 3*. Tübingen: Mohr (Siebeck), 1995.

Hague, S. T. "אָרוֹן." In *New International Dictionary of Old Testament Theology & Exegesis*, edited by Willem VanGemeren, 1:500–10. Grand Rapids: Zondervan, 1997.

Hallo, W. W., and K. L. Younger, editors. *The Context of Scripture*. 3 Vols. Leiden: Brill, 1997–2002.

Hamilton, G. J. "Alphabet." Unpublished and undated paper.

————. "Development of the Early Alphabet." PhD diss., Harvard University, 1985.

Haran, Menahem. "Book-Scrolls in Israel in Pre-Exilic Times." *Journal of Jewish Studies* 33 (1982) 161–73.

————. "Seething a Kid in Its Mother's Milk." *Journal of Jewish Studies* 30 (1979) 23–35.

Harrelson, Walter J. *The Ten Commandments and Human Rights*. Rev. ed. Macon, GA: Mercer University Press, 1997.

Harrison, R. K. *Introduction to the Old Testament*. Grand Rapids: Eerdmans, 1969.

Hartley, John E. "Clean and Unclean." In *International Standard Bible Encyclopedia*. Rev. ed. Edited by G. W. Bromiley, 1:718–23. Grand Rapids: Eerdmans, 1979.

————. *Leviticus*. Word Biblical Commentary 4. Dallas: Word, 1992.

Hartman, L. F., and S. D. Sperling. "God, Names of." In *Encyclopaedia Judaica*. 2nd ed. Edited by F. Skolnik, 7:672–76. Farmington Hills, MI: Gale, 2007.

Hartsock, Nancy C. M. *Money, Sex, and Power: Toward a Feminist Historical Materialism*. New York: Longman, 1983.

Hasel, G. "The Polemic Nature of the Genesis Cosmology." *Evangelical Quarterly* 46 (1974) 81–102.

Healey, J. F. "Dagon." In *Dictionary of Deities and Demons in the Bible*, edited by K. van der Toorn, B. Becking, and P. W. van der Horst, 216–19. Rev. ed. Leiden: Brill, 1999.

————. "Tirash תירוש." In *Dictionary of Deities and Demons in the Bible*, edited by K. van der Toorn, B. Becking, and P. W. van der Horst, 871–72. Rev. ed. Leiden: Brill, 1999.

Heidel, A. *The Babylonian Genesis*. 2nd ed. Chicago: University of Chicago Press, 1954.

Herrmann, W. "El." In *Dictionary of Deities and Demons in the Bible*, edited by K. van der Toorn, B. Becking, and P. W. van der Horst, 274–80. Rev. ed. Leiden: Brill, 1999.

————. "Jahwe und des Menschen Liebe zu ihm zu Dtn. VI 4." *Vetus Testamentum* 50 (2000) 47–54.

————. "Rider Upon the Clouds." In *Dictionary of Deities and Demons in the Bible*, edited by K. van der Toorn, B. Becking, and P. W. van der Horst, 703–5. Rev. ed. Leiden: Brill, 1999.

Hess, Richard S. *Amarna Personal Names.* American School of Oriental Research Dissertation Series 9. Winona Lake, IN: Eisenbrauns, 1996.

Hill, A. E. "רָמַס." In *New International Dictionary of Old Testament Theology & Exegesis.* Edited by Willem VanGemeren, 3:1126–27. Grand Rapids: Zondervan, 1997.

Himbaza, I. *Le Décalogue et l'histoire du texte: Etudes des formes textuelles du Décalogue et leurs implications dans l'histoire du texte de l'Ancien Testament.* Orbis biblicus et orientalis 207. Göttingen: Vandenhoeck & Ruprecht, 2004.

Hoffman, Joel M. *In the Beginning: A Short History of the Hebrew Language.* New York: New York University Press, 2004.

Hoftijzer, J., and K. Jongeling. *Dictionary of the North-West Semitic Inscriptions.* New York: Brill, 1995.

Holladay, W. "Jeremiah and Moses: Further Observations." *Journal of Biblical Literature* 85 (1966) 17–27.

Hossfeld, F.-L. *Der Dekalog: Seine späten Fassungen, die originale Komposition und seine Vorstufen.* Orbis biblicus et orientalis 45. Göttingen: Vandenhoeck & Ruprecht, 1982.

Houston, Walter. *Purity and Monotheism: Clean and Unclean Animals in Biblical Law.* Journal for the Study of the Old Testament Supplement Series 140. Sheffield: Sheffield Academic, 1993.

Huehnergard, J. "On the Etymology and Meaning of Hebrew *nabi'.*" *Eretz-Israel* 26 (1999) 88*–93*.

Huffmon, H. B. *Amorite Personal Names in the Mari Texts: A Structural and Lexical Study.* Baltimore: John Hopkins University Press, 1965.

————. "The Covenant Lawsuit in the Prophets." *Journal of Biblical Literature* 78 (1959) 285–95.

Hugenberger, Gordon. *Marriage as a Covenant: Biblical Law and Ethics as Developed from Malachi.* Biblical Studies Library. Winona Lake, IN: Eisenbrauns, 1998.

Hurowitz, Victor. *I Have Built You an Exalted House: Temple Building in the Bible in the Light of Mesopotamian and Northwest Semitic Writings.* Journal for the Study of the Old Testament Supplement Series 115. Sheffield: Sheffield Academic Press, 1992.

Hurtado, Larry W. *One God, One Lord: Early Christian Devotion and Ancient Jewish Monotheism.* London: SCM, 1988.

Hutter, M. "Adam als Gärtner und König (Gen 2:8, 15)." *Biblische Zeitschrift* 30 (1986) 258–62.

Hwang, Jerry. *The Rhetoric of Remembrance: An Investigation of the "Fathers" in Deuteronomy.* Siphrut: Literature and Theology of the Hebrew Scriptures. Winona Lake, IN: Eisenbrauns, forthcoming.

Jackley, John L. *Below the Beltway: Money, Sex, Power, and Other Fundamentals of Democracy in the Nation's Capital.* Washington, DC: Regnery, 1996.

Jackson, B. S. "A Feminist Reading of the Decalogue(s)." *Biblica* 87 (2006) 542–54.

Jacobs, L. "Shema, Reading of." In *Encyclopaedia Judaica.* 2nd ed. Edited by Fred Skolnik, 14:1370–74. Farmington Hills, MI: Gale, 2007.

Janzen, J. G. "The Claim of the Shema." *Encounter* 59 (1998) 243–57.

————. "On the Most Important Word in the Shema (Deuteronomy VI 4–5)." *Vetus Testamentum* 37 (1987) 280–300.

Janzen, W. *Old Testament Ethics: A Paradigmatic Approach.* Louisville: Westminster John Knox, 1994.

Jastrow, M. *A Dictionary of the Targumim, Talmud Babli, Yerushalmi and Midrashic Literature.* New York: Judaica, 1971.

Jenni, E. "אָדוֹן *ādôn.*" In *Theological Lexicon of the Old Testament,* edited by E. Jenni and C. Westermann, and translated by M. E. Biddle, 1:23–29. Peabody, MA: Hendrickson, 1997.

Jepsen, Alfred. "Beiträge zur Auslegung und Geschichte des Dekalogs." *Zeitschrift für die alttestamentliche Wissenschaft* 149 (1967) 277–304.

Johnson, Robert M. "'The Least of the Commandments': Deuteronomy 22:6–7 in Rabbinic Judaism and Early Christianity." *Andrews University Seminary Studies* 20 (1982) 205–15.

Johnstone, W. "The Ten Commandments: Some Recent Interpretations." *Expository Times* 100 (1989) 453–59, 461.

Josberger, Rebekah. "Between Rule and Responsibility: The Role of the *'āb* as Agent of Righteousness in Deuteronomy's Domestic Ideology." PhD diss., Southern Baptist Theological Seminary, 2007.

Josephus, Flavius. *Jewish Antiquities.* Loeb Classical Library. Cambridge: Harvard University Press, 1978.

Joüon, Paul. *A Grammar of Biblical Hebrew.* Translated by T. Muraoka. Subsidia Biblica 14/1–14/2. Rome: Editrice Pontificio Istituto Biblio, 1991.

Kaiser, Walter C., Jr. "The Current Crisis in Exegesis and the Apostolic Use of Deuteronomy 25:4 in 1 Corinthians 9:8–10." *Journal of the Evangelical Theological Society* 21 (1978) 3–18.

———. "Leviticus." In *The New Interpreter's Bible,* edited by L. E. Keck et al., 1:985–1191. Nashville: Abingdon, 1994.

Kalluveettil, Paul. *Declaration and Covenant: A Comprehensive Review of Covenant Formulae from the Old Testament and the Ancient Near East.* Rome: Biblical Institute Press, 1982.

Kaufman, Stephen. "The Structure of the Deuteronomic Law." *Maarav* 1 (1979) 105–58.

Keel, O. *Das Böcklein in der Milch seiner Mutter und Verwandtes im Lichte eines altorientalischen Bild-motifs.* Orbis biblicus et orientalis 33. Freiburg: Universitätsverlag, 1980.

———. *Jahwe-Visionen und Siegelkunst: Eine neue Deutung der Majestätschilderung in Jes 6, Ez 1 und Sach 4.* Stuttgarter biblische Beiträge 84/85. Stuttgart: Katholisches Bibelwerk, 1977.

———. *The Symbolism of the Biblical World: Ancient Near Eastern Iconography and the Book of Psalms.* Translated by T. J. Hallett. New York: Seabury, 1978.

Keiser, T. A. "The Song of Moses as a Basis for Isaiah's Prophecy." *Vetus Testamentum* 55 (2005) 486–500.

Kellermann, D. "עָלָה." In *Theological Dictionary of the Old Testament,* edited by G. J. Botterweck and H. Ringgren, and translated D. E. Green, 11:97–113. Grand Rapids: Eerdmans, 2001.

Keneally, Thomas. *Moses the Lawgiver.* New York: Harper & Row, 1975.

King, P. J., and L. E. Stager. *Life in Biblical Israel.* Library of Ancient Israel. Louisville: Westminster John Knox, 2001.

Kitchen, Kenneth A. *On the Reliability of the Old Testament.* Grand Rapids: Eerdmans, 2003.

Kittel, R. *Geschichte des Volkes Israel.* 6th ed. Stuttgart: Kohlhammer, 1932.

Kline, Meredith G. "The Two Tables of the Covenant." *Westminster Theological Journal* 22 (1960) 133–46.

Knierim, R. "The Composition of the Pentateuch." In *The Task of Old Testament Theology: Substance, Method, and Cases*, 351–79. Grand Rapids: Eerdmans, 1995.

Knoppers, Gary. "The Deuteronomist and the Deuteronomic Law of the King: A Re-examination of a Relationship." *Zeitschrift für die alttestamentliche Wissenschaft* 108 (1996) 329–46.

———. "Rethinking the Relationship between Deuteronomy and the Deuteronomistic History." *Catholic Biblical Quarterly* 63 (2002) 393–415.

Koehler, Ludwig, and Walter Baumgartner. *The Hebrew and Aramaic Lexicon of the Old Testament*. Translated and edited by M. E. J. Richardson. Leiden: Brill, 2001.

Kooij, A. van der. "The Ending of the Song of Moses: On the Pre-Masoretic Version of Deut 32:43." In *Studies in Deuteronomy in Honour of C. J. Labuschagne*, edited by F. G. Martínez, 93–100. Vetus Testamentum Supplement Series 53. Leiden: Brill, 1994.

Kornfeld, W. "Reine und unreine Tiere im Alten Testament." *Kairos* 7 (1965) 134–47.

Köstenberger, Andreas. *God, Marriage, and Family: Rebuilding the Biblical Foundation*. Wheaton, IL: Crossway, 2004.

Kruse, Colin G. "Law." In *New Dictionary of Biblical Theology: Exploring the Unity and Diversity of Scripture*, edited by T. D. Alexander et al., 629–36. Downers Grove, IL: InterVarsity, 2000.

Kugel, J. L. *The Idea of Biblical Poetry: Parallelism and Its History*. Baltimore: Johns Hopkins University Press, 2004.

———. "Poetry." In *Harper's Bible Dictionary*, edited by Paul J. Achtemeier, 804–6. San Francisco: Harper & Row, 1985.

Kühlewein, J. "בַּעַל *ba'al* owner." In *Theological Lexicon of the Old Testament*, edited by E. Jenni and C. Westermann, and translated by M. E. Biddle, 1:247–51. Peabody, MA: Hendrickson, 1997.

Kuntz, P. G. *The Ten Commandments in History: Mosaic Paradigms for a Well-Ordered Society*. Grand Rapids: Eerdmans, 2004.

Labuschagne, C. J. *The Incomparability of Yahweh in the Old Testament*. Pretoria Oriental Series 5. Leiden: Brill, 1966.

———. "The Song of Moses in Deuteronomy 32—Logotechnical Analysis." Online: http://www.labuschagne.nl/2b.deut32.pdf.

———. "The Song of Moses: Its Framework and Structure." In *Dructu Oris Sui: Essays in Honour of A. van Selms*, edited by I. H. Eybers et al., 85–98. Leiden: Brill, 1971.

———. "'You Shall not Boil a Kid in its Mother's Milk': A New Proposal for the Origin of the Prohibition." In *The Scriptures and the Scrolls*, edited by F. G. Martínez, 6–17. Vetus Testamentum Supplement Series 49. Leiden: Brill, 1992.

Lambert, W. G. "Ancestors, Authors, and Canonicity." *Journal of Cuneiform Studies* 11 (1957) 1–14.

———. *Babylonian Wisdom Literature*. Oxford: Clarendon, 1960.

———. "A Catalogue of Texts and Authors." *Journal of Cuneiform Studies* 16.3 (1962) 59–77.

———. "The Cosmology of Sumer and Babylon." In *Ancient Cosmologies*, edited by C. Blacker and M. Loewe, 42–62. London: Allen & Unwin, 1975.

———. "Himmel." In *Reallexikon der Assyriologie und Vorderasiatischen Archäologie*, edited by M. P. Streck, 4:411–12. Berlin: de Gruyter, 1975.

Lang, B. "The Number Ten and the Antiquity of the Fathers: A New Interpretation of the Decalogue." *Zeitschrift für die alttestamentliche Wissenschaft* 118 (2006) 218–38.

Langdon, Stephen. *Babylonian Penitential Psalms*. Paris: Geuthner, 1927.

Leaney, A. R. C. *The Rule of Qumran and its Meaning*. New Testament Library. London: SCM, 1966.

Lee, Andrew. "The Narrative Function of the Song of Moses in the Contents of Deuteronomy and Genesis-Kings." PhD diss., University of Gloucestershire, 2010.

Lee, Won. "The Exclusion of Moses from the Promised Land: A Conceptual Approach." In *The Changing Face of Form Criticism for the Twenty-First Century*, edited by Marvin A. Sweeney and Ehud Ben Zvi, 217–39. Grand Rapids: Eerdmans, 2003.

Leibert, Julius. *The Lawgiver*. New York: Exposition, 1953.

Leichty, Earle. "The Colophon." In *Studies Presented to A. Leo Oppenheim*, edited by Robert D. Biggs and John A. Brinkman, 147–54. Chicago: Chicago University Press, 1964.

Leiman, S. Z. *The Canonization of Hebrew Scripture: The Talmudic and Midrashic Evidence*. 2nd ed. Transactions of the Connecticut Academy of Arts and Sciences. New Haven: Connecticut Academy of Arts and Sciences, 1991.

Lemaire, André. "Writing and Writing Materials." In *Anchor Bible Dictionary*, edited by D. N. Freedman, 6:999–1008. Garden City, NY: Doubleday, 1992.

Leuchter, Mark "Why is the Song of Moses in the Book of Deuteronomy?" *Vetus Testamentum* 57 (2007) 295–317.

Levinson, Bernard M. *Deuteronomy and the Hermeneutics of Legal Innovation*. Oxford: Oxford University Press, 1998.

Lewis, T. J. "Teraphim תרפים." In *Dictionary of Deities and Demons in the Bible*. Edited by K. van der Toorn, B. Becking, and P. W. van der Horst, 844–50. Rev. ed. Leiden: Brill, 1999.

Liddell, H. G., and R. Scott. *A Greek-English Lexicon*. Rev. ed. Edited by H. S. Jones and R. McKenzie. Oxford: Clarendon, 1996.

Liedke, G. "חקק *ḥqq* einritzen, festsetzen." In *Theologisches Handwörterbuch zum Alten Testament*, edited by E. Jenni and C. Westerman, 1:626–34. Munich: Kaiser, 1971.

Lienhard, S. J. *Exodus, Leviticus, Numbers, Deuteronomy*. Ancient Christian Commentary on Scripture. Old Testament 3. Downers Grove, IL: InterVarsity, 2001.

Lim, Johnson Teng Kok. "The Sin of Moses in Deuteronomy." *Asia Journal of Theology* 17 (2001) 250–66.

Littauer, M. A., and J. H. Crouwel. "Chariots." In *Anchor Bible Dictionary*, edited by D. N. Freedman, 1:888–92. Garden City, NY: Doubleday, 1992.

Lohfink, N. "אֶחָד *'echādh*." In *Theological Dictionary of the Old Testament*, edited by G. J. Botterweck and H. Ringgren, and translated by G. W. Bromiley, 1:196. Grand Rapids: Eerdmans, 1964.

———. "Der Bundesschluss im Land Moab: Redaktionsgeschichtliches zu Dt 28,69–32,47." *Biblische Zeitschrift* 6 (1962) 32–56.

———. "Dt 26,17–19 und die 'Bundesformel.'" In *Studien zum Deuteronomium und zur deuteronomischen Literatur I*, 228–35. Stuttgarter biblische Aufsatzbände 8. Stuttgart: Katholisches Bibelwerk, 1990.

———. *Great Themes from the Old Testament*. Translated by R. Walls. Edinburgh: T. & T. Clark, 1982.

———. "Kennt das Alte Testament einen Unterschied von 'Gebot' und 'Gesetz'? Zur biblelteologischen Einstufung des Dekalogs." *Jahrbuch für Biblische Theologie* 4 (1989) 63–89.

———. "Zur deuteronomischen Zentralizationsformel." *Biblica* 65 (1984) 297–329.

————. "Zur Fabel in Dtn 31–32." In *Konsequente Traditionsgeschichte: Festschrift für Klaus Baltzer zum 65. Geburtstag.* Edited by R. Bartelmus, T. Krüger, and H. Utschneider, 255–79. Orbis biblicus et orientalis 126. Freiburg: Universitätsverlag, 1993.

Lohfink, N., and G. Braulik. "Deuteronomium 4,13 und der Horebbund." In *Für immer verbündet: Studien zur Bundestheologie der Bibel,* edited by C. Dohmen and C. Frevel, 27–36. Stuttgarter Bibelstudien 211. Stuttgart: Katholisches Bibelwerk, 2007.

Lohse, B. *Martin Luther's Theology.* Minneapolis: Fortress, 1999.

Lord, Carnes. *The Modern Prince: What Leaders Need to Know Now.* 2nd ed. New Haven, CT: Yale University Press, 2003.

Loretz, O. "Die *Einzigkeit* Jahwes (Dtn 6,4) im Licht der ugaritischen Ball-Mythos." In *Vom Alten Orient zum Alten Testament: Festschrift W. F. von Soden.* Edited by M. Dietrich and O. Loretz, 215–304. Neukirchen-Vluyn: Neukirchener, 1995.

————. *Ugarit-Texte und Thronbesteigigungspsalmen: Die Metamorphose des Regenspenders Baal-Jahwe (Ps 24, 7–10; 29; 47; 93; 95–100 sowie Ps 77, 17–20; 114).* Ugaritisch-biblische Literatur 7. Münster: Ugarit, 1988.

Lunn, Nicholas. *Word-Order Variation in Biblical Hebrew Poetry: Differentiating Pragmatics and Poetics.* Paternoster Biblical Monographs. Eugene, OR: Wipf & Stock, 2006.

Luther, Martin. *Lectures on Deuteronomy.* Luther's Works 9. Minneapolis: Concordia, 1960.

Luyten, Jos. "Primeval and Eschatological Overtones in the Song of Moses (Dt 32, 1–43)." In *Das Deuteronomium,* edited by N. Lohfink, 341–47. Leuven: Leuven University Press, 1985.

Malamat, Abraham. "'Love Your Neighbor as Yourself': What it Really Means." *Biblical Archaeology Review* 16.4 (1990) 50–51.

————. "'You Shall Love Your Neighbor As Yourself ': A Case of Misinterpretation?" In *Die Hebräische Bibel und ihre zweifache Nachgeschichte: Festschrift für Rolf Rendtorff zum 65. Geburtstag,* edited by E. Blum et al., 111–15. Neukirchen-Vluyn: Neukirchener, 1990.

Maraqten, M. *Die semitischen Personennamen in den alt–und reischsaramäischen Inschriften aus Vorderasien.* Hildesheim: Olms, 1988.

Martens, E. A. "Accessing Theological Readings of a Biblical Book." *Andrews University Seminary Studies* 34 (1996) 223–37.

Martin, Ralph P. *James.* Word Biblical Commentary 48. Waco, TX: Word, 1988.

Martínez, Florentino G., and Eibert J. C. Tigchelaar. *The Dead Sea Scrolls Study Edition.* Leiden: Brill, 1997.

Maxwell, J. C. *The 21 Irrefutable Laws of Leadership: Follow Them and People Will Follow You.* Nashville: Nelson, 1998.

Mayes, A. D. H. *Deuteronomy.* New Century Bible. Grand Rapids: Eerdmans, 1981.

McBride, S. Dean, Jr. "Polity of the People of God: The Book of Deuteronomy." *Interpretation* 41 (1987) 229–44.

————. "The Yoke of the Kingdom: An Exposition of Deut. 6:4–5." *Interpretation* 27 (1973) 273–306.

McCarter, P. K., Jr. *I Samuel: A New Translation with Introduction, Notes and Commentary.* Anchor Bible 8. Garden City, NY: Doubleday, 1980.

McCarthy, Carmel, editor. *Deuteronomy.* Biblia Hebraica Quinta 5. Stuttgart: Deutsche Bibelgesellschaft, 2007.

McConville, J. G. *Deuteronomy.* Apollos Old Testament Commentary. Downers Grove, IL: InterVarsity, 2002.

———. *Grace in the End: A Study in Deuteronomic Theology.* Grand Rapids: Zondervan, 1993.

———. *Law and Theology in Deuteronomy.* Sheffield: JSOT Press, 1984.

———. "Singular Address in the Deuteronomic Law and the Politics of Legal Administration." *Journal for the Study of the Old Testament* 97 (2002) 19–36.

McConville, J. Gordon, and J. G. Millar. *Time and Place in Deuteronomy.* Journal for the Study of the Old Testament Supplement Series 179. Sheffield: Sheffield Academic Press, 1984.

McKenzie, S. L. "Deuteronomistic History." In *Anchor Bible Dictionary*, edited by D. N. Freedman, 2:160–68. Garden City, NY: Doubleday, 1992.

Meier, S. A. *Speaking of Speaking: Marking Direct Discourse in the Hebrew Bible.* Vetus Testamentum Supplement Series 46. Leiden: Brill, 1992.

Mendenhall, George. "The Conflict between Value Systems and Social Control." In *Unity and Diversity: Essays in the History, Literature, and Religion of the Ancient Near East*, edited by Hans Goedicke and J. J. M. Roberts, 169–80. Baltimore: Johns Hopkins University Press, 1975.

Merrill, Eugene H. *Deuteronomy.* New American Commentary. Nashville: Broadman & Holman, 1994.

Mettinger, Tryggve N. D. *No Graven Image? Israelite Aniconism in Its Ancient Near Easter Context.* Coniectanea biblica Old Testament Series 42. Stockholm: Almqvist & Wiksell, 1995.

Milgrom, Jacob. "Profane Slaughter and a Formulaic Key to the Composition of Deuteronomy." *Hebrew Union College Annual* 47 (1976) 1–17.

Millar, J. G. "Living at the Place of Decision: Time and Place in the Framework of Deuteronomy." In *Time and Place in Deuteronomy*, J. G. Millar and J. G. McConville, 15–88. Journal for the Study of the Old Testament Supplement Series 179. Sheffield: Sheffield Academic Press, 1994.

———. *Now Choose Life.* Grand Rapids: Eerdmans, 1998.

Millard, Alan R. "Books in the Late Bronze Age in the Levant." In *Past Links: Studies in the Languages and Cultures of the Ancient Near East. Fs. Anson Rainey*, edited by S. Izre'el et al., 171–81. Israel Oriental Studies 18. Winona Lake, IN: Eisenbrauns, 1998.

———. "Mass Communication and Scriptural Proclamation: The First Step." *Evangelical Quarterly* 2 (1978) 67–70.

———. "La prophetie et l'ecriture: Israël, Aram, Assyrie." *Revue de l'histoire des religions* 202 (1985) 125–44.

———. *Reading and Writing in the Time of Jesus.* Sheffield: Sheffield Academic Press, 2000.

Miller, Cynthia L. "Pivotal Issues in Analyzing the Verbless Clause." In *The Verbless Clause in Biblical Hebrew: Linguistic Approaches*, edited by Cynthia L. Miller. Winona Lake, IN: Eisenbrauns, 1999.

Miller, J. W. *The Origins of the Bible: Rethinking Canon History.* New York: Paulist, 1994.

Miller, P. D. *Deuteronomy.* Interpretation. Louisville: John Knox, 1990.

———. "Deuteronomy and the Psalms: Evoking a Biblical Conversation." *Journal of Biblical Literature* 118 (1999) 3–18.

———. "'Moses My Servant': The Deuteronomic Portrait of Moses." *Interpretation* 41 (1987) 245–55.

————. "The Place of the Decalogue in the Old Testament and Its Law." In *The Way of the Lord: Essays in Old Testament Theology,* 3–16. Grand Rapids: Eerdmans, 2004.

————. "The Sufficiency and Insufficiency of the Commandments." In *The Way of the Lord: Essays in Old Testament Theology,* 17–36. Grand Rapids: Eerdmans, 2004.

————. *The Ten Commandments.* Interpretation. Louisville: Westminster John Knox, 2009.

Miller, Robert D., II. "The 'Biography' of Moses in the Pentateuch." In *Illuminating Moses: A History of Reception,* edited by Jane Beal. Commentaria Series. Leiden: Brill, forthcoming.

Moberly, R. W. L. "Toward an Interpretation of the Shema." In *Theological Exegesis: Essays in Honor of Brevard S. Childs,* edited by C. Seitz and K. Greene-McCreight, 124–44. Grand Rapids: Eerdmans, 1999.

————. "Yahweh is One: The Translation of the Shema." In *Studies in the Pentateuch,* edited by J. A. Emerton, 209–15. Vetus Testamentum Supplement Series 41. Leiden: Brill, 1990.

Monson, John. "The New 'Ain Dara Temple: Closest Solomonic Parallel." *Biblical Archaeology Review* 26.3 (2000) 20–35, 67.

Moo, Douglas J. "Nature in the New Creation: New Testament Eschatology and the Environment." *Journal of the Evangelical Theological Society* 49 (2006) 449–88.

Moore, Russell D. "After Patriarchy, What? Why Egalitarians Are Winning the Gender Debate." *Journal of the Evangelical Theological Society* 49 (2006) 569–76.

Moskala, J. *The Laws of Clean and Unclean Animals in Leviticus 11: Their Nature, Theology, and Rationale (an Intertextual Study).* Adventist Theological Society Dissertation Series. Berrien Springs, MI: Adventist Theological Society, 2000.

Murphy, Frederick J. *Early Judaism: The Exile to the Time of Jesus.* Peabody, MA: Hendrickson, 2002.

Mutius, Hans-Georg von. "Sprachliche und religionsgeschichtliche Anmerkungen zu einer neu publizierten samaritanischen Textfassung von Deuteronomium 6,4." *Biblische Notizen* 101 (2000) 23–26.

Nelson, R. *Deuteronomy: A Commentary.* Old Testament Library. Louisville: Westminster John Knox, 2002.

Neusner, Jacob. *The Treasury of Judaism: A New Collection and Translation of Essential Texts.* Vol. 2, *The Life Cycle.* Studies in Judaism. Lanham, MD: University Press of America, 2008.

New International Webster's Comprehensive Dictionary of the English Language. Deluxe Encyclopedic Edition. Naples, FL: Trident, 1996.

Nicholson, E. W. *Deuteronomy and Tradition: Literary and Historical Problems in the Book of Deuteronomy.* Philadelphia: Fortress, 1967.

————. *God and His People: Covenant Theology in the Old Testament.* Oxford: Clarendon, 1986.

Niehaus, J. J. "The Deuteronomic Style: An Examination of the Deuteronomic Style in the Light of Ancient Near Eastern Literature." PhD diss., University of Liverpool, 1985.

Nielsen, E. "The Song of Moses (DT 32): A Structural Analysis." *Ephemerides theologicae Lovanienses* 72 (1996) 5–22.

————. *The Ten Commandments in New Perspective: A Traditio-historical Approach.* Studies in Biblical Theology, 2nd Series 7. Naperville, IL: Allenson, 1968.

————. "'Weil Jahwe unser Gott ein Jahwe ist' (Dtn. 6,4f)." In *Law, History, and Tradition: Selected Essays by Eduard Nielsen,* 106–18. Copenhagen: Gads, 1983.

Nigosian, Solomon A. "Linguistic Patterns of Deuteronomy 32." *Biblica* 78 (1997) 206–24.

———. "The Song of Moses (DT 32): A Structural Analysis." *Ephemerides theologicae lovanienses* 72 (1996) 5–22.

Nissinen, Martti. *Prophets and Prophecy in the Ancient Near East.* Atlanta: Society of Biblical Literature, 2003.

Nohrnberg, James. *Like unto Moses: The Constituting of an Interruption.* Bloomington, IN: Indiana University Press, 1995.

Noonan, J. T., Jr. "The Muzzled Ox." *Jewish Quarterly Review* 70 (1980) 172–75.

Noth, Martin. *The Deuteronomistic History.* Translated by D. Orton. Journal for the Study of the Old Testament Supplement Series 15. Sheffield: JSOT Press, 1981.

———. *Überlieferungsgeschichtliche Studien.* 2nd ed. Tübingen: Niemeyer, 1957.

Olson, Dennis T. *Deuteronomy and the Death of Moses: A Theological Reading.* Overtures to Biblical Theology. Minneapolis: Fortress, 1994.

Oppenheim, A. Leo. *Ancient Mesopotamia: Portrait of a Dead Civilization.* Rev. ed. Chicago: University of Chicago Press, 1977.

Otto, Eckart. *Das Deuteronomium.* Beihefte zur Zeitschrift für die alttestamentliche Wissenschaft 284. Berlin: de Gruyter, 1999.

———. "Mose der erste Schriftgelehrte: Deuteronomium 1,5 in der Fabel des Pentateuch." In *L'Ecrit et L'Esprit: Etudes d'Histoire du texte et de théologie biblique en hommage à Adrian Schenker*, edited by D. Böhler, I Himbaza, and P. Hugo, 273–84. Orbis biblicus et orientalis 214. Göttingen: Vandenhoeck & Ruprecht, 2005.

———. "Revisions in the Legal History of Covenant Code, Deuteronomy, Holiness Code and the Legal Hermeneutics of the Torah." Paper delivered to the Society of Biblical Literature, New Orleans, November 23, 2009.

———. *Theologische Ethik des Alten Testaments.* Theologische Wissenschaft 3/2. Stuttgart: Kohlhammer, 1994.

Oxford English Dictionary. Compact Edition. Oxford: Oxford University Press, 1971.

Pardee, D. "Dawn and Dusk (The Birth of the Gracious and Beautiful Gods)." In *The Context of Scripture*, edited by W. W. Hallo, vol. 1, 274–83. Leiden: Brill, 1997.

Parker, S. B., editor. *Ugaritic Narrative Poetry.* Society of Biblical Literature Writings from the Ancient World 9. Atlanta: Scholars, 1997.

Parpola, Simo. "The King as God's Son and Chosen One." In *Assyrian Prophecies.* State Archives of Assyria 9. Helsinki: Helsinki University Press, 1997.

———. *Letters from Assyrian and Babylonian Scholars.* State Archives of Assyria 10. Helsinki: Helsinki University Press, 1993.

Parpola, S., and K. Watanabe. *Neo-Assyrian Treaties and Loyalty Oaths.* State Archives of Assyria 9. Helsinki: Helsinki University Press, 1988.

Patrick, Dale. *Old Testament Law.* Atlanta: John Knox, 1985.

Perlitt, L. *Bundestheologie im Alten Testament.* Wissenschaftliche Monographien zum Alten und Neuen Testament 36. Neikirchen-Vluyn: Neukirchener, 1969.

Peters, George. *Biblical Theology of Missions.* Chicago: Moody, 1972.

Phillips, Anthony. *Ancient Israel's Criminal Law: A New Approach to the Decalogue.* New York: Schocken, 1970.

———. "The Decalogue: Ancient Israel's Criminal Law." In *Essays on Biblical Law*, 2–24. London: T. & T. Clark, 2002.

———. "A Fresh Look at the Sinai Pericope." In *Essays on Biblical Law*, 25–48. London: T. & T. Clark, 2002.

Philo. *De Specialibus Legibus.* In *Philonis Alexandrini opera quae supersunt*, 5:1–265. Reprint. Berlin: de Gruyter, 1962.

————. *On the Decalogue*. Loeb Classical Library. Cambridge: Harvard University Press, 1984.

Pleins, J. David. *The Social Visions of the Hebrew Bible: A Theological Introduction*. Louisville: Westminster John Knox, 2001.

Pohlmann, K.-P. *Ezechiel Studien: Zur Redaktionsgeschichte des Buches und zur Frage nach den ältesten Texten*. Beihefte zur Zeitschrift für die alttestamentliche Wissenschaft 202. Berlin: de Gruyter, 1992.

Polaski, Donald C. "Moses' Final Examination: The Book of Deuteronomy." In *Postmodern Interpretations of the Bible—A Reader*, edited by A. K. M. Adam, 29–41. St. Louis: Chalice, 2001.

Polzin, R. *Moses and the Deuteronomist: A Literary Study of the Deuteronomistic History*. New York: Seabury, 1980.

Porten, Bezalel. *Archives from Elephantine*. Berkeley: University of California Press, 1968.

Pressler, Carolyn. *The View of Women Found in the Deuteronomic Family Laws*. Beihefte zur Zeitschrift für die alttestamentliche Wissenschaft 216. Berlin: de Gruyter, 1993.

Preuss, H. D. "גּלּוּלִים." In *Theological Dictionary of the Old Testament*, edited by G. J. Botterweck and H. Ringgren, and translated by G. W. Bromiley, 3:1–5. Grand Rapids: Eerdmans, 1965.

————. *Die Verspottung fremder Religionen im Alten Testament*. Beihefte zur Zeitschrift für die alttestamentliche Wissenschaft 12. Stuttgart: Kohlhammer, 1971.

Pritchard, James B., editor. *Ancient Near Eastern Texts Relating to the Old Testament*. 3rd ed. Princeton: Princeton University Press, 1969.

Propp, W. H. C. *Exodus 19–40: A New Translation with Introduction and Commentary*. Anchor Bible 2A. Garden City, NY: Doubleday, 2006.

Rabinowitz, L. I. "Cosmology." In *Encyclopaedia Judaica*. 2nd ed. Edited by F. Skolnik, 5:231–32. Farmington Hills, MI: Gale, 2007.

Rad, G. von. *Deuteronomy: A Commentary*. Old Testament Library. Philadelphia: Westminster, 1966.

————. *The Problem of the Hexateuch and Other Studies*. London: SCM, 1966.

————. *Studies in Deuteronomy*. Studies in Biblical Theology 9. London: SCM, 1953.

Ratner, R., and B. Zuckerman. "'A Kid in Milk?': New Photographs of KTU 1:23, line 14." *Hebrew Union College Annual* 57 (1986) 15–60.

Redford, Donald B. "Hyksos." In *Anchor Bible Dictionary*, edited by D. N. Freedman, 3:341–44. Garden City, NY: Doubleday, 1992.

Reines, Alvin J. "Commandments, The 613." In *Encyclopaedia Judaica*. 2nd ed. Edited by F. Skolnik, 5:760–83. Farmington Hills, MI: Gale, 2007.

Rendsburg, G. A. "The Mock of Baal in 1 Kgs 18:27." *Catholic Biblical Quarterly* 50 (1988) 414–17.

Rendtorff, Rolf. *The Covenant Formula: An Exegetical and Theological Investigation*. Translated by M. Kohl. Edinburgh: T. & T. Clark, 1998.

Richter, Sandra. *The Deuteronomistic History and the Name Theology: lĕšakkēn šĕmô šām in the Bible and the Ancient Near East*. Beihefte zur Zeitschrift für die alttestamentliche Wissenschaft 318. Berlin: de Gruyter, 2002.

Ringgren, H. "Monotheism." In *The Interpreter's Dictionary of the Bible*. Supplementary Volume, edited by K. Crim, 602–4. Nashville: Abingdon, 1978.

Rodd, Cyril S. *Glimpses of a Strange Land: Studies in Old Testament Ethics*. Edinburgh: T. & T. Clark, 2001.

Rofé, A. "The End of the Song of Moses (Deuteronomy 32:43)." In *Liebe und Gebot: Studien zum Deuteronomium, Festschrift zum 70. Geburtstag von Lothar Perlitt,* edited by R. G. Kratz and H. Spieckermann, 164–72. Göttingen: Vandenhoeck & Ruprecht, 2000.

———. "The Tenth Commandment in the Light of Four Deuteronomic Laws." In *The Ten Commandments in History and Tradition,* edited by Ben-Zion Segal and G. Levi, 45–54. Jerusalem: Magnes, 1990.

Römer, Thomas. "Moses outside the Torah and the Construction of a Diaspora Identity." *Journal of Hellenic Studies* 8 (2008) 1–12.

Rose, M. *5. Mose 12–25: Einführung und Gesetze.* Zürcher Bibel-kommentare. Zurich: Theologischer, 1994.

Rösel, Martin. "Names of God." In *Encyclopedia of the Dead Sea Scrolls,* edited by L. H. Schiffman and J. C. VanderKam, 2:600–602. Oxford: Oxford University Press, 2000.

Rosenfield, Paul. *The Club Rules: Power, Money, Sex and Fear—How It Works in Hollywood.* New York: Warner, 1992.

Roth, Martha. T. *Law Collections from Mesopotamia and Asia Minor.* 2nd ed. Society of Biblical Literature Writings from the Ancient World 6. Atlanta: Scholars, 1997.

Rubin, Gretchen Craft. *Power, Money, Fame, Sex: A User's Guide.* New York: Atria, 2001.

Rudman, D. "When Gods Go Hungry: Mesopotamian Rite Clarifies Puzzling Prophecy." *Bible Review* 18.3 (2002) 37–39.

Safrai, Shmuel, and Michael Avi-Yonah. "Temple: Structure." In *Encyclopaedia Judaica.* 2nd ed. Edited by F. Skolnik, 19:611–16. Farmington Hills, MI: Gale, 2007.

Saggs, H. W. F. *The Greatness That was Babylon: A Sketch of the Ancient Civilization of the Tigris-Euphrates Valley.* London: Sidgwick & Jackson, 1962.

Sailhamer, John H. *The Pentateuch as Narrative: A Biblical-Theological Commentary.* Library of Biblical Interpretation. Grand Rapids: Zondervan, 1992.

Salvesen, Alison. "Early Syriac, Greek and Latin Views of the Decalogue." In *The Decalogue through the Centuries: From the Hebrew Scriptures to Benedict XVI,* edited by J. Greenman and T. Larsen. Louisville: Westminster John Knox, forthcoming.

Sanders, Deion. *Power, Money & Sex: How Success Almost Ruined My Life.* Nashville: Word, 1999.

Sanders, James A. *Torah and Canon.* Philadelphia: Fortress, 1972.

Sanders, P. *The Provenance of Deuteronomy 32.* Old Testament Studies 37. Leiden: Brill, 1996.

Sandy, D. Brent. *Plowshares & Pruning Hooks: Rethinking the Language of Biblical Prophecy and Apocalyptic.* Downers Grove, IL: InterVarsity, 2002.

Sawyer, John F. A. *Sacred Languages and Sacred Texts.* New York: Routledge, 1999.

Schaper, J. "The 'Publication' of Legal Texts in Ancient Judah." In *The Pentateuch as Torah: New Models for Understanding Its Promulgation and Acceptance,* edited by G. N. Knoppers and B. M. Levinson, 225–36. Winona Lake, IN: Eisenbrauns, 2007.

Schiffmann, L. H. "Phylacteries and Mezuzot." In *Encyclopedia of the Dead Sea Scrolls,* edited by L. H. Schiffmann and J. C. VanderKam, 2:675–77. Oxford: Oxford University Press, 2000.

———. "Some Laws Pertaining to Animals in Temple Scroll Column 52." In *Legal Texts and Legal Issues: Proceedings of the Second Meeting of the International Organization for Qumran Studies Cambridge 1995: Published in Honour of Joseph M. Baumgarten.* Edited by M. Bernstein, 167–78. Studies on the Texts of the Desert of Judah 23. Leiden: Brill, 1997.

Schmid, Herbert. *Die Gestalt des Mose: Probleme atlttestamentlicher Forschung unter Berücksichtigung der Pentateuchkrise.* Erträge der Forschung 237. Darmstadt: Wissenschaftliche Buchgesellschaft, 1986.

Schmidt, Werner H. *Die Zehn Gebote im Rahmen alttestamentlicher Ethik.* Erträge der Forschung 281. Darmstadt: Wissenschaftliche Buchgesellschaft, 1993.

Schreiner, Thomas R. *The Law and Its Fulfillment: A Pauline Theology of Law.* Grand Rapids: Baker, 1993.

———. *Romans.* Baker Exegetical Commentary on the New Testament. Grand Rapids: Baker, 1998.

Scurlock, JoAnn. "Animal Sacrifice in Ancient Mesopotamian Religion." In *History of the Animal World in the Ancient Near East.* Edited by Billie Jean Collins, 389–97. Handbook of Oriental Studies 64. Leiden: Brill, 2002.

Searle, John. *Speech Acts: An Essay in the Philosophy of Language.* Cambridge: Cambridge University Press, 1969.

Segal, Ben-Zion, and G. Levi, editors. *The Ten Commandments in History and Tradition.* Jerusalem: Magnes, 1990.

Segal, Eliezer. "Justice, Mercy, and a Bird's Nest." *Journal of Jewish Studies* 42 (1991) 176–95.

Seitz, G. *Redaktionsgeschichtliche Studien zum Deuteronomium.* Beiträge zur Wissenschaft vom Alten und Neuen Testament 93. Stuttgart: Kohlhammer, 1971.

Seux, M. J. *Épithètes royales akkadiennes et sumériennes.* Paris: Letouzey et Ané, 1967.

Simian-Yofre, H. "עוד." In *Theological Dictionary of the Old Testament*, edited by G. J. Botterweck and H. Ringgren, and translated by D. W. Scott, 10:495–515. Grand Rapids: Eerdmans, 1999.

Sivan, H. *Between Woman, Man, and God: A New Interpretation of the Ten Commandments.* Journal for the Study of the Old Testament Supplement Series 401. London: T. & T. Clark, 2004.

Ska, Jean-Louis. "From History Writing to Library Building: The End of History and the Birth of the Book." In *The Pentateuch as Torah: New Models for Understanding Its Promulgation and Acceptance*, edited by G. N. Knoppers and B. M. Levinson, 145–69. Winona Lake, IN: Eisenbrauns, 2007.

Skehan, Patrick W. "A Fragment of the 'Song of Moses' (Deut 32) from Qumran." *Bulletin of the American Schools of Oriental Research* 136 (1954) 12–15.

———. "The Structure of the Song of Moses in Deuteronomy (Deut 32:1–43)." *Catholic Biblical Quarterly* 13 (1951) 153–63.

Skehan, Patrick W., and Alexander A. Di Lella. *The Wisdom of Ben Sira: A New Translation with Notes.* Anchor Bible 39. New York: Doubleday, 1987.

Smend, Rudolf. *Die Bundesformel.* Theologische Studien 68. Zurich: EVZ, 1963.

Smircich, L., and G. Morgan. "Leadership: The Management of Meaning." *Journal of Applied Behavioral Science* 18 (1982) 257–73.

Smith, Mark S. *The Early History of God: YHWH and Other Deities in Ancient Israel.* San Francisco: Harper & Row, 1987.

———. "Matters of Space and Time in Exodus and Numbers." In *Theological Exegesis: Essays in Honor of Brevard S. Childs*, edited by C. Seitz and K. Greene-McKnight, 182–207. Grand Rapids: Eerdmans, 1999.

Soden, W. Von, editor. *Akkadisches Handwörterbuch.* 3 vols. Wiesbaden: Karrassowitz, 1965–81.

Sohn, Seock-Tae. *The Divine Election of Israel.* Grand Rapids: Eerdmans, 1991.

————. "'I Will Be Your God and You Will Be My People': The Origin and Background of the Covenant Formula." In *Ancient Near Eastern, Biblical, and Judaic Studies in Honor of Baruch A. Levine*, edited by R. Chazan, W. W. Hallo, and L. H. Schiffman, 355–72. Winona Lake, IN: Eisenbrauns, 1999.

Sonnet, Jean-Pierre. *The Book within the Book: Writing in Deuteronomy*. Leiden: Brill, 1997.

Sonsino, Rifat. "Forms of Biblical Law." In *Anchor Bible Dictionary*, edited by D. N. Freedman, 4:252–54. Garden City, NY: Doubleday, 1992.

Spronk, Klaas. "The Picture of Moses in the History of Interpretation." In *The Interpretation of Exodus: Studies in Honour of Cornelis Houtman*, edited by R. Roukema et al., 253–64. Leuven: Peeters, 2006.

Stamm, J. J. *The Ten Commandments in Recent Research*. Studies in Biblical Theology. 2nd Series 2. Naperville, IL: Allenson, 1967.

Stewart, David A. *Money, Power, and Sex*. New York: Libra, 1965.

Stolz, F. "Monotheismus in Israel." In *Monotheismus im alten Israel und seiner Umwelt*, edited by O. Keel, 163–74. Biblische Beiträge 14. Fribourg: Schweizerisches Katholisches Bibelwerk, 1980.

Stuart, D. K. *Exodus*. New American Commentary 2. Nashville: Broadman & Holman, 2006.

————. *Studies in Early Hebrew Meter*. Missoula, MT: Scholars, 1976.

Thiessen, Matthew. "The Form and Function of the Song of Moses (Deuteronomy 32:1–43)." *Journal of Biblical Literature* 123 (2004) 401–24.

Thompson, J. A. *The Book of Jeremiah*. New International Commentary on the Old Testament. Grand Rapids: Eerdmans, 1980.

————. *Deuteronomy: An Introduction and Commentary*. Tyndale Old Testament Commentaries. Downers Grove, IL: InterVarsity, 1974.

Tigay, J. *Deuteronomy*. Jewish Publication Society Torah Commentary. Philadelphia: Jewish Publication Society, 1996.

————. *You Shall Have No Other Gods: Israelite Religion in the Light of Hebrew Inscriptions*. Harvard Semitic Monographs 31. Atlanta: Scholars, 1986.

Toorn, Karel van der. *Scribal Culture and the Making of the Hebrew Bible*. Cambridge: Harvard University Press, 2007.

————. "Sheger." In *Dictionary of Deities and Demons in the Bible*, edited by K. van der Toorn, B. Becking, and P. W. van der Horst, 760–62. Rev. ed. Leiden: Brill, 1999.

Tov, Emanuel. *Textual Criticism of the Hebrew Bible*. 2nd rev. ed. Minneapolis: Fortress, 1992.

Trible, Phyllis. *Texts of Terror: Literary-Feminist Readings of Biblical Narratives*. Overtures to Biblical Theology. Philadelphia: Fortress, 1984.

Turner, Philip. *Sex, Money and Power: An Essay on Christian Ethics*. Cambridge, MA: Cowley, 1985.

Uehlinger, C. "Leviathan." In *Dictionary of Deities and Demons in the Bible*, edited by K. van der Toorn, B. Becking, and P. W. van der Horst, 511–15. Rev. ed. Leiden: Brill, 1999.

Van Dyke, Fred, editor. *Redeeming Creation: The Biblical Basis for Environmental Stewardship*. Downers Grove, IL: InterVarsity, 1996.

VanderKam, J. C. *The Dead Sea Scrolls Today*. Grand Rapids: Eerdmans, 1994.

Van der Merwe, C. H. J., J. A. Naudé, and J. H. Kroeze. *A Biblical Hebrew Reference Grammar*. Biblical Languages—Hebrew 3. Sheffield: Sheffield Academic Press, 2004.

VanGemeren, Willem, editor. *New International Dictionary of Old Testament Theology & Exegesis*. 5 vols. Grand Rapids: Zondervan, 1997.

Vanhoozer, Kevin J. *Is There a Meaning in This Text? The Bible, the Reader, and the Morality of Literary Knowledge*. Grand Rapids: Zondervan, 1998.

Veijola, T. "Höre Israel! Der Sinn und Hintergrund von Deuteronomium VI 4–9." *Vetus Testamentum* 42 (1992) 528–41.

Vermes, Geza. "Pre-Mishnaic Jewish Worship and the Phylacteries from the Dead Sea." *Vetus Testamentum* 9 (1959) 65–72.

Vogt, Peter. *Deuteronomic Theology and the Significance of Torah: A Reappraisal*. Winona Lake, IN: Eisenbrauns, 2006.

Vokes, F. E. "Creeds in the New Testament." *Studia Evangelica* 6 (1973) 582–84.

———. "The Ten Commandments in the New Testament and in First Century Judaism." In *Studia Evangelica 5*, edited by F. L. Cross, 146–54. Berlin: Akademie, 1968.

Vriezen, T. C. "Das hiph'il von *āmar* in Deut 26,17.18." *Jaarbericht van het Voorasiatische-Egyptisch Geselschap Ex oriente lux* 17 (1964) 207–10.

Walker, C., and M. B. Dick. "The Induction of the Cult Image in Ancient Mesopotamia: The Mesopotamian *mispî* Ritual." In *Born in Heaven, Made on Earth: The Making of the Cult Image in the Ancient Near East*, edited by M. B. Dick, 55–121. Winona Lake, IN: Eisenbrauns, 1999.

Waltke, Bruce K. "Canonical Process Approach to the Psalms." In *Tradition and Testament: Essays in Honor of Charles Lee Feinberg*, edited by J. S. Feinberg and P. D. Feinberg, 3–19. Chicago: Moody, 1981.

———. "Oral Tradition." In *A Tribute to Gleason Archer: Essays on the Old Testament*, edited by W. C. Kaiser Jr. and R. F. Youngblood, 17–34. Chicago: Moody, 1986.

Waltke, Bruce K., with Charles Yu. *An Old Testament Theology: An Exegetical, Canonical, and Thematic Approach*. Grand Rapids: Zondervan, 2007.

Walton, John H. "Interpreting the Bible as an Ancient Near Eastern Document." In *Israel: Ancient Kingdom or Late Invention*, edited by Daniel I. Block, 298–327. Nashville: Broadman & Holman, 2008.

———. "The Place of the *hutqattel* within the D–Stem Group and Its Implications in Deuteronomy 24:4." *Hebrew Studies* 32 (1991) 7–17.

Watanabe, C. E. *Animal Symbolism in Mesopotamia: A Contextual Approach*. Wiener Offene Orientalistik 1. Vienna: Institute für Orientalistik, University of Vienna, 2002.

Watts, James W. "The Legal Characterization of Moses and the Rhetoric of the Pentateuch." *Journal of Biblical Literature* 117 (1998) 415–26.

———. *Psalm and Story: Inset Hymns in Hebrew Narrative*. Sheffield: JSOT Press, 1992.

———. *Reading Law: The Rhetorical Shaping of the Pentateuch*. Biblical Seminar 59. Sheffield: Sheffield Academic Press, 1999.

———. "Rhetorical Strategy in the Composition of the Pentateuch." *Journal for the Study of the Old Testament* 68 (1995) 3–22.

Weinfeld, M. "The Decalogue: Its Significance, Uniqueness, and Place in Israel's Tradition." In *Religion and Law: Biblical-Judaic and Islamic Perspectives*, edited by E. B. Firmage et al., 3–47. Winona Lake, IN: Eisenbrauns, 1990.

———. "Deuteronomy." In *Anchor Bible Dictionary*, edited by D. N. Freedman, 2:168–83. Garden City, NY: Doubleday, 1992.

———. *Deuteronomy 1–11: A New Translation with Introduction and Commentary*. Anchor Bible 5. Garden City, NY: Doubleday, 1991.

———. *Deuteronomy and the Deuteronomic School*. 1972. Reprint. Winona Lake, IN: Eisenbrauns, 1992.

————. "Divine Intervention in War in Ancient Israel and in the Ancient Near East." In *History, Historiography, and Interpretation: Studies in Biblical and Cuneiform Literature*, edited by Hayim Tadmor and M. Weinfeld, 124–31. Jerusalem: Magnes, 1983.

————. "Social and Cultic Institutions in the Priestly Source against Their Ancient Near Eastern Background." *Proceedings of the Eighth World Congress of Jewish Studies* (1983) 105–11.

————. "The Uniqueness of the Decalogue and Its Place in Jewish Tradition." In *The Ten Commandments in History and Tradition*, edited by Ben-Zion Segal and G. Levi, 1–44. Jerusalem: Magnes, 1990.

Weiss, Meir. "The Decalogue in Prophetic Literature." In *The Ten Commandments in History and Tradition*, edited by Ben-Zion Segal, 67–81. Jerusalem: Magnes, 1990.

Weitzman, S. *Song and Story in Biblical Narrative: The History of a Literary Convention in Ancient Israel.* Indianapolis: Indiana University Press, 1997.

Wellhausen, J. *Die Composition des Hexateuchs und der historischen Bücher des Alten Testaments.* Berlin: Reimer, 1889.

————. *Prolegomena to the History of Israel.* 1885. Reprint. Cleveland: World, 1957.

Wells, Tom, and Fred Zaspel. *New Covenant Theology: Description, Definition, Defense.* Frederick, MD: New Covenant Media, 2002.

Wenham, Gordon J. *The Book of Leviticus.* New International Commentary on the Old Testament. Grand Rapids: Eerdmans, 1979.

————. "Deuteronomy and the Central Sanctuary." *Tyndale Bulletin* 22 (1971) 103–18.

————. "The Ethics of the Psalms." In *Interpreting the Psalms: Issues and Approaches*, edited by D. Firth and P. S. Johnston, 175–94. Downers Grove, IL: InterVarsity, 2005.

Wennberg, Robert N. *God, Humans, and Animals: An Invitation to Enlarge Our Moral Universe.* Grand Rapids: Eerdmans, 2003.

Westbrook, Raymond. "Prohibition on Restoration of Marriage in Deuteronomy 24:1–4." In *Studies in Bible 1986*, edited by S. Japhet, 387–405. Scripta hierosolymitana 31. Jerusalem: Magnes, 1986.

Wevers, John William. *Notes on the Greek Text of Deuteronomy.* Septuagint and Cognate Studies 39. Atlanta: Scholars, 1995.

Whitekettle, R. "Where the Wild Things Are: Primary Level Taxa in Israelite Zoological Thought." *Journal for the Study of the Old Testament* 93 (2001) 17–37.

Whitelam, K. W. "Israelite Kingship: The Royal Ideology and Its Opponents." In *The World of Ancient Israel: Sociological, Anthropological and Political Perspectives*, edited by R. E. Clements, 119–39. Cambridge: Cambridge University Press, 1991.

Widengren, Geo. *The Ascension of the Apostle and the Heavenly Book.* Uppsala: Lundequistska Bokhandeln, 1950.

Wiebe, J. M. "The Form, Setting and Meaning of the Song of Moses." *Studia Biblica et Theologica* 17 (1989) 119–63.

Wilkinson, L., editor. *Earthkeeping in the Nineties: Stewardship of Creation.* 3rd ed. Eugene, OR: Wipf & Stock, 2003.

Will, George. "Ending the 'Feminization' of Politics." *The Courier-Journal*, 29 January 2004, A7.

Williamson, P. R. "Covenant." In *Dictionary of the Old Testament: Pentateuch*, edited by T. D. Alexander and D. W. Baker, 139–55. Downers Grove, IL: InterVarsity, 2003.

Willis, T. M. "'Eat and Rejoice Before the Lord': The Optimism of Worship in the Deuteronomic Code." In *Worship and the Hebrew Bible: Essays in Honour of John T. Willis*, edited by Rick R. Marrs, 276–94. Journal for the Study of the Old Testament Supplement Series 284. Sheffield: JSOT Press, 1999.

Wilson, Gerald H. *Psalms*. Vol. 1. NIV Application Commentary. Grand Rapids: Zondervan, 2002.

Wilson, Ian. "Merely a Container? The Ark in Deuteronomy." In *Temple and Worship in Biblical Israel*, edited by J. Day, 212–49. London: T. & T. Clark, 2007.

―――. *Out of the Midst of the Fire*. Society of Biblical Literature Dissertation Series 151. Atlanta: Scholars, 1995.

Wolde, Ellen van. "Does *'innâ* Denote Rape? A Semantic Analysis of a Controversial Word." *Vetus Testamentum* 52 (2002) 528–44.

Wright, Christopher J. H. *Deuteronomy*. New International Biblical Commentary. Peabody, MA: Hendrickson, 1996.

―――. *An Eye for an Eye: The Place of Old Testament Ethics Today*. Downers Grove, IL: InterVarsity, 1983.

―――. *God's People in God's Land: Family, Land, and Property in the Old Testament*. Grand Rapids: Eerdmans, 1990.

―――. *The Mission of God: Unlocking the Bible's Grand Narrative*. Downers Grove, IL: InterVarsity, 2006.

―――. *Old Testament Ethics for the People of God*. Downers Grove, IL: InterVarsity, 2004.

―――. "Ten Commandments." In *International Standard Bible Encyclopedia*. Rev. ed. Edited by G. W. Bromiley, 4:786–90. Grand Rapids: Eerdmans, 1988.

―――. *Walking in the Ways of the Lord: The Ethical Authority of the Old Testament*. Downers Grove, IL: InterVarsity, 1995.

Wright, G. E. "The Lawsuit of God: A Form-Critical Study of Deuteronomy 32." In *Israel's Prophetic Heritage*, edited by B. W. Anderson et al., 26–67. New York: Harper, 1962.

Wright, J. E. *The Early History of Heaven*. New York: Oxford University Press, 2000.

Wright, N. T. *The Climax of the Covenant: Christ and the Law in Pauline Theology*. Minneapolis: Fortress, 1993.

―――. "Monotheism, Christology and Ethics: 1 Corinthians 8." In *The Climax of the Covenant: Christ and the Law in Pauline Theology*, 120–36. Edinburgh: T. & T. Clark, 1991.

Würthwein, Ernst. *The Text of the Old Testament*. Translated by E. F. Rhodes. 2nd ed. Grand Rapids: Eerdmans, 1995.

Wyatt, N. "Astarte." In *Dictionary of Deities and Demons in the Bible*, edited by K. van der Toorn, B. Becking, and P. W. van der Horst, 109–14. Rev. ed. Leiden: Brill, 1999.

―――. "Oil יצהר." In *Dictionary of Deities and Demons in the Bible*, edited by K. van der Toorn, B. Becking, and P. W. van der Horst, 640. Rev. ed. Leiden: Brill, 1999.

―――. *Religious Texts from Ugarit: The Words of Ilimilku and His Colleagues*. Biblical Seminar 53. Sheffield: Sheffield Academic Press, 1998.

Xella, P. "Resheph." In *Dictionary of Deities and Demons in the Bible*, edited by K. van der Toorn, B. Becking, and P. W. van der Horst, 700–703. Rev. ed. Leiden: Brill, 1999.

Yadin, Y. "New Gleanings on Resheph from Ugarit." In *Biblical and Related Studies Presented to Samuel Iwry*, edited by Ann Kort and Scott Morschauser, 259–74. Winona Lake, IN: Eisenbrauns, 1985.

Yeivin, I. *Introduction to the Tiberian Masorah*. Translated and edited by E. J. Revell. Masoretic Studies 5. Missoula, MT: Scholars, 1980.

Zevit, Z. "Jewish Biblical Theology: Whence? Why? And Whither?" *Hebrew Union College Annual* 76 (2005) 289–340.

Index of Modern Authors

Index of Selected Subjects

Index of Scripture References

Old Testament

~

New Testament